Praise for *Strategic Risk Management*

"The authors of *Strategic Risk Management: New Tools for Competitive Advantage in an Uncertain Age* have produced a well-written, entertaining, and thought-provoking compendium of ideas and stimulating insights into strategic planning and the related risk management implications. There is a wealth of interesting risk management case studies in well-known organizations to demonstrate their views. I thoroughly enjoyed reading this and believe it will be helpful to all risk managers and executives to assess and possibly rethink their own methodologies."
—John Fraser, former Chief Risk Officer, Hydro One Networks Inc.

"Technology has made the world smaller and more unified, but it has also created a fragmented and complex environment for business. Volatility, ambiguity, and uncertainty face today's business leaders. This book takes a thoughtful and insightful look at strategic risk management—specifically, the gap between those formulating strategy and those who are providing the execution layers. For any business leader looking for a competitive advantage, this book will provide you with real-life examples of those who have found a way to make it happen."
—Mike Petroff, business executive and MBA professor

"A groundbreaking book for executives that provides the missing piece for solving the strategic planning puzzle!"
—Corey Gooch, Senior Director, Ankura

"*Strategic Risk Management: New Tools for Competitive Advantage in an Uncertain Age* is the essential text for understanding the concept and practice of strategic risk management. Through clear definitions of risk terminology and application of concepts, to engrossing real-life examples from Yogi Berra to Walt Disney and from Intel to ESPN, the well-pedigreed authors have provided a rich source of information that can help all risk practitioners add value to their organization."
—Ken Baker, Corporate Manager, ERM, City of Edmonton

PAUL C. GODFREY, EMANUEL LAURIA, JOHN BUGALLA, AND KRISTINA NARVAEZ

STRATEGIC RISK MANAGEMENT

NEW TOOLS FOR COMPETITIVE ADVANTAGE IN AN UNCERTAIN AGE

BK

Berrett–Koehler Publishers, Inc.

Berrett-Koehler Publishers, Inc.
1333 Broadway, Suite 1000
Oakland, CA 94612-1921
Tel: (510) 817-2277
Fax: (510) 817-2278
www.bkconnection.com

ORDERING INFORMATION
Quantity sales. Special discounts are available on quantity purchases by corporations, associations, and others. For details, contact the "Special Sales Department" at the Berrett-Koehler address above.
Individual sales. Berrett-Koehler publications are available through most bookstores. They can also be ordered directly from Berrett-Koehler: Tel: (800) 929-2929; Fax: (802) 864-7626; www.bkconnection.com.
Orders for college textbook / course adoption use. Please contact Berrett-Koehler: Tel: (800) 929-2929; Fax: (802) 864-7626.

Distributed to the U.S. trade and internationally by Penguin Random House Publisher Services.

Berrett-Koehler and the BK logo are registered trademarks of Berrett-Koehler Publishers, Inc.

Printed in the United States of America

Berrett-Koehler books are printed on long-lasting acid-free paper. When it is available, we choose paper that has been manufactured by environmentally responsible processes. These may include using trees grown in sustainable forests, incorporating recycled paper, minimizing chlorine in bleaching, or recycling the energy produced at the paper mill.

Library of Congress Cataloging-in-Publication Data

Names: Godfrey, Paul C., author.
Title: Strategic risk management : new tools for competitive advantage in an uncertain age / Paul C. Godfrey, Emanuel Lauria, John Bugalia, Kristina Narvaez.
Description: First edition. | Oakland, CA : Berrett-Koehler Publishers, [2020] | Includes bibliographical references and index.
Identifiers: LCCN 2019033042 | ISBN 9781523086955 (hardcover) | ISBN 9781523086962 (pdf) | ISBN 9781523086979 (epub)
Subjects: LCSH: Risk management.
Classification: LCC HD61 .G63 2020 | DDC 658.15/5--dc23
LC record available at https://lccn.loc.gov/2019033042

25 24 23 22 21 20   10 9 8 7 6 5 4 3 2 1

Cover Design: Rob Johnson, Toprotype.com
Interior design and composition: Seventeenth Street Studios
Copy editing: Todd Manza
Photo & illustration credits: see page 221

For Robin—PCG

For Marsha—JAB

For Geri—EVL

For Kevin, Katelyn, Korryn, Kristyn, and Kameron—KLN

CONTENTS

PREFACE

This book traces its origin to the connecting skills of Kristina Narvaez. Kristina began working with John Bugalla in 2010 at an enterprise risk management (ERM) workshop. They started discussing the potential impacts that the then new Securities and Exchange Commission Rule 33-9089 and Dodd-Frank Section 165(c) would have on how the C-suite would report their risk management practices to the board of directors. What followed was a decadelong collaboration that has produced two dozen articles in a wide range of publications, including two books. The major themes of our articles are the role of ERM within corporate governance structures and need to link risk management with corporate strategy.

John and Manny Lauria share a common history, having worked together many years ago in the Chicago office of the insurance broker Marsh & McLennan. Both shared a passion for serving large multinational clients and relished the challenge of developing original, creative risk management solutions to seemingly intractable challenges. Building on that experience, the two have more recently collaborated on numerous articles and consulting projects that inform and assist firms motivated to explore the move from ERM to strategic risk management (SRM). Their work reflects the practical realities of making the linkage between corporate strategy and risk management, the importance of getting strategic risk communication right at the board level, how to evaluate emerging risks, and how SRM can narrow the strategy–execution performance gap.

Kristina met Paul Godfrey in 2015, when she began teaching strategy courses at Brigham Young University, where Paul works. They connected over the power of risk management thinking to frame and understand many of the strategic choices that executives made. Dr. Godfrey's academic research focused on how risk management thinking could explain and justify why firms engage in philanthropy and various forms of corporate social responsibility. These activities provide firms with something like an insurance policy, a reservoir of goodwill among stakeholder groups, which they can draw upon when bad things happen. He and his colleagues showed that firms engaging in corporate social responsibility weathered the financial shocks of crises better than firms without such insurance.

As she does so well, Kristina connected all of us, and we began talking about our vision of risk management and its importance for firms. Those conversations revealed two common perspectives. First, risk management logic and thinking are powerful tools for crafting and implementing better strategy. Executives who link risk and strategy create a stronger, more defensible, and more durable competitive advantage. We also posited that the risk management function, when properly deployed, provides executives with a way to execute strategy more effectively.

Our second common worldview centered on the current state of the art in risk management, ERM. Regulatory strictures such as Sarbanes-Oxley (2002), the Committee of Sponsoring Organizations of the Treadway Commission guidelines for risk (2004), and Dodd-Frank (2010) had provided organizations with incentives, both carrots and sticks, to deepen their attention to and improve their management of risks, particularly those risks that threatened the firm as a whole. John, Kristina, and Manny saw progress but were frustrated because, as the years passed, ERM morphed from advanced risk management with the potential to link to strategy into just another compliance function within the firm. ERM, rather than helping managers look out the front windshield, forced them to look in the rearview mirror.

We shared a final reality: just as risk management had become mired in past actions, so too had it fallen into the traditional trap of defining risk as all the bad things that can happen to a firm. This made, and continues to make, little sense to us, because our training and backgrounds in finance and strategy model risk as a Janus-like entity with a downside, peril face and an upside, opportunity one. The past is the wrong place to look for opportunity—it always, and only, resides in the future.

Paul helped the risk experts better understand the language, logic, and models of strategy, and they gave him a crash course in the tools and techniques of risk management, especially ERM. That was 2016. What we collectively saw then, and continue to see now, is a tremendous need to link strategy, decision making, and risk. This is in no small measure because business is becoming riskier, both in terms of perils and of opportunities. Those conversations, as they sometimes tend to do, led to the idea that we should write a book about these important linkages, although, when the "write a book" concept comes up, the usual response is to say "What a great idea," and then nothing happens. Writing a book is hard work. We took the opposite tack and started writing text, developing models, and synthesizing our hundred-plus years of collective experience with risk and strategy to make that conversation real. What you hold in your hands is the output of that work.

If it takes a village to raise a child, then it takes a number of colleagues, critics, experts, and friends to write a book. There are many people to acknowledge and thank for their help. For Paul, that list begins with Craig Merrill at BYU, who years ago encouraged and enabled the study of risk management as a helpful way to think about strategic decision making. The support of colleagues in the BYU Marriott School of Business, not limited to but especially members of the strategy group and management departments, has made this book possible and made it better. Neal Mallet, Steve Piersanti, Jeevan Sivasubramaniam, and the entire staff at Berrett-Koehler have worked hand in glove with us to make a readable, engaging book. Sam, Lilly, Charlie, Kate, and Grant Godfrey have proved incredibly patient through the process, and my conversations with them have added new insights and perspective. Finally, and most importantly, thanks to Robin. I am always better because of your encouragement, feedback, love, and support.

For John, whose career spans the longest time, the list of acknowledgments and thanks could run for pages. In terms of the current project, John thanks Corey Gooch. The two work together at Aon and currently work on several consulting projects.

Manny expresses appreciation and thanks to Rich Phillips and Lars Matthiassen in the J. Mack Robinson College of Business at Georgia State University, as well as his colleagues in the Department of Risk Management and Insurance and at the Risk Management Foundation. These GSU relationships directly influenced the writing of this book in no small way. Conrad Ciccotello at the Daniels College of Business at the University of Denver is a sounding board nonpareil and a mentor who always seems to sharpen his thinking. Sincere thanks to Julian Smiley, friend, partner, and leader, for his enduring support in so many ways. Jonathan, Courtney, and Ashley Lauria ask insightful questions beyond either their years or their experience, often prompting consideration of complex issues from fresh perspectives. Geri, you are my better half by far, a constant source of wisdom, encouragement, and great faith. Your loving support means everything to me. And most of all, to God be the glory forever!

Kristina Narvaez acknowledges Steve Cain, who was her first mentor and the risk manager at Utah Transit Authority twenty years ago. Thanks go out to Jeff Rowley, who is the risk manager at Salt Lake County; Tim Rodriguez at Revere Health; Wendell Bosen; Fred Doehring at the Utah Department of Transportation; Dan Hair, who is the retired chief risk officer at Workers Compensation Fund; Carol Fox, who is the vice president of strategic initiatives at the Risk and Insurance Management Society and has organized these wonderful events; and Dr. Betty Simkins and John Fraser, for their joint work on our book *Implementing Enterprise Risk Management: Case Studies and Best Practices*, published by Wiley in 2015. A shout-out goes to Kristina's colleagues at Hanover Stone Solutions—Tim Morris, Donna Galer, Max Rudolph, and John Kelly—for their support. Last but not least, I want to thank Leo Costantino, who is the risk manager for the Los Angeles Community College District, and Carrie Frandsen, who is the enterprise risk manager for the University of California system, for the opportunity to teach courses in the UCLA Extension's Enterprise Risk Management certificate program.

INTRODUCTION

How We Got into This Mess, and the Need for New Tools

Heavyweight champion Mike Tyson once quipped, "Everyone has a plan until they get punched in the mouth." Wise words for boxers. Even wiser words, perhaps, for executives, who face increased uncertainty when their business gets punched in the mouth by unexpected change. Most executives develop some type of longer-range strategic plan. Almost all have shorter-term operating performance objectives that demonstrate to their numerous stakeholders that they have a pathway to operational and financial success. But when punched in the mouth by shifting customer demands, competitor moves, or changes in cost, these plans can quickly prove ineffectual. Far too many companies then begin to improvise like street fighters.

Improvisation may work well in the ring, but few successful business strategies—which often require years of investment to create and implement—emerge on the fly. In what follows, we argue that, just as good boxers learn to anticipate punches by knowing enough about the sport and their opponents and to see the signals of an oncoming flurry and respond, executive teams must pay careful attention to *strategic risks*. These risks threaten or extend their core competitive advantages or viability. When these are managed explicitly, firms are better equipped to anticipate and respond to competitive or market punches. Unfortunately, plans may fail to survive because of self-inflicted wounds, too, if those responsible for creating strategy fail to fully comprehend the risks or are too distant from execution.

However, linking strategy tightly with risk management is a powerful means to drive performance improvement.

Customers, competitors, and costs aren't fixed stars in any market; they behave more like wandering planets. As they shift, they create strategic risks. Like planetary movement, many of those changes happen slowly, giving teams sufficient time to plot their trajectory and act accordingly. Strategic risk management, as we argue here, provides leaders with a modern-day astrolabe, a set of principles, processes, and tools that allow them to monitor those wanderings, gauge their position, and chart a course to continued success.

. . . . .

What we propose in this book represents the further evolution of risk management, one that differs in scale and scope from what has come before. All business entails risk. Wise managers work not just to eliminate, mitigate, or transfer risk but also to leverage it. It's been this way since the dawn of time. An ancient account of risk management appears in Genesis 41, when the Hebrew steward Joseph bought and stored seven years of Egyptian grain harvests in anticipation of a great famine. Joseph's handling of the famine saved his family and his adopted country and led to a huge promotion: a foreigner became the regent to Pharaoh. Egypt was the undisputed world superpower. Babylon was just a town between in the swampy marsh between two rivers, Greece and Rome just a collection of olive orchards. Egypt thrived for another half millennium because someone in power recognized and managed risk.

Risk management evolved from Joseph's simple stockpiling of assets in anticipation of future perils. Fast forward a few millennia, and those willing to bear risk devised ways to profit from those who loathed the threat of peril inherent in any commercial venture. Risk-tolerant entrepreneurs offered contracts that allowed risk-averse customers to transfer risk for a fee based on the probability that such perils would become real, material losses. Insurance evolved from contracts on a few oceangoing ships in the mercantilist era into a $5 trillion dollar global industry by 2017.[1]

If you went to business school and took a class in risk and insurance, you learned that insurance is a tool in a larger kit we refer to as traditional risk management (TRM). Those tools include the choice to *avoid* risk by not engaging in certain activities—think of those retailers who refuse to sell firearms. Companies may choose to *manage* risks by reducing their likelihood—think safety training programs and protocols—or by mitigating the impacts of loss when risk becomes realized—for example, installing a fire suppression system in a warehouse. Managers *transfer* much risk through insurance contracts, financial hedges, warranties, and other guarantees that shift the consequences of risk to another party. In some instances, executives choose to *retain* risk because the gains from the activity outweigh the potential losses, even if those losses can't be mitigated or transferred to others.

That class would have helped you understand two more important elements of risk management. First, risks come in two flavors: *pure* risks that bring only the threat of loss and *speculative* ones that offer potential gains as well as losses. Fire, flood, and earthquake represent pure risks for everyone except insurers. Financial strategies such as hedging or real estate investing represent speculative risks. Second, you would have learned that your willingness to pay for risk management depends on the probability of the risk being realized. If the cost of insurance or management exceeded the probability of loss, you'd retain risks. When risks can't be quantified and priced, then the tools of TRM are of little use.

Insurance and other elements of TRM protect a firm against discrete, actuarially predictable risks. Companies implement TRM through specialists, such as insurance brokers, financial traders, and safety officers. Each has the skill and tools to manage downsides traceable to single activities or functions within the firm. By the middle of the twentieth century, most businesses had a formalized risk management program led by these specialists.[2] Today, TRM plays a vital role in most organizations of any size.

As the twentieth century drew to a close, globalization, financial market complexity, supply chain interdependencies, and cross-functional organizational structures had spawned additional categories of risk, which the tools of TRM proved unable to handle. These companywide or *enterprise* risks, whether pure or speculative, defied management by any one subunit in the firm because they originated in the interactions of different units. Consequently, companies were increasingly exposed to interconnected risks and losses for which no formal response was available. Recognizing this challenge, the Committee of Sponsoring Organizations of the Treadway Commission (COSO), a consortium of the world's leading accounting associations, was birthed, and it issued *Enterprise Risk Management—Integrated Framework* in 2004.[3]

As ERM developed and matured, it brought together from various organizational silos professionals responsible for overseeing risk, often under the ultimate guidance of the board of directors and increasingly led by a new executive, the chief risk officer (CRO). A painful time of testing for the nascent ERM process came during the financial sector crisis in 2008. Consider AIG and its credit default swap (CDS) position at that time.[4] A CDS acts like an insurance policy on a bond or other financial instrument. If an issuer defaults on its obligation, then the holder of a CDS has the loss covered by the writer and seller of the CDS.

CDSs became increasingly popular in the years before the financial crisis. Historical evidence of financial instrument default suggested very, very low risk, and the price of a CDS was equally low. A CDS transaction provided cheap insurance against default for buyers—and a license to print money for sellers. Sellers made a tiny amount on each one but had almost zero risk of loss. CDSs played a major role in the 2008 meltdown, when defaults in the subprime mortgage and mortgage-backed security markets defied history and took off.

Most investment banks, including Bear Stearns, Lehman Brothers, Goldman Sachs, and Morgan Stanley, had divisions that sold CDS instruments, and others that bought them. There were winners and losers in the mix, depending on whether the bank was buying, selling, or both. Individual banking divisions were either paying out or were being paid when defaults occurred. Despite several high-profile bankruptcies, most of these institutions had enough diversification in their portfolios to weather the storm, although they sustained significant damage.

AIG, however, the largest reinsurer in the country, stood alone among its peers. AIG sold only CDSs. For AIG, what had been a giant revenue stream for many years now threatened not only its existence but also that of its customers. If AIG couldn't meet its CDS obligations, then its customers risked default. Stepping in to bail out AIG, the U.S. Financial Stability Oversight Council poured $85 billion into the company to forestall a potential catastrophic market failure.

ERM wasn't foolproof, of course, and it didn't necessarily prevent banks—or, for that matter, manufacturing firms, real estate operations, or service businesses—from trouble during the financial crisis. Based on this experience and other critical commentary, it was becoming clear that ERM was well intended but wasn't designed to properly encompass the big strategic risks that eventually threaten survival. Unless ERM linked to and operated in sync with a firm's strategy, its effectiveness would be limited.

In September 2017, COSO released an updated framework for ERM, *Enterprise Risk Management—Integrating with Strategy and Performance*. This revised framework reflects the reality that ERM too often fails to inform strategic decision making. A well-stated emphasis on "integrating with strategy" captures the hope of realizing the original vision of ERM: that effective risk management is an integral element of strategy formulation and implementation.

Why had ERM failed to integrate with strategy the first time around? What got us into this mess? We see the convergence of two factors. First, ERM came on the scene as U.S. companies adapted to a new compliance regime, the Sarbanes-Oxley Act, in 2002, which required executive teams to pay greater attention to how their financial reporting and internal audit systems worked and recorded results. It had no discernible impact on what risks those teams chose to take. By the end of the decade, executives would face additional governmental mandates, this time explicitly including risk management, in the form of the Dodd-Frank Wall Street Reform and Consumer Protection Act of 2010. Factor one, then, was strong external pressure for compliance, and compliance protocols are very poor at creating competitive advantage.

Second, COSO was a creation of the accounting industry. Its vision of ERM was naturally biased toward that profession, resonating particularly well with the Big Four accounting firms. Firms already relied on their auditors, external and internal, to help navigate reporting requirements, so adding ERM to the burgeoning list of tasks made sense. Most companies outside of financial services didn't have a formal ERM program or internal audit, and the office of the chief financial officer (CFO) provided a ready place for these. Factor two, therefore, was a strong tendency to default ERM to accounting and internal audit.

Accounting professionals—and we have many who are former students and current colleagues—echo and reinforce this next statement: accountants, and the tools they employ, are well suited to looking backwards, not forward. Those wearing the proverbial "green eyeshades" do a great job of calculating the current score, yet they lack the skills to predict what the score might be later. Most ERM programs are able to provide postmortems on previous actions. They create lengthy registers of current risks and they do a yeoman's job of meeting the demands of regulatory compliance. ERM in its original form tells executives where they've been, through the rearview mirror. But executives really want to know what threats and opportunities lie ahead.

Success today and tomorrow requires driving while looking squarely out the front windshield. We employ the language, mind-sets, and tools of strategic management to create a simple notion of strategic risk. We also offer a set of strategic tools and organizational actions that allow executives to assess and respond to future risks—the big ones that imperil or enable strategic health. How would you rather drive?

Strategic risk management helps executive teams think coherently and effectively about strategy and risk. SRM inextricably links the two. When leaders design and implement a strong SRM program, they help to address another major reason why strategies fail: the gap between strategy and its execution, the difference between a formulated strategy's projected benefits and the ones it actually delivers. This gap is prima facie evidence that plans rarely withstand a solid punch in the mouth, and this results in organizations realizing about two-thirds of their stated financial objectives.[5] Some may argue that attaining 60% to 70% of performance objectives is acceptable. To us, it sounds like an excuse for accepting competitive mediocrity. After all, 70% on a college exam is roughly a gentleman's C grade.

The strategy–execution gap has many causes, including faulty structural arrangements that lead to a unidirectional handoff of strategy from those responsible for its formulation to those tasked with its implementation. A communication chasm can develop between the two groups that precludes effective execution. Next, strategists too often fail to recognize and plan for new assets and processes essential to on-the-ground execution of the strategy, or they dramatically underestimate the scale of investment needed to build those capabilities. Implementers are then subjected to budget fights that further stymie execution. Executives driven by short-term thinking assume and adhere to an unreasonable time horizon for implementation, which ensures mediocrity at best and outright failure at worst. Finally, strategy makers may presume the existence of knowledgeable and skilled human, social, and organizational capital that may not exist. Execution hits another pothole if the talent doesn't materialize. The list of execution failures goes on and on.

We wish we could eliminate the strategy–execution gap in its entirety. We can't, though; it's just too big and too multifaceted. At the risk of overselling our ideas, our experience suggests that linking the strategy and risk management processes in a firm goes a long way toward closing the divide. SRM processes, done effectively, overcome the major driver of the gap, which is the disconnect between those making and those implementing a strategy. SRM helps to pierce the hierarchical layers and bureaucratic rigidities that isolate executives and keep them from seeing how their competitive environment is, and may be, evolving in ways that create strategic risks. SRM includes a set of structural arrangements that weave strategy formulation and implementation together in the assessment of and response to strategic risks. Supporting these arrangements requires communication pathways and protocols that enable two-way feedback between the C-suite and those on the ground. Consistent and meaningful communication between these groups closes the gap. Most importantly, we'll describe how to align culture around both strategy and implementation in a way that harmonizes the two.

Why do we need new ways of managing risks, particularly strategic ones? Because, in the words of Yogi Berra, which summarizes our experiences over several years, "The future ain't what it used to be." Far more frequent and often unexpected punches in the mouth are commonplace. Business is more volatile, uncertain, complex, and ambiguous than ever before. We see managers taking more, not fewer, punches. The best way to win in this environment is to drive with both eyes focused out the front windshield. Though the future can't ever be perfectly predicted, smart leaders using SRM are far better positioned to anticipate and shape it wherever possible.

As the drama of our book unfolds, you'll encounter several characters, concepts and themes. Before we dive in, we'll take a moment to introduce them.

Chief risk officer. A corporate executive charged with responsibility for all the risk management functions of the organization. Usually a member of the senior executive team.

Chief strategy officer. A corporate executive responsible for strategy development, strategic planning, budgeting, and resource allocation. In many companies, this role is played by the chief executive officer (CEO).

Enterprise risk management. A set of knowledge, skills, and tools that allow firms to manage organization-wide risks.

Risk. Events or exposures that create variability and volatility in performance. Risks may be pure, downside only, or speculative, having both upside and downside potential outcomes. Risks can be accurately modeled and reduced to a set of probabilistic outcomes.

Strategic risk management. A set of principles, processes, teams, and tools that allow firms to manage strategic risks, which are those uncertainties, events, and exposures that create threats to—or opportunities to expand—their core competitive advantages.

Traditional risk management. A set of knowledge, skills, and tools that allow firms to manage individual risks.

Uncertainty. A future state that cannot be accurately modeled or reduced to a set of probabilistic outcomes.

Uncertainty absorption. A natural organizational tendency and set of protocols that replace real uncertainty in the environment with estimates or forecasts that create an "illusion of certainty."

Here, we've set the stage for strategic risk management by explaining why the existing tools and practices, TRM and ERM, prove inadequate to the task ahead. In the next chapter, we clarify and explain the essential need to combine risk and strategy. To do so, we look back on an industry, television broadcasting, at a time when it began to experience significant change. An inflection point happened in the late 1970s, when innovation and competition turned a sleepy oligopoly of three major broadcast networks into a cutthroat competitive jungle now filled with millions of competitors.[6] Some leveraged that strategic risk to build amazing companies and wealth; others struggled to make sense of and adapt to the change. We begin our story of SRM with the tale of one of the real winners in the industry.

CHAPTER 1

Strategic Risk Management: Competitive Advantage in an Uncertain World

At 4:19 a.m. on January 18, 1978, the roof of the Hartford Civic Center collapsed under the weight of the previous day's heavy snowfall. Just a few hours before, more than five thousand fans had cheered as the University of Connecticut Huskies men's basketball team upset the University of Massachusetts Minutemen, 56–49. By 4 a.m. the building was empty, and luckily no lives were lost.[1]

Damage to the property proved substantial, and it took two years to bring the building back on line. The disaster forced the building's tenants to find new homes. Among the disenfranchised were the World Hockey Association's New England Whalers, who moved thirty miles north to finish the season in Springfield, Massachusetts. Sadly, on the ice they went from a stellar 26–13–3 record before the relocation to a mediocre 18–18–2 after.[2] Most season ticket holders remained loyal, but the Whalers' individual game revenue declined because the Springfield Civic Center seated two thousand fewer fans each night.

The Hartford Civic Center seems like the perfect introduction for a book about strategic risk management. But it's not. We have a hazard (the snow event), a loss event (the roof collapse), risk transfer (the City of Hartford certainly had insurance on the building), and loss mitigation (the Whalers moved to Springfield). Nonetheless, the collapsed roof represented an *operational risk*, not a strategic one. Operational risks threaten an organization's ability to deliver products and services and short-term earnings. *Strategic risks*, on the other hand, are actions or events, and the uncertainty they generate, that foundationally threaten or enhance a company's competitive advantage, its pursuit of strategic aspirations, or its viability as a going concern.

Operational risks, like excessive snowfall and the attendant damages, follow a known probability distribution. Storms of varying intensity occur annually, which enables actuaries to estimate the likelihood of excessive snow events and to price hazard coverage accordingly. Likewise, executives can choose from a menu of well-known options to control weather-related risk and to minimize or mitigate its effects. Strategic risks, on the other hand, don't reduce to a set of probabilistic outcomes; they incorporate and reflect fundamental uncertainty about potential outcomes.

Operational risks create tactical difficulties and financial losses. Strategic risks encompass more than just financial losses, however. These risks put a company's fundamental *competitive advantage and their future viability* in play. The events in Hartford impaired the Whalers' operations and revenue stream but did not affect their strategic advantages. The team survived the 1977–1978 season and finished second in the World Hockey Association playoffs that spring. They returned to Hartford in 1980 and would play another eighteen years as a member of the National Hockey League before moving to North Carolina to become the Hurricanes, where they continue to compete.

Our book makes a simple argument: *when executive teams link strategy and its risks, they'll better create new—and protect existing—business value in an increasingly uncertain world*. That value arises from two sources. First, the strategy–risk link invites a systematic, future-focused assessment of threats and opportunities, which we'll refer to throughout this book as "driving while looking out the front windshield." Second, that link closes the gap between strategy formulation and its execution as executives focus on *who* manages strategic risks and *how* they respond to them.

· · · · ·

For one employee of the Whalers, the collapse of the Civic Center roof created strategic risk. Bill Rasmussen had been the Whalers' director of communication for nearly four years. Rasmussen loved sports, having played baseball at DePauw University and for the U.S. Air Force. He cut his business teeth working in Westinghouse's advertising department and subsequently founded, grew, and sold his own advertising fulfillment firm. Rasmussen then returned to his first love, but this time in the role of broadcaster and entrepreneur. In one venture, he assembled a mini network of small, rural Massachusetts stations to broadcast University of Massachusetts football and basketball games, doing the play-by-play at night and selling advertising by day. That venture failed, as did others, and Rasmussen eventually landed with the Whalers, in 1974. When the Whalers' revenues tanked, the team decided that a director of communications was a luxury. The owner fired Bill over the Memorial Day weekend of 1978.[3]

The forty-five-year-old broadcaster and entrepreneur met with a group that hoped to use the emerging medium of cable TV to broadcast Whalers games, sports news, and other local entertainment to Connecticut households. Rasmussen added to the idea and envisioned a network that would broadcast University of Connecticut men's basketball games across the state. He, along with his son Scott, named their idea Entertainment and Sports Programming Television, or ESP-TV, and went to work. Rasmussen threw his indomitable energy into the venture, and it would have been hard to find anyone with a stronger résumé in entrepreneurial, small-market sports broadcasting.

With Rasmussen's connections to Connecticut's sports community, from the Whalers and the University of Connecticut Huskies to the smaller colleges and minor leagues sprinkled throughout the Constitution State, finding programming content appeared doable. The real challenge lay in distribution. Rasmussen's original plan called for ESP-TV to produce five hours of programming each night. Using satellite transmission, a new technology, the company would beam content to local providers, who would then send it over coaxial cable to subscribers' homes. But when Bill and Scott sat down with Al Parinello, the RCA sales executive in charge of selling satellite transponder time, their plans changed.

RCA priced its transponders to encourage continuous transmission, to prove the value of the nascent model and recover the sunk cost of their satellite. Parinello laid out the pricing model: ESP-TV could pay $250 per hour for five hours of transmission each night, or $38,750 per month. Alternately, it could pay $48 an hour, or $35,712 per month, for continuous, 24/7 transmission.[4] Bill recognized a good deal when he saw one. ESP-TV mushroomed from a small venture serving a few thousand Connecticut Yankees into a nationwide sports network.

ESP-TV exemplifies our notion of strategic risk, in that it was a de novo venture full of opportunity, threat, and uncertainty. Uncertainty on the demand side arose because ESP-TV represented a radical new, untried product. National sports programming consisted of a few hours of live events on Saturday and Sunday afternoons, and a rare weekday game. By 1979, the Big Three broadcast networks (ABC, CBS, and NBC) aired 1,356 hours of sports programming. While that sounds like a lot, it worked out to a little over eight hours per week for each network.[5] Local sports programming might include local event broadcasts, but the bulk came in two to three minutes of sports segments during the nightly news. ESP-TV would offer 168 hours per week, *seven times* the combined networks' current coverage. No one could estimate how many viewers would watch sports all day, every day—or even for part of a day that wasn't a weekend.

Could two thousand or so fragmented—and primarily rural—cable companies attract enough viewers each day, week, and month to make ESP-TV attractive to sponsors? Advertisers paid good money for slots on major network broadcasts because the scarcity and elite matchups that characterized sports programming guaranteed millions of eyeballs in the prime eighteen-to-forty-nine age demographic. But all sports, all the time? Such an extreme level of programming had never been offered, and demand was completely uncertain.

On the supply side, ESP-TV faced similar strategic uncertainty. How would they fill 168 hours each week? How would they pay for that much content? The Big Three spent almost a billion dollars for broadcast rights, spread across college sports, which was controlled through the monopolist National Collegiate Athletic Association, and every major professional league: the National Football League, Major League Baseball, the National Basketball Association, the Professional Golfers' Association, and even the Professional Bowlers Association. Despite all this available content, though, each network only broadcast eight hours each week, and scarcity translated into huge profits for the sports divisions. ESP-TV needed to fill seven times that much time with whatever scraps the major networks let fall from their table. Also, ESP-TV, with hardly any cash on hand, had to pay as little as possible. If ESP-TV couldn't fill the time, the consequences were obvious and dire: no viewers, no advertisers, and the venture would die a quick and unremarkable death.

Round-the-clock programming represented substantial downside strategic risk, but with huge upside potential competitive advantage. If ESP-TV could fill those hours, attract viewers, and garner advertising dollars, it would become the only network of its kind. More importantly, they had a product that, from the perspective of the Big Three, couldn't be replicated. For the networks, sports telecasts represented a very profitable side business, but only a side business. Sports could never dominate the schedule, since the networks had too many audiences—men, women, and children—who enjoyed other types of programming. The Big Three would always fill their days with soap operas, serials, newscasts, and movies, and to do otherwise would alienate core audiences and advertisers. Practically speaking, 24/7 sports programming represented economic suicide for the Big Three.

Rasmussen had almost no control over viewer behaviors, but a lot of control over content. By the summer of 1979, he and son Scott had secured a contract with the NCAA to broadcast "nonpremier" sporting events, the scraps the networks didn't want. They also negotiated an initial advertising agreement with Budweiser and garnered a $10 million investment from an unlikely source, Getty Oil. Getty had found itself awash in cash after the oil price hikes of the late 1970s, and Getty vice president Stuart Evey, a huge sports fan and future-focused investor, saw the seed of competitive advantage in ESP-TV.[6] Rechristened ESPN, the venture prepared to debut on air with its own in-house sports report: *SportsCenter*.

SportsCenter cost only a fraction of what was required to produce a live sporting event. Production costs were also kept to a minimum by using a permanent set and a single camera, or two at the most. A skeleton crew of anchors, a director, camera operators, and a few production assistants were hired. ESPN paid only production costs, without the rights fee it paid to broadcast sporting events. If *SportsCenter* cost little to produce, it cost almost nothing to *reproduce*. For the cost of a few videotapes and an operator, ESPN could rerun the original broadcast to fill dead spaces throughout the day.

SportsCenter launched on Saturday, September 7, 1979. Longtime broadcaster and ESPN new hire Lee Leonard proclaimed salvation to starved fans everywhere with his opening line: "If you're a fan, *if* you're a fan, what you'll see in the next minutes, hours, and days to follow may convince you you've gone to sports heaven." He then anointed tiny Bristol, Connecticut, home of the fledgling network, the center of the sporting universe.[7]

Leonard's opening words proved prophetic on both counts. ESPN struggled to find its foothold, but as the years went by, millions of American sports fans tuned in to *SportsCenter*, often multiple times each day, to get their piece of sports heaven. Tiny Bristol became the center of the sports universe, ESPN grew into one of the most valuable brands in entertainment, and the network generated profits that eventually made it the crown jewel of the Walt Disney Company, its corporate parent.[8]

A New Age: VUCA and a World of Strategic Risk

The launch of ESPN illustrates what we mean by strategic risk. Television broadcasting had been a bucolic business in the three decades since the advent of the medium in the early 1940s. NBC and CBS began as national radio networks in the 1920s and had successfully incorporated the new technology into their existing business model. ABC got its start when the U.S. government required NBC to spin off some of its radio holdings in the 1940s. Networks enjoyed the protection of the Federal Communications Commission, which limited the number of stations in each market and the overall number of broadcast frequencies in exchange for the networks providing free programming, news reporting, and other services to the entire nation. In 1976, 78.2 million people, or 92% of the viewing public, tuned in to the Big Three for their evening entertainment.[9]

The year 1976 also marked the beginning of the industry's transition from idyllically calm to hellishly turbulent. The cause was technological and regulatory changes in the early 1970s that allowed two additional broadcast platforms, cable and satellite, to flourish and prosper.[10] The industry in short order exemplified what staff at the U.S. Army War College would later term VUCA—volatile, uncertain, complex, and ambiguous. In just under a decade, the Big Three saw its share of viewers fall to 75%, and then to just 50% by the early 1990s. Bruce Springsteen memorialized the chaos in his classic 1992 song "57 Channels (and Nothin' On)."

Today, every business in every industry faces a rapidly accelerating VUCA world, and the trend line indicates more of this, rather than less, in the future. Technological advances alone account for increasing amounts of VUCA and are responsible for waves of disruptive innovation confronting executives. At one end of the scale is escalating VUCA wrought by global conditions, such as geopolitical instability, interconnected financial markets, regulatory responses to the climate change debate, and renegotiated international trade agreements. At the other end are microeconomic considerations of equal intensity: more sophisticated and nontraditional competitors entering markets, big data analytics, and constantly shifting consumer preferences. These elements combine to surround far too many decisions with uncertainty, and ambiguous signals from communities, customers, investors, and suppliers make differentiating signal from noise a difficult ongoing task.

VUCA elements reinforce each other in a virtuous circle/vicious cycle sort of way. For example, the actions of more competitors lead to more volatile outcomes, and so on. Volatility, complexity, and ambiguity—as well as the underlying actions and events that engender them—create and magnify uncertainty, or the inability to predict the future with any sense of accuracy. Uncertainty runs the gamut from minor and temporary worries (How will forecasted weather swings impact this season's deliveries?) to significant concerns (How will tariff and trade wars impact investments in global supply chains?). Uncertainty around these significant concerns gives rise to strategic risk.

Risk Versus Uncertainty

Uncertainty differs from risk, and that difference sets strategic risks apart from the way executives and experts traditionally think about risk. The work of Frank Knight, an early twentieth-century economist at the University of Chicago, helps us understand this crucial difference. Knight pioneered the study of entrepreneurship, one of the riskiest and most rewarding types of business activity. For Knight, the potential entrepreneur faces many potential challenges in setting up shop. Some challenges represent risk, others uncertainty.

Certain challenges involve potential hazards. Will inventory be damaged by flood or fire? What interest rate will I pay to finance that inventory?

Others provide opportunities for gain, as in the case of a hard-bid project taking less time to complete than anticipated, the difference creating profit. Knight defined both challenges as risks because the likelihood of the outcomes was volatile, given that interest rates fluctuate and projects run into snags, but they do so in largely predictable ways. Based on past experience, an entrepreneur could calculate the probability of fire or flood, or that work would be done in a compressed time frame. "Risk" means that an event follows a known probability distribution. A wise entrepreneur estimates the likelihood of a risky event and plans accordingly through traditional methods such as insurance or risk mitigation programs.

But entrepreneurs face *uncertainty* as well as risk. Will the company solve the technical challenges of getting a new product to market? Will customers like it? Will enough of them pay enough to turn a profit? Uncertainties, like risks, exhibit volatility because they have multiple potential outcomes. However, the entrepreneur has no historical data from which to predict the likelihood of any outcome, and the more radical the innovation, the more uncertain the outcome. Uncertain events can't be estimated from known probability distributions, so the only way to reduce uncertainty is to act and enter the business.

Strategic risks arise from, and center on, uncertainty. A new business will either pay off or not, but because of the unique nature of the situation, neither entrepreneurs nor actuaries can estimate the outcome in advance. Entrepreneurs succeed to the extent that they manage and master uncertainty.

ESPN certainly did so. Bill Rasmussen assumed that viewers had not reached their saturation point for sports, although uncertainty hung over this assumption because no one had ever offered 24/7 programming. ESPN's team embraced uncertainty, jumped in, and then figured out ways to manage and reduce uncertainty. They did so in a way that created a significant and sustained competitive advantage.

Uncertainty, Competitive Advantage, and Strategy

Put simply, strategic risk concerns strategy. A firm's *strategy* is the set of resource allocation decisions that help a firm create and sustain a competitive advantage over its rivals in the pursuit of its strategic ambitions. A firm with a competitive advantage generates more profit that its rivals; captures greater market share; commands greater loyalty and respect from customers, employees, and other stakeholders; or capitalizes on market changes more rapidly. Competitive advantage allows a firm to win. Strategic risks are those that threaten—or amplify—a firm's competitive advantage over rivals. It turns out that the tool kits available through TRM and ERM prove inadequate to cope with the nature of uncertainty that impacts competitive advantage.

Much has been written about strategy and strategic management. Indeed, a search for book titles containing the words "strategic management" returns more than ten thousand hits on Amazon. For us, winning strategies in a VUCA world come as leaders answer four questions and allocate resources based upon those answers. We'll briefly describe those questions here, and readers who want a deeper dive will find more in appendix A. Two of the questions focus on the development of strategy, and the other two on its deployment.

The primary question of *developing* competitive advantage is *what* unique value will we offer customers? Why will we win? Customers engage products or services because they have work they need to do, or jobs to be done. Competitive advantage accrues to those companies that can help customers do jobs in unique ways through differentiated product features and benefits, or by doing those jobs more cheaply than other options. ESPN focused on helping customers do their "sports entertainment" job. *SportsCenter* provided a clear answer to ESPN's unique value question. The show offered viewers quantifiably more sports news—thirty minutes compared to three minutes—and a qualitatively different experience, one that covered a broader range of sports and featured longer pieces with greater depth and insight.

After executives know what their unique value will be, they focus on the next question: *How* will we create that unique value? Firms create value by configuring their assets (resources) and processes (capabilities) to support activities (such as manufacturing, sales, or service) that deliver that value to customers. Cable TV provided one answer to the question of how ESPN would deliver value, since it defined the distribution channel.

A second answer to that question gets at the core of *SportsCenter*'s enduring advantage. In the earliest days, when reruns were many and viewers few, the show's anchors adopted a philosophy of innovation: "No one is watching anyway, so try something new." *SportsCenter* developed a culture in which the hosts mattered. They did more than just read the news; they injected commentary, humor, and often satire into the show to make the value of *SportsCenter* truly unique. Humor contributed greatly to an iconic brand that viewers loved.

The first question about the *deployment* of a strategy is *where* will we compete? The traditional answer has been to think in terms of industries or markets, but life in a VUCA world invites another answer: jobs to be done. ESPNs original business plan focused on a narrow market niche (Connecticut sports fans); however, Bill Rasmussen leaped at the opportunity to compete nationally. Over time, ESPN expanded its customer reach into new programming, such as *SportsCentury* and *30 for 30*, a set of documentaries about sports stars, into print media (*ESPN Magazine*), and even into restaurants (ESPN Zone). Each of these moves deepened competitive advantage as the network helped customers do jobs such as dining out in sports-related ways.

Strategy's final question—*Why* can't competitors imitate or create a substitute for our competitive advantage?—ensures that competitive advantage persists over time. Unique value creates immediate competitive advantage and profits, but when it is easily copied by competitors, unique value transforms into a commodity yielding competitive parity. ESPN enjoyed a durable advantage. It didn't face serious competition until the Fox Broadcasting Company (another upstart network) founded its own sports network fifteen years later, in 1994. Rasmussen and his successors employed competitive judo against the Big Three; ABC, CBS, and NBC couldn't match ESPN's all-sports offering without alienating their core audiences.[11] Breadth, depth, and edginess created a powerful connection with viewers of ESPN that other networks, and even Fox, couldn't match. ESPN was, and for a long time remained, the undisputed leader in sports television.

We live and hope to compete in a VUCA world, where uncertainty abounds. Some of that uncertainty gets at the heart of strategy and competitive advantage, and it can impact, for better or worse, a company's current answers to strategy's four questions. Such is the reality of the world we live in. Living in a VUCA world, however, creates a problem for both individuals and organizations, because we all hate uncertainty and do our best to eliminate or avoid it.

An Old Problem: Uncertainty Avoidance and Absorption

*H*ate is a strong word, and we're sure that people don't truly hate uncertainty. We would bet, though, based our own experiences and those of our students, colleagues, and executive clients, that most people strongly dislike uncertainty. When it comes to individual decision making, uncertainty doesn't mesh well with a seemingly hardwired desire of our brains for solid anchors to our decisions. Individual aversion to uncertainty gets amplified when we come together in an organizational setting. Indeed, the gears of collective decision making grind to a halt when the question "What do we expect to happen?" gets answered with "We don't know." We'll briefly examine the drivers of individual and organizational responses to uncertainty.

Individuals and Uncertainty Avoidance: The Illusion of Certainty

Dislike of uncertainty stems from two of its most prominent features: the lack of predictability and the lack of control it signifies.[12] Both of these create mental stress, which has two effects. First, stress reduces our effectiveness in making decisions. Under conditions of high stress, our cerebral cortex, the seat of rational thought and the part of our brain that makes us different from animals, gives way to the hippocampus and amygdala, the parts of the brain that generate emotion. When stressed, we replace reasoned decision making with fear and aggression.[13] Most of us realize that these two attitudes don't lend themselves to good decisions, leading to the second effect: we engage in mental gymnastics to replace real uncertainty with an illusory, yet believable, assertion of certainty. We replace a range of equally likely potential outcomes with a single-point estimate.

Humans employ a powerful tool to craft that estimate: the past. We scan our history for events similar to the current state and its potential futures, and then we invoke the assumption that the past predicts the future. What happened last time becomes our default belief about what will happen this time around.[14] We fail to think critically about the past and gloss over two questions: How similar to the past is the current situation? On what dimensions do the two situations differ? When looking out the front windshield causes too much stress, we look in the rearview mirror in the vain hope that it will illuminate the road ahead.

An example illustrates this behavior and its impact. A few days after the horrific and shocking events of September 11, 2001, one of us visited our aging mother to check in. As you might expect, the conversation turned to the attacks, and mother warned of a country at war and an economy transforming to wartime production, which would include rationing of essential items and the reassignment of people and assets to weapons manufacturing. Mom was seven years old when the bombing of Pearl Harbor took place, in 1941, and the similarities between the two attacks—a surprise attack on U.S. soil and the use of airplanes—fueled her predictions. She failed, in the stress and fear of that intense moment, to identify differences between the two situations. For example, the nation-state of Japan initiated Pearl Harbor, whereas the non-nation-state terrorist group Al Qaeda struck in 2001. Also, note the massive difference in the size and scale of the U.S. economy sixty years after Pearl Harbor. Looking in the rearview mirror encouraged her to make a set of dire predictions, none of which turned out to be correct.[15]

When the past generates a false sense of certainty, we eliminate perceived unpredictability, and that gives us the illusion of control. In our example here, our teammate was encouraged to stockpile foods and prepare for a world with limited gasoline, butter, and chocolate. Had he done so, resources would have been allocated around a future that never materialized. He chose not to listen to his mother in this case, and with all due respect, and to eschew actions based on illusory certainty.

Organizations and Uncertainty: Absorption at Every Level

Nobel Laureate Herbert Simon, the 1978 prize winner in Economic Sciences, and his colleague James March thought a lot about how uncertainty impacts organizational, as opposed to individual, decision making. Their research led them to identify a clear pattern they named *uncertainty absorption*. Uncertainty absorption represents a rational response by those who gather and process information about unfolding events. In this light, they perceive executive decision makers' aversion to uncertainty and their desire to make decisions based on point forecasts, no matter how tenuous, rather than to consider a wide range of possible and unpredictable outcomes.

Simon and March wrote that "uncertainty absorption takes place when inferences are drawn from a body of evidence and the inferences, instead of the evidence itself, are then communicated."[16] Decision makers often don't work with facts or the on-the-ground reality. Instead, they work with the interpretations and inferences made about meaning and trajectory by those gathering and analyzing facts and data. They also don't usually want to know what *might* happen, preferring to focus on what someone thinks *will* happen. This phenomenon takes place at every organizational tier, from the supervisory to the executive. Managers have little desire to tell the boss "I really don't know." It makes them sound like they either haven't done the work to figure out what's going on or lack the courage to make the tough calls good leaders have to make. In either case, prospects for promotion may in reality sink as the truth of "I don't know" leaves their lips.

At each step of the managerial hierarchy, inferences and interpretations, the carriers of the illusion of certainty, move future outcomes from possible to plausible to probable. Wide ranges of potential outcomes reduce to point forecasts. Inference and interpretation act as a VUCA-neutralizing agent, scrubbing the following from facts and reality: the *volatility* and magnitude differences between potential outcomes and the fundamental *uncertainty* about which outcomes are more likely than others, the *complexity* of the fundamental interrelatedness among different elements and the nuances that account for specific contexts or admit the fuzzy nature of the facts, and *ambiguity*, as multiple meanings and interpretations give way to a single narrative.

Organizations, like individuals, invoke the past as a framework to create an illusion of certainty. But organizations, compared to individuals, have more potential pasts to draw on. They might draw on the histories of individual members, the institutional memory of the organization recorded in formal documentation and informal narratives, and the experiences of any number of key stakeholders such as competitors, suppliers, or investors. Analysts and managers get to choose which rearview mirror to look out of as they create the illusion of certainty.

Pressure for certainty, or at least predictability, exists at every level of an organization. It usually increases as information escalates. Senior executives rarely have enough contact with day-to-day markets and operations to see emerging uncertainty, so as this information progresses upward, more and more uncertainty gets absorbed. What began on the sales floor as a range of potential outcomes contingent on multiple factors becomes a neat and tidy point forecast when it arrives at the C-suite. Unfortunately, this dramatically narrowed forecast means that the final decision maker "is severely limited in his [or her] ability to judge [the inferences' and interpretations'] correctness."[17] They know neither the facts themselves nor the uncertainty that littered the path as the interpretation moved upward.

Uncertainty absorption has another deadly consequence for organizations, in that it helps to create and perpetuate the gap between strategy and its execution. Successful execution requires that those making strategy and resource allocation decisions have a solid understanding of the on-the-ground reality. However, uncertainty absorption means that strategy gets made by people with a curated version of reality. As executives are further detached from the day-to-day reality, the gap between strategy's objectives and the actions that realize them becomes wider. Illusions of certainty lead to poor answers to strategy's four questions and to misguided implementation processes that affect strategic plans, capital and operating budgets, mergers and acquisitions, or hiring and training protocols.

We may not truly hate uncertainty, but we do dislike it and the stress it generates in our own lives. We don't check that disdain at the office door; we just fold our personal uncertainty avoidance into an elaborate bureaucratic ritual of uncertainty absorption. We hope for stress-free lives of predictability and control; however, the realities of a VUCA world crash that party and leave decision makers in a difficult situation.

The Fundamental Question (and Answer)

Living in a VUCA world is tough, even for those individuals and organizations that manage to thrive in it. Regardless, the tandem processes of uncertainty avoidance and absorption magnify the threats, and dampen the opportunities, of strategic risks to all. Leaders must overcome resistance and learn to accurately assess and manage uncertainty if they hope to survive, let alone thrive, in an uncertain age. This raises the critical question: How can executives and their firms learn to embrace uncertainty? Our answer: by adopting a strategic risk management program.

Strategic risk management is a set of principles, processes, teams, and tools that allow firms to manage strategic risks, which are those uncertainties, events, and exposures that create threats to—or opportunities to expand—their core competitive advantages. First and foremost, SRM embodies an *organizational* response to uncertainty. The chief risk officer, a position enacted by the Dodd-Frank Act to ensure risk management compliance for large bank holding companies and endorsed by industry standards such as the COSO II framework, leads the SRM team and all other risk functions in the organization. The CRO can't work in isolation, however. SRM only works when people in all functions at all levels get involved in the process, either providing input about strategic risks or helping to manage them. SRM needs to stand on equal footing with the other critical strategy systems of the firm: budgeting, corporate development, mergers and acquisitions, human capital management, product development, and strategic planning.

The rest of this book outlines how organizational leaders design and implement the principles and processes, staff the teams, and utilize the tools to manage strategic risk. Chapter 2 begins the process by more richly defining what we mean by strategic risk. Before they can be managed, SRM leaders and their teams must understand strategic risks, those critical areas of uncertainty that threaten their firms' ability to gain and maintain a competitive advantage and that arise from the interaction of three elements: changes in the external or market environment, a firm's response to those changes, and the development of that change–response relationship over time. Boards, executives, and all organizational leaders need this understanding as well, in order to differentiate strategic risks from the ones they already know about and for which they have oversight responsibility.

Chapter 3 then lays out the fundamental principles that guide SRM. To effectively combine strategy and risk management, boards and executive teams need to adopt, in most cases, a new mental map, which is a set of assumptions, cause-and-effect relationships, and worldviews. These high-level mental maps—we use the metaphor of a thirty thousand–foot perspective—invite leaders to see how SRM complements their existing efforts in risk management and strategy. They also have to see how SRM extends current organizational capabilities related to creativity, environmental scanning, and horizontal and vertical communication within the firm.

Chapter 4 descends to ten thousand feet, where *processes* guide the daily work of the executive team, including the CRO, CEO, CFO, and chief strategy officer (CSO). Successful SRM programs integrate the work of these executives toward the "strategy complex" of the enterprise. Leaders can't merely bolt on additional activities called SRM and hope to create long-term value, so we identify the significant touch points where managers can weave the unique threads of SRM into the fabric of the existing strategy architecture. Here is where the link between strategy and risk becomes real and robust.

In chapter 5, we identify the characteristics of the SRM team, a dedicated group, working under the direction of and reporting to the CRO, that coordinates and carries out the work of SRM. These teams systematically search for weak signals in the firm's market, industry, and broader environment that portend potential strategic risks. As we describe, the team complements their external scanning with rich and frequent interactions with business units or functions potentially impacted by those emerging risks. The team maps those potential strategic risks onto the Strategic Uncertainty Decision Map, a tool unique to our model of SRM. This map gives the SRM team, and the senior leaders to whom they report, a quick and easy way to interpret relevant weak signals and emerging strategic risks.

Chapter 6 provides leaders with more tangible tools to assess and manage emerging strategic risks. We'll present three tools that, when used in concert, facilitate deep understanding of emerging strategic risks and uncertainties in sensible, action-oriented ways and enable effective management. As risks mature, uncertainty begins to resolve and the nature of the impact becomes more calculable. Scenario planning exercises empower teams to identify potential futures and to outline the general contours of possible outcomes. Scenario plans give decision makers structured space to think expansively about general response strategies, activities that would create value across multiple potential futures.

Wargaming is the second tool in the SRM kit, with the goal of action plan creation targeted at a concrete version of a future scenario. Using stakeholder role-play techniques over several iterations of action–reaction exercises, teams develop a response pattern and observe the consequences of their hypothetical investments for the behavior of others. This type of simulation aids in understanding default mind-sets, fostering trial and error in a low-cost environment.

Our Strategic Risk Ownership Map complements the Strategic Uncertainty Decision Map. As strategic risks evolve, the organization moves from monitor-and-understand mode to manage-and-respond mode. This map identifies which organizational actors have direct responsibility for managing and responding to strategic risks and provides some detail about specific actions and timelines. It offers a snapshot of the internal risk management processes under way at any given point in time, connecting those implementing strategies with those responsible for its formulation. In so doing, we aim to close the strategy–execution gap.

Chapter 7 applies the tools of SRM to an emerging set of strategic risks: the transformational changes taking place in the automobile industry. We focus on three related changes that have the power to fundamentally alter our economic and social lives—the development of autonomous vehicles, the rise of ridesharing as a viable alternative to vehicle ownership, and the shift from petroleum to electricity as a fuel. We consider how these uncertainties create strategic risks for three companies, none of which produce automobiles, and show how the logic and tools of SRM can help them successfully adapt to a radically new world.

There is a hard reality embedded in setting up an effective SRM system: it requires large amounts of time, energy, and human and financial capital. Nonetheless, the potential payoffs far exceed the costs. While establishing an effective system is difficult enough, keeping that system running and contributing to winning strategic outcomes requires sustained effort. Chapter 8 takes on the two biggest obstacles to SRM becoming a meaningful and lasting organizational contributor: culture and communication.

Risk and culture, whether implicitly or explicitly recognized, are inextricably intertwined in organizations. Years of consulting work have shown us that, beyond the processes and committees, cultural attitudes toward risk itself can ultimately make or break an ERM program. Peter Drucker admonished us to remember that "culture eats strategy for breakfast." It is therefore reasonable to conclude that leaders must weave SRM into the cultural fabric of the organization. Since existing management control processes contribute to circumscribing the full cultural tapestry, this also means interlacing risk considerations directly into those processes. Absent such an assimilation, SRM is destined to have a limited shelf life.

Promoting rigorous and ongoing consideration of uncertainty is a big leap for organizations that normally default to uncertainty absorption habits. Cultures often can impede the serious consideration of strategic risks through a series of cautionary tales and taboos against extolling the potential gains from uncertainty.

Culture also underlies communication, the second important element for creating a truly dynamic system. It instructs workers on what types of information should be shared, and when, and acts as a powerful filter of the flow to senior management. Cultural norms also speak to who should carry messages upward, and they install credibility and legitimacy checks for discerning what's worth hearing and what's not. Sustainable SRM programs work within and leverage culture and its norms to embed themselves into the everyday life of the firm. We introduce a final tool, the Risk Reporting Matrix, to frame and guide these efforts.

Chapter 9 presents our concluding thoughts on SRM and the fusion between strategy and risk as we go to press. Much of what we propose is intended to have timeless value. Other elements will serve as timely prompts to move forward and begin the journey to SRM. We have faith that you'll implement the timely now and find continued value in the timeless.

Conclusion

In the beginning, Bill Rasmussen had no idea whether enough viewers would tune in to make ESPN viable. He felt, along with his investors, that the potential for competitive advantage justified making the attempt. *SportsCenter* neutralized the greatest strategic risks to the fledgling network through low costs and sufficient programming content to build a solid viewer base. We know now that *SportsCenter* helped ESPN resolve customer uncertainty in its favor, in a big way. ESPN became the undisputed leader in sports television. We also know, today, that ESPN's position is anything but secure, due in no small part to the rise of social media and video streaming. Viewers may get for free what they once paid to access. ESPN faces a different set of strategic risks that could undo the network or could open the door to a new level of excellence.

Your company may have much in common with ESPN. You may be, metaphorically, in 1979, looking to neutralize a clear threat to your survival or to capitalize on uncertainty to create a competitive advantage. You may mirror ESPN today and face an emerging set of strategic risks about the viability of your core competitive advantages, brought on by new competitors in the world of online and on-demand media.

Wherever you are, strategic risks abound. We believe that by facing and responding to those risks with the tools we provide in this book, your organization can leverage strategic risks in a way that builds competitive advantage. We'll begin our study by looking at a company with a long history of facing and mastering strategic risk: the Walt Disney Company.

CHAPTER 2

Strategic Risk: Uncertainties That Impact Competitive Advantage

We introduced the concept of strategic risks in chapter 1. In this chapter, we'll clearly define strategic risks and explain the three interrelated elements that transform uncertainty into strategic risk: external changes, a company's responses to those changes, and the passage of time. Strategic risks can threaten competitive advantage, or it can create opportunities to extend or strengthen it. Our discussion begins with the Walt Disney Company and two strategic risks it faced in the mid-1980s.

· · · · ·

Michael Eisner assumed the title of chief executive officer of the Walt Disney Company, and Frank Wells became the company's chief operating officer (COO), on September 15, 1984. Disney had barely survived a hostile takeover attempt and, after paying a $328 million ransom to corporate raider Saul Steinberg, the board knew that the company needed new leadership. Stanley Gold, advisor to Roy Disney in the battle for the Magic Kingdom, articulated the need: "What's been wrong with [Disney] over the past twenty years is that it hasn't been run by the crazies. It needs to be run by the crazies again. . . . We're talking about creative crazies. That's what we ought to have. We can always hire MBA talent."[1]

Technically, master of business administration talent did not drive the company to disaster, as none of Disney's senior leaders had MBAs. Nonetheless, an MBA mind-set that valued tactical management over strategic thinking and short-term financial returns over creative risk taking had brought Disney to the brink of breakup. The mind-set had taken hold almost two decades earlier, in December of 1966, with the unexpected death of Walt Disney, the company's "creative crazy." Walt's successors Roy Disney (CEO 1929–1971), Don Tatum (CEO 1971–1976), Card Walker (CEO 1976–1983), and son-in-law Ron Miller (CEO 1983–1984) lacked that inventive spark. Disney devolved from a forward-looking, out-the-windshield company to one that peered through a rearview mirror, obsessed with implementing Walt's dreams and visions rather than creating new ones.

Walt's last dream was to develop a new theme park in Florida and rectify a mistake the company had made in the early 1950s. Industry experts at the time referred to the project that later became Disneyland as "Disney's Folly," a destination theme park where families could come and immerse themselves in a magic kingdom through rides, attractions, and encounters with the fabled Disney characters roaming the park.[2] The experts had a point, one that made sense if you looked in the rearview mirror. Amusement parks were a local draw. Without an efficient system to move people around the country, it seemed unlikely that Walt's venture would reach beyond its roots in southern California. The Dwight D. Eisenhower National System of Interstate and Defense Highways—the U.S. interstate system—was just a set of drawings, as were the plans for commercial jet aircraft. Disneyland seemed destined for only limited success.

Walt financed the project himself, through selling television content to the upstart ABC network, and scraped together enough to purchase 160 acres of orange groves in Anaheim and to finance construction. Disneyland opened in July of 1955 and welcomed sixty thousand paying visitors the first month. Walt proved his critics very wrong; Disneyland was an immediate, unprecedented success. By 1960, a short five years after opening day, more than 20 million people had visited the park, exceeding the population of the entire state of California at the time.[3] Success brought a new round of challenges, however. A series of inexpensive motels, fast-food restaurants, neon signs, and shops selling cheap merchandise soon rimmed Disneyland, and the company did not own enough land to create its own lodging and dining options at the scale the park required. Disney had, ironically, underinvested in real estate.

Walt would not make the same mistake twice. By June 1965, when a reporter for the *Orlando Sentinel* broke the story, Disney had surreptitiously purchased more than twenty-seven thousand acres of Florida swampland for a total of about $5.5 million, or close to $200 per acre. Whatever the next park would eventually become, it could occupy a footprint almost 170 times larger than the original Disneyland site.[4] Overnight, Disney became a real estate development company first and a creative company second. With Walt's death, that transformation accelerated, as Roy Disney and other leaders had little creative talent to offer. Real estate development was in their corporate wheelhouse, and they settled into a comfortable strategy of completing Walt's dream park.

By 1984, the company had developed 3,500 acres and set aside another 7,500 acres as a nature preserve. That left approximately sixteen thousand acres of undeveloped Florida land sitting on the balance sheet. From a financial standpoint, disposal of those acres would generate around $2 billion in revenue, for a capital gain of 400%. Content, films, and TV brought in more than $160 million a year, though this revenue stream masked the underutilization of its impressive library of twenty-five animated features, 119 live-action films, and more than five hundred cartoons and TV episodes.[5] *Snow White* and *The Rescuers*, both reissued in 1983, brought in $51 million, just under one-third of the unit's box office receipts. Put simply, the combined company's performance, in terms of return on assets, underperformed what each of its units could earn separately.

Disney shares at the time traded in the neighborhood of $50, far short of an estimated liquidation value of $100 per share. Investor Saul Steinberg noted the gap, acquired about 12% of Disney stock, and pursued a hostile takeover. He planned to sell the once storied but now cratered film division and its extensive, dormant library, divest the unused Florida land, and keep the theme parks and their $200 million of annual net income for his troubles. Disney, widely recognized as a true American icon, now faced the existential threat of being broken up and sold piecemeal. Over the next four months, Disney fought for its life as an independent company. Part of that battle involved changes in the C-suite, replacing a team mired in the past with one intent on creating a vibrant future.

Eisner and Wells, the "creative crazies" hired to save Disney, looked to the film library as the first place to unlock value. They felt that the key might lie in the emerging home video market, with sales to video rental outlets and directly to consumers. By 1984, a new technology, the VCR, appeared ready to take off. A "format war" over competing technology platforms VHS and Betamax had been raging. As 1984 drew to a close, VHS emerged victorious, with an approximately 80% market share of annual unit sales, up from nothing a decade earlier.

VCR sales had grown from twenty thousand units in 1975 to more than 29 million units in 1984. Estimates indicated that one in ten American homes owned a VCR, and the number was expected to grow over the next few years.[6] The number of video rental stores had grown dramatically, too, from seven thousand in 1982 to twenty thousand, although many of these were mom-and-pop grocery stores that rented just a few titles. Industrywide, videocassette sales for 1983 totaled $330 million, which was one-eighth of the domestic box office receipts for the year. Optimistic projections had the market growing to $1 billion by 1990.[7]

Even so, this video market had a significant downside. First and foremost, as Walt had learned with the loss of his initial character, Oswald the Lucky Rabbit, in 1927, ownership of copyrights and other intellectual property was crucially important to competitive advantage. If Disney gave up control of copyrights, it risked its most valuable strategic asset—its stable of characters. Piracy was a big concern, and the VCR was, in one sense, nothing more than a convenient tool to ease the life of an intellectual property rogue. A single, revenue-generating copy might turn into hundreds of nonrevenue copies. Disney also worried about cannibalization. If viewers could rent the movies at home, or worse yet own them, they would find little reason to attend the periodic theatrical rereleases of the Disney classics. In that sense, the company would be jeopardizing a long-term income stream, by way of reissue, for an assumed smaller gain in current income.

But home video had an upside as well. Most of the more than 650 titles in the Disney vault earned nothing. Releasing them for home viewing would provide an immediate boost to Disney's anemic film revenues. Even a modest release effort could equal or exceed the revenue generated by the existing strategy of timed reissue. Indeed, 1984's rerelease of *The Jungle Book* had brought in $20 million during a four-week run, and Disney believed it could garner $100 million through the release of the classic in the home video market.[8]

Instead of cannibalizing future sales of Disney films, home video might present economies of scope and create customers hungry for more Disney products, from merchandise to a dedicated cable channel to theme park visits. Rather than dilute the brand, Disney videos in the home would give customers a daily touch point with Disney magic. Finally, as the number of VCRs in the United States increased, the risk of piracy should actually decrease, given the wide availability of the original versions.

Eisner and Wells opted for the upside potential, and Disney entered the home video market in a big way over the next few years. *Pinocchio* (1985) sold well at a list price of $29.95. Clever marketing themes, such as "Bring Disney home for good," helped create demand for *Sleeping Beauty* (1986), and access to sales channels through mass retailers like Target and Walmart propelled *Cinderella* to $100 million in sales in 1988. In 1985, Disney estimated the upside of the total home video market at $1 billion by 1990; by 1992, Disney's own home video unit generated $1.1 billion in revenue. Total industry sales topped $5.1 billion in 1990, and in 1997, seven of the top ten videocassette titles came from Disney.[9]

Strategic Risk

For us, Disney's experience illustrates the nature and notion of strategic risk. A *strategic risk* is any exposure (event, occurrence, or situation) and the associated uncertainty that foundationally threatens or enhances a company's competitive advantage or its viability as a going concern. An exposure is the combined interaction of external events and internal responses over a long period of time. Both of Disney's strategic risk exposures followed this same pattern.

Several interactions over time laid the groundwork for the Steinberg takeover crisis. While the market loved *Disneyland* (an external event), Disney was short on land, which led the company to go "long" on land in Florida, both in acquisition and in management attention (a string of internal actions), and to realize the appreciation of the acreage (the passage of time). Risk managers tend toward discrete risk classifications in their thinking, whether these are brand, ethical, financial, natural disaster, operational, political, reputational, or technology classifications (to name a few). Virtually any type of risk can metastasize into a threat or materialize as an opportunity. Risks become strategic when they have the magnitude and centrality to threaten or enhance the core competitive advantage of the firm.

External Change: The PEST Model

Francis J. Aguilar (1932–2013) taught at the Harvard Business School for more than three decades.[10] His book *Scanning the Business Environment*, based on his award-winning 1967 doctoral dissertation, explained how senior management operating in a complex world "gains relevant information about events occurring outside the company in order to guide the company's future course of action."[11] He developed an acronym to highlight four critical sources of strategic information, ETPS, which stood for *economic, technological, political,* and *social* forces. Analysts, consultants, and scholars would later rearrange those letters into an easy mnemonic, PEST. Each PEST element represents a "tectonic plate" in the underlying structure of markets and meets our criteria for a source of strategic risk by capturing important sources of change in the external environment.

The *political* plate includes changes originating in government. Forces driving political change begin with philosophical and policy orientations, and at the highest level of abstraction they reflect a preference for libertarianism versus activism. These preferences become embodied in the executive, legislative, and judicial branches as well as in the administrative state, finding expression in enacted laws and regulations. Regulatory policies, legislative actions, and the attendant judicial interpretations create and maintain long-term constraints that define the boundaries for permissible business models, practices, and strategies.

Economic elements of the model begin with the microeconomic realities of supply and demand for goods and services, production costs, market prices, consumer incomes, demand curves, and elasticities. Market structure and industry segmentation fit here and define competitive attractiveness according to the threat of entry, competitive rivalry, the presence of substitute products, supplier power, and buyer power. Macroeconomic trend elements such as global trade balances, inflation, interest rates, gross domestic product growth, and unemployment also bring about strategic threats and opportunities.

The *social* category houses demographic and other fixed features of a society and includes data concerning birth rates, levels of educational attainment, income distribution, and other markers of class distinction. Consumer tastes and preferences fit here as well. Everyday factors such as urban versus suburban living, family size, and marital status aggregate to impact markets and create stability or volatility in industries from automobiles to housewares to zippers. As deeply held societal values and norms—close cousins of tastes and preferences—evolve over time, social tectonics will give rise to strategic uncertainty.

Technological change deals with advancements that either assist or replace people in the production and delivery of goods and services. Industrial invention (first-time creation) and innovation (improvements to existing products) both drive technological change. The speed and rate of meaningful innovation, such as between successive generations of a product, impacts the sustainability of existing strategies, while the overall speed and trajectory of invention signals strategic risks to the viability of current sources of competitive advantage.

Three of these forces—politics, economy, and technology—can be considered "hardware" environmental factors, having specific, clearly measurable, tangible manifestations, such as written regulations (politics), interest rates or money (economy), and microprocessors (technology). Together, PET determines the supply-side fitness of strategies. Disney's video library valuation, for instance, depends on the robustness of the intellectual property protections offered by governments, consumer demand for their family of animated characters, and the company's flexibility in dealing with technological innovations such as VCRs or, later, digitization.

The social factor denotes a "software" environmental force, which is broader, more difficult to measure, and often incorporates intangible elements such as national mood or customer tastes and preferences. Social change primarily acts on the demand side, as attitudes, norms, and values all work to mold and modify what constitutes "value" in exchange. Value can have both permanent and temporary elements, and company strategies can seek to exploit either. Disney's strategy in the past and present relies on relatively stable attitudes and values that define family entertainment in animated films or in visits to its parks and vacation properties. In contrast, its live-action remakes depend on hitting more fleeting preferences for comedies, dramas, and adventure films.

EXTERNAL ELEMENTS AND DOWNSIDE STRATEGIC RISKS

The PEST components of the environment define and shape both the demand and the supply conditions that managers face as they formulate and then implement strategies. In a real sense, the PEST elements provide the firm with a set of guardrails that define appropriate answers to strategy's four questions.

Changes in any PEST element moves those guardrails, which invites new answers to the four questions. When those guardrails narrow and become more rigid, past strategic choices made by managers create the conditions for exposure to the emergence of strategic risks.

Disney's leaders made choices over the 1960s and 1970s about how quickly to develop their land in Florida and how deeply to focus their energy on real estate. They chose to develop the land methodically and to focus their attention heavily on growing the theme park business. In many ways, Disney's choices reflect the benign and bountiful U.S. economic environment of the 1950s and 1960s. Investors valued revenue growth, and executives felt little pressure to be hyperefficient managers of the assets on their books. For Disney, theme parks had better prospects and more appeal than a stagnant film division.

By the mid-1970s, however, the economic world turned from beneficent to hostile. Stagflation, the toxic combination of high inflation and low growth, rising global competition, oil price shocks, and a flat stock market created a new mind-set among investors, and profits became paramount. This rising economic concern, coupled with a powerful financial technology instrument, the high-yield (junk) bond, and an existing set of politicolegal doctrines about the fiduciary duties of corporate managers, birthed an aggressive model and actor: the hostile takeover and the corporate raider.

Disney's decisions to heavily prioritize the progress of Walt Disney World made strategic sense in the somnambulant business environment of the previous decades. By the early 1980s, Disney had created and delivered huge value to consumers with profit-producing theme parks, and as a result, it had generated a cash-rich balance sheet. A fat balance sheet, when paired with nonproducing land assets, a film library, and a stable of branded characters that gathered more dust than dollars, formed a perfect bull's-eye target on Disney's corporate back. The door of opportunity to liberate revenues, cash flows, and earnings was opened and fueled the takeover bid.

EXTERNAL ELEMENTS AND UPSIDE STRATEGIC RISKS

Environmental change both narrows and widens guardrails. VCRs were not just a technological innovation; their appearance also represented a shift in the political, economic, and social landscape. VCR technology expanded opportunities to sell movies, although the major studios failed to see this possibility at first. Instead, they viewed consumers' ability to record content for home use as a violation of copyright protections and sought legal remedies. Through the 1984 ruling in *Sony v. Universal*, a political factor change occurred.[12] The U.S. Supreme Court established that the "time shifting" capability that VCRs provided—that is, the ability to record a program for later viewing—did not violate copyright protections.

Time shifting was also an economic change. It allowed consumers to do a significant job in a very different way, since they could now view programming on their own schedule rather than on the schedule dictated by the networks. Time shifting fit with social changes that had created a much more mobile and time-constrained set of consumers. As the national freeway system opened up in the 1950s and 1960s, so did opportunities for consumers to travel faster and farther to reach entertainment options, such as amusement parks or collegiate and professional sporting events. Newfound mobility and more choices, combined with the entry of many women into the workforce in the 1970s, increased the scarcity—and the value—of family time for entertainment and relaxation.

The film industry viewed the VCR as a strategic threat, in terms of potential copyright violation, pirating of content, and the potential cannibalization of theater visits. Theater attendance had been on a steady decline, in percentage terms, since the end of World War II. In 1945, 60% of Americans visited theaters weekly, both for entertainment and for the newsreels that provided information about the war. By 1983, the year before the Disney takeover crisis, that number had dwindled to 10%.[13] VCRs represented one more reason for people to not go to the movies; hence the fierce opposition from studio executives.

These executives failed to see the potential upside the VCR offered. Television viewership had actually driven much of the decline in theater visits. In 1945, fewer than ten thousand homes had a television and 60% of Americans went the movies every week. A decade later, more than 30 million homes had a TV and movie attendance had dropped by half. By 1960, 90% of American households had a television but fewer than one in five went to the movies every week. In the early 1980s, most homes had multiple television sets and the home became the entertainment epicenter.[14]

Home video, a market Disney would help to build aggressively throughout the 1980s, meshed with a strong and long-term customer preference for consuming entertainment at home. If managed adeptly, studios might leverage this alternative method of doing an important job in ways that complemented, rather than cannibalized, their theatrical release schedule. To navigate the transition, Disney relied on a series of decisions that broke sharply with how former leaders thought about and managed risk.

Internal Responses

A firm's internal responses to shifts in the PEST forces constitutes the second generator of strategic risk. As companies respond to these changes, uncertainty absorption begins. Our experience reveals three common actions that emerge, each consistent with the principles of uncertainty absorption: *deny*, *define away*, and *detach*. Each of these *D*s creates an illusion of certainty in the face of an uncertain future.

DENY

A primary response we've seen (with senior leaders not exempt) is simple and outright denial. Too many executives create illusory strategic certainty through one of two logic chains: either the risk will never materialize or, if it does, it will have no substantial effect on strategy. When in this mode, it's highly doubtful that the organization has invested in risk management tools beyond what traditional risk management offers. Denial differs greatly from a careful analysis of whether the consequences of risk fit within an existing risk appetite framework, and it almost never considers the capacity of the organization to withstand or benefit from uncertainty. Denial offers a shortcut to thinking about risk. Outright denial won't always be acceptable, which leads to the second response.

DEFINE AWAY

Uncertainty becomes somewhat diminished here, as all risk is forced to align operationally. Real, material uncertainty and substantial risks do exist, but the leaders tend to expect functional silos to respond to and manage threats. Interest rate risk impacts finance, compliance risk is the domain of audit, business development risk hits marketing and sales, and people and process risks concern individual business units. Absent gross mismanagement, these functional risks normally won't morph into system-wide uncertainty. Other risks that are larger in scope, such as political risks, affect a limited number of functional units, and they in turn must shield the whole firm.

It took ERM as a sense-making process to break through silos, to connect risks and communicate about them across the organization, to introduce appetite and capacity considerations into risk discussions, and to reposition corporate insurance buying as one of many, and not the primary, solution. We recognize ERM as a great leap forward, indeed. Yet one unintended consequence was a disconnect in its original design and deployment, which short-circuits effectiveness and contributes to the third response.

DETACH

When executives attempt to mitigate risks solely through traditional means, to handle them operationally at the functional/business unit level, or to rely on an ERM program as the sole answer to organizational uncertainty, there still is a "last mile" problem: the lack of a hardwired connection between risk management and strategy formulation. This gives rise to what we characterize as a *detach* position. Detach builds on the illusory but very real belief that a deep consideration of risks to and risks of strategic commitments narrows the range of options executives will be able to consider. When leaders detach strategy from risk, they run the risk of expanding the strategy–execution gap. Most TRM approaches and ERM programs have little influence on strategic decision making because their place in the hierarchy constrains them to audit, compliance, or control functions. Paradoxically, detach engages executive teams in uncertainty absorption as they filter out VUCA in strategies, budgets, and directives sent to those below them.

INTERNAL DECISIONS AND DOWNSIDE STRATEGIC RISKS

Deny, define away, and detach form a management behavior triumvirate that exposes firms to progressively increasing downside strategic risk. This response pattern assumes that the current state of the organization equips it as well for the future as it does for today. That can only be true if, first, current activities actually do fit with the PEST environment and, second, if the current environment won't change in any substantive way. As we noted earlier, the essence of strategic risk lies in the fact that one or more elements of the PEST model have changed. Even though the change might appear slight today, it has the potential to become consequential in the future.

When Walt Disney died, in 1966, the company lost a founder who drove the company by looking out the front windshield. Whether out of respect for the founder, a lack of confidence, or a skill set steeped in finance and administration, Roy Disney and his successors navigated the future by looking in the rearview mirror. They seemed to ponder "What would Walt have done?" If Walt saw no risk in a huge land purchase, then why should they? Developing the Florida project completely occupied their energy, their time, and many, many dollars. With so much on their minds, the risk of the size of the purchase proved easy to compartmentalize, even by the late 1970s, when troubling stories of junk bond financing and Wall Street raiders should have brought laser-like attention to their own balance sheet.

Disney's leaders fell into a myopic trap around the internal demands of real estate development, which had dire consequences for its film entertainment business. Roy arranged for a $400 million loan in 1965 to begin developing the Florida property. It was a merely a down payment on a total cost to open the Florida park that exceeded $1.2 billion.[15] In contrast, Disney had spent only $6 million, in 1964, to produce *Mary Poppins*, its highest-grossing film to date.[16] This investment differential foreshadowed internal resource allocation at the company for the next two decades.

INTERNAL DECISIONS AND UPSIDE STRATEGIC RISKS

Denial, define away, and detach behaviors inhibit the ability to prepare for and alleviate downside risk. They also constrain leaders' abilities to see and then act on the upside potential surrounding strategic uncertainty. Executives rarely deny the *possibility* of an opportunity. They may, as a matter of convenience, invoke a current-state decision-making calculus to evaluate the *plausibility* or *probability* that their company can, or should, try to exploit it. Disney executives shared the industry sentiment that inspired the suit against VCR technology, a view that saw no opportunity, only threat. The threat manifested itself in the loss of current box office receipts, should moviegoers choose video, and in the future lost revenue from the rerelease of classic films.

By 1984, the lack of winning new productions and the reliance on reissues kept the door of Disney's film vault locked and heavily guarded. Rereleases represented a large chunk of the division's total revenue and, given that Disney had already amortized the production costs of these films decades before, contributed to outsize film profits. The logic of reissue had ossified around a long-term model that produced predictable revenues through tightly controlled showings. *Pinocchio* brought in $26 million at the box office with its 1984 reissue, and the firm could bank on that same revenue, adjusted for inflation and population growth, every seven years or so, when the next generation of kids was ready for the movie.

VCRs presented an entirely different value proposition. Disney might get close to $26 million from a single release of *Pinocchio* on home video, but with the potential loss of the future revenue stream. Nonetheless, Eisner and Wells, needing revenue now rather than seven years hence, decided to enter home video in a big way. In 1985, the company put *Pinocchio* out on home video and, with very little marketing support, sold six hundred thousand copies at $29.95, for a gain of $18 million.[17] Disney had learned an important lesson, one that unveiled a modern cadence for Hollywood producers. Movies in the theater drove demand for home video, so now it would be theater first, home video soon thereafter. Disney would employ the sequence repeatedly, to great benefit.

Seeking the upside opportunities of strategic risks calls for truly tough-minded decision making. It demands the willingness to confront and work past those existing frames, sacred cows, and closely held assumptions that denial, define away, and detach seek to protect. In tandem, decision makers have to recalibrate potential downsides to see these opportunities clearly. If the VCR had been a bust, Disney still could have reissued *Pinocchio* seven years later, with little worry about cannibalization from cassettes that operated on a failed technological platform.

Many upside strategic risks begin this way, as small bets on emerging technologies, untested business models, or small pockets of customer demand. Early entry is often the preferred route. It may offer little in the way of initial revenue growth ($18 million on $1.5 billion in total Disney revenue is just over 1%) but much in terms of learning and the ability to shape the eventual nature of the external opportunity. Those initial decisions prove critical, because they set the company on a developmental trajectory, which brings us to the third pillar of strategic risk, the importance of time.

The Passage of Time

The Disney story illustrates a third essential feature of strategic risks: they mature and manifest over time. Walt and his team began their search for land in Florida in 1964, and those seeds took two decades to flower into a takeover threat. Sony developed the first consumer-grade VCR in 1969, but it would take fifteen years to resolve the technological issues (the format war) and the political ones (around the legality of the VCR) and create a viable market for home video. Time lags are inherent to strategic risks, whether positive or negative. Early seeds slowly bloom and mature into full-blown exposures, impacted by the process of *path dependence*.

Path dependence is the simple assumption that history matters, that today's actions and decisions influence those of tomorrow. Consider three investments, A, B, or C. The principle of path dependence means that our resolution to pursue A today (choosing one among several options) influences whether B or C is the better choice tomorrow. B makes option D more attractive in the next phase, while C implies E. Investment D leads to F, E to G, and so on. The decision at A initiates a route that, over time, deepens into rut and finally becomes a canyon as "nonadjacent" investments—such as choosing F after C—become prohibitively expensive.

LOCK-IN AND LOCK-OUT

Investments along a given pathway lead to lock-in. Lock-in results from two different processes, the economic one just described and a cognitive process that matters for both individuals and organizations. Simply put, we get better at what we do more of. Adam Smith recognized this learning process as a valuable by-product of the division of labor. When people focus on a single or small number of related tasks, they become more efficient.[18] They'll also experiment with other ways of doing things, and this combination of efficiency and innovation generates performance gains. Personal satisfaction and fulfillment reinforce this loop, as we all tend to do more of what we like, so pathways become ruts and eventually canyons.

Financial and learning aspects of path dependence mean that lock-in deepens competitive advantages. Brands become more valuable, and relationships with customers more intimate, when a company locks in. Average costs fall because each marginal investment builds on a complementary core, and relationships with suppliers and partners become more productive. Lock-in improves strategic position and financial performance. Superior performance cements the commitment to strategy as it begets the self-reinforcing belief in the "goodness" of the strategy and the wisdom of management in executing it.

The economics of lock-in have a flip side, though: lock-out. Just as path dependence makes one set of investments more attractive, it also makes other investment options less attractive. If a company has limited resources to invest in the future—and management time and attention is a limited resource—then locking in to one path naturally locks the company out of alternative ones. Jumping pathways proves difficult, getting out of ruts more difficult, and getting out of a canyon exponentially harder. Lock-in enhances chosen competitive advantages at the same time as it degrades, through lock-out, the potential value along abandoned pathways.

Disney's experience in film provides the quintessential example of lock-out. The company chose to invest heavily in theme parks, which led to significantly reduced investments in filmed entertainment and the gutting of Disney's core business of animated films. Film and TV as a share of revenue fell from 55% in 1965 to barely 13% in 1983. Motion pictures generated only $79 million, $63 million of which came from three reissues: *The Rescuers*, *The Sword in the Stone*, and *Snow White and the Seven Dwarfs*. When the crisis hit, in 1984, Disney generated zero dollars in box office revenue from new animation.[19]

PATH DEPENDENCE AND DOWNSIDE STRATEGIC RISK

Downside strategic risk, exposures that destroy competitive advantage and threaten viability of the business, arises because path dependence replaces flexibility with strategic rigidity. Path dependence turns dark when lock-in and lock-out discourage, and eventually prevent, departure from the path, which has now become a crevasse. When the company finds itself deep inside a strategic gorge, PEST changes make business life treacherous.

Walt's Florida land grab set in motion a series of decisions that elevated real estate development and caused filmed entertainment to languish. The passage of time cemented these decisions, but time played one more role in the crisis that would face Disney two decades later. When the Orlando purchase closed, Disney pledged $400 million to turn the swamp into an international vacation destination. In turn, local officials allowed Disney to become its own municipality, the Reedy Creek Improvement District. The company committed to engineer a fifty-five-mile system of canals to control water levels on the site, to build an electrical power facility, and to set up a system to remove garbage.[20]

Over time, and as a consequence of developing the 7,500 acres that would become Walt Disney World, the value of the rest of the Disney parcel, as well as land in neighboring Orlando, rose. Orlando and the surrounding

Orange County population grew 30% and 37%, respectively, in the decade from 1970 to 1980.[21] In-migration and the development of Disney World naturally combined to lift property values. Disney's balance sheet, following standard accounting rules, recorded the value of the land at its purchase price, somewhere north of $5 million. By 1984, the undeveloped land around Disney World carried a $2 billion liquidation value—four hundred times the amount recorded on the balance sheet.[22]

That $2 billion liquidation value acted as bait to hostile takeover sharks such as Saul Steinberg. Disney shares were trading between $50 and $65 during Steinberg's pursuit. The company had just under 38 million shares outstanding, which adds up to a market value of $1.9 billion to $2.5 billion.[23] Disney could be acquired on the cheap, with most of the sales price recovered by selling just the undeveloped land in Florida, without exploiting the value literally locked up in the film vault. Disney was an extremely attractive target to Wall Street, and the passage of time enhanced, rather than diminished, the company's perverse beauty.

PATH DEPENDENCE AND UPSIDE STRATEGIC RISK

The upside of path dependence comes as companies make commitments over time that competitors won't follow early and then can't replicate as time goes by. Path dependence also generates upside strategic risk—the opportunity to create or extend competitive advantage—because it helps resolve demand, supply, and use uncertainty. New business opportunities succeed when their functionality creates a win for customers, either by doing a current job better or by performing a necessary job that couldn't be done at all before. When new products or services emerge, the use value is an unknown. That uncertainty remains until a sufficient number of customers have enough experience with it to determine what jobs the product or service really does better than its competitors.

During the Beta/VHS format war, use value uncertainty took center stage. The two technologies cost about the same and offered similar picture quality. Sony made its Beta cassettes smaller, betting that customers preferred compactness. JVC offered a larger cassette that had double the recording/playback capacity of Beta, initially two hours versus one, and then four versus two. At the dawn of the VCR era, there was no video rental market; the first store opened in late 1977, three years after VCR machines first appeared. Interestingly, the R (recorder) in VCR drove early sales, and the ability to double recording time created substantial use value because it matched the two-hour movies or three-hour sporting events that early adopters wanted to record. Longer playback time mattered more than compact size.

Use uncertainty was settled as early as 1978, when VHS achieved a 60% market share. Next, demand uncertainty—how many customers wanted the value the product offered—could be resolved. With a dominant technology now established, the market exploded. From 1977 to 1983, just before Disney entered the market, annual sales of VCRs grew from 763,000 units to 18.2 million units, with VHS enjoying a 75% share. As Eisner and Wells assumed the helm at Disney, they bet that the home video market would be huge and that VHS would be the dominant format. Their entry into the home video market helped work out the last critical uncertainty: supply uncertainty. Consumers would soon find ample titles, some made exclusively for home video, to justify the investment in a VCR. By 1989, global sales of VCRs hit 45 million units.[24]

Home video represented a major strategic opportunity for Disney. When Eisner and Wells took over, Disney's total revenue stood at $1.5 billion; within eight years, their home video business generated $1.1 billion on its own. It also drove merchandise purchases and created excitement to visit the parks. Margins were extremely high because the company had amortized the production costs of Disney classics years ago. Copying tapes was cheap and easy, and increased marketing expenses were more than offset. As a result, Disney's return on assets increased from 4% in 1984 to 7% in 1992.

Conclusion

Eisner and Wells built on their early successes at Disney. They oversaw the creation of a new generation of great stories, memorable music, and lovable characters, including Ariel (*The Little Mermaid*); Simba, Timon, and Pumbaa (*The Lion King*); and Belle (*Beauty and the Beast*). They would also expand Disney's creative reach into seemingly "crazy" businesses, such as Broadway plays, Disney on Ice, and the Disney Cruise Line. When Michael Eisner retired, in 2005, Disney's annual revenues had grown from $1.5 billion to $30.8 billion (a 2,000% increase), net income had risen from $294 million to $4.5 billion (up 1,600%), Disney shares sold for $28.40

versus $1.33 in 1984 (adjusted for splits), and the company's market value stood at $57.4 billion, up from $1.9 billion in 1984, a gain of 3,000%.[25]

As we've detailed here, much of Disney's success came from managing strategic risks. Eisner oversaw a media company at a time when technology dramatically expanded the potential richness and reach of the industry. Eisner and Wells embodied craziness, in contrast to the pervasive "MBA logic" that had guided Disney since Walt's death. Perhaps their most valuable contribution was in fashioning a different mental map, or way of viewing the entertainment business. We'll talk more about mental maps in the next chapter, and we begin with an example of how the wrong mental model can torpedo otherwise solid risk management efforts.

CHAPTER 3

SRM at Thirty Thousand Feet: Assumptions, Mental Maps, and Principles

Strategic risk management is a set of principles, processes, teams, and tools that allow firms to manage strategic risks, which are those uncertainties, events, and exposures that create threats to—or opportunities to expand— their core competitive advantages. This chapter takes up the first element of SRM: principles. SRM requires a new management mind-set, or mental map, to link strategy and risk. That mental map builds from four compass points: focus on unknowns, clarify risk capacity and appetite, integrate SRM with other risk functions, and embed SRM in the "strategy complex" of the firm. We begin with a story of a company that employed the wrong mental map.

. . . . .

Shareholders of Man Financial Global (MF Global) rejoiced in March of 2010, when the firm announced the hiring of Jon Corzine as its new CEO. Their exuberance sent shares of the commodities trader skyrocketing more than 10% in a single day.[1] Corzine, former co-CEO of Goldman Sachs, U.S. senator, governor of New Jersey, and successful financial markets trader, had been recruited by one of MF's key investors, Chris Flowers, and other members of the MF board.[2] They saw Corzine as the remedy to the malaise that set in after a trading scandal hit the firm in 2008. The stock gained another 26% in the first three weeks following the celebrity CEO's arrival.[3] Investors looked forward to a new day and a return to profitability for the firm.

MF Global had gone public in 2007, when the British hedge fund Man Group divested its commodities brokerage and futures clearing operation. By 2008, MF's 97 million shares traded at a respectable $31.47, for a capitalization of $3.8 billion. Shares fell 28% when the company announced, in February of that year, that an MF trader in Memphis had lost $141.5 million in rogue trades of wheat futures. The firm's shares continued to tumble, falling almost 80% from their peak before the scandal. MF's regulator, the Commodity Futures Trading Commission, found that "from 2003 to 2008, MF Global failed in four separate instances to ensure that its risk management, supervision and compliance programs comported with its obligations to supervise diligently its business."[4]

The commission directed MF Global to hire outside consulting firms to advise the board about its failed risk management, supervision, and compliance programs. These consultants advised MF to create a robust enterprise risk management program. Included in the recommendations was the advice to hire an experienced chief risk officer, a position that was filled in August 2008. Michael Roseman initiated a full-fledged ERM program, and the firm's investors injected new capital to beef up the balance sheet. The firm also hired a new CEO, Bernie Dan, the former chair of the Chicago Board of Trade.

Dan's hiring coincided with the gale force winds of the 2008–2009 financial crisis and the ensuing Great Recession, and MF's business and stock price continued to languish. Dan resigned in March of 2010, leaving the firm adrift and unprofitable; the commissions the company earned from its core business, the execution of futures trades, did not even cover expenses.[5] The future of the company looked bleak, and, in desperation, the board searched for a strong CEO who could lead the firm back to prosperity. That encouraged Flowers to reach out to Corzine, a larger-than-life former trader.

MF needed a CEO and Corzine needed money, since he'd spent roughly $134 million of his own funds to finance his senate and gubernatorial aspirations. Corzine accepted the MF job after considering it for just three days. MF desperately needed to boost its almost penny-stock share price, as regulators threatened the firm with a further downgrade of its debt to pure junk status, a move that would cripple the small firm's ability to raise capital. Corzine looked forward to returning to his first love, financial trading.

Corzine's trading would happen within with the confines of a textbook ERM program and risk governance measures designed to fuel prudent growth. Roseman reported directly to Corzine, worked in the C-suite, and had unfettered access to the board, all best practices for ERM. Roseman advised the board about whether its operations and trades fit within the board-approved risk appetite and tolerance frameworks. He also established an escalation process, should a need to increase the company's risk appetite and tolerance positions arise due to opportunities resulting from changing financial market conditions.

Corzine immediately realized that the mundane commodities brokerage business would never be the engine that could propel the firm forward. He set about turning MF into a miniature Goldman, an investment bank engaged in its own proprietary trading. Trading began when Corzine personally led the firm into European sovereign debt, the short-term bonds offered by European countries to finance their operations. These bonds carried attractive interest rates, due to the precarious state of finances in many countries as the impact of the financial crisis rippled across the globe. If MF bought the bonds and held them to maturity, the firm would quickly exhaust the meager cash generated by its still barely profitable operations, and MF would have to carry the bonds as assets on the balance sheet. MF needed assets. The problem with the bonds was the mark-to-market rule, which meant that the firm would have to book losses from negative changes in asset values. To sidestep these problems, Corzine employed an esoteric transaction structure to build his position.

Corzine used the bonds as collateral to borrow the money to buy them, a method known as repo-to-maturity (RTM). Accounting rules allowed holders of RTMs to book the potential profits from the transaction—the difference in interest paid by the bonds and the interest paid to the lenders—in the period of the transaction. The RTM structure would generate immediate profits to satisfy the rating agencies, who would then grant MF better credit terms. Quick profits would also boost the stock price and provide potential investors and trading partners with renewed confidence in the firm. Sovereign debt carried risks, but it also allowed MF to quickly report a profit.

In normal times, sovereign debt is extremely low risk. These instruments are issued by nation states that never default, yielding low returns. But

2010 was not normal times, and several European countries, led by Greece, were teetering on the brink of default. The market demanded an interest premium on European sovereign debt to cover this risk. Corzine was convinced that the high interest rates European nations had to pay for their debt ignored the fact that European countries would bail each other out and prevent a default. In fact, in June 2010, the European Union had created the European Financial Stability Facility (EFSF), a bailout fund that would reassure nervous investors about the risk of lending to potentially insolvent states.[6] Indeed, as the problems at MF Global played out, the underlying default risk of the firm's holdings never materialized. Corzine was proved right about that situation. However, he forgot the sage advice attributed to John Maynard Keynes: "The market can remain irrational longer than you can remain solvent."[7]

Irrationality and solvency risk would play out in two ways: margin calls and time to liquidate. Because MF used the bonds to collateralize their own purchase, to cover any shortfalls in the value of the bonds, the firm would have to post margin collateral, in the form of cash or securities, with the London Clearing House (LCH), the firm executing the transactions. The margin started out at a mere 3% of the outstanding bond value, but LCH reserved the right to increase its margin call if the threat of national default rose or if LCH had doubts about MF's quality as a borrower.[8] The RTM structure also created liquidation risk for MF. Since it didn't actually own the bonds, the firm couldn't simply sell its position in the spot market. In the case of a crisis, it might take MF Global weeks, not days, to unwind its position.

By the fall of 2010, MF Global—largely in the person of Jon Corzine—had invested just over $1 billion in European sovereign debt. That position grew to $3.5 billion in early 2011, which sparked action by Roseman. He went to the board with his concerns, and, in a classic showdown, Corzine challenged the board to continue with the purchases or find a new CEO. Either Roseman's or Corzine's vision would carry the day. The board sided with Corzine, and Roseman left the firm in late January. The new CRO, Michael Stockman, saw little risk in the sovereign debt purchases, given the EFSF. MF Global continued to buy bonds through the summer of 2011, eventually assuming a net unhedged position of $6.4 billion.[9]

The risk of country default never materialized, but the other two risks did. Economic conditions in Europe continued to look bleak, and LCH slowly raised its margin calls on MF's holdings as the bonds slipped in value. By the summer of 2011, when the board finally put a stop to bond purchases, the company had $550 million tied up in LCH. Such a large sum created angst about the firm's overall liquidity among MFs rating and regulatory agencies. One of those agencies, the Financial Industry Regulatory Authority, informed MF in late August that the firm would have to set aside an additional $225 million to cover potential losses, which further burdened its cash-strapped balance sheet. By October 2011, margin risk had created an existential crisis at MF—the firm didn't have the cash to withstand any further shocks.

Liquidity risk finished off the firm. Faced with increasing margin calls and a debt rating downgrade, MF realized that its only hope for survival lay either in expeditiously unwinding its positions or in finding a buyer for the firm. The complexity of the actual trades for the European RTMs, some eighty-seven in all, meant that the company required weeks to generate cash. It had days. The firm could not liquidate its position quickly enough. As MF careered toward insolvency, its financial officers apparently crossed a red line. They dipped into customer accounts for a total of $1.6 billion to cover losses on sales and other margin calls. MF became the first trading firm to violate the sacred legal principle of never trading with customers' money. When that news broke, potential buyers of MF fled.

On Halloween of 2011, MF Global filed for bankruptcy. Its bet on growth had gone completely bust.

MF Global died from strategic risk, when the actions of LCH foundationally threatened MFs viability as a going concern. The core uncertainty lay in the differing judgments of Corzine and the managers at LCH about how to respond to the underlying default risk of sovereign debt. Corzine's days in politics had led him to believe, correctly, that the EFSF would prevent default on the sovereign bonds. But he mistakenly assumed that LCH would anchor its liquidity demands to the actual risk of default. LCH, however, adjusted the margin calls based on the *perceived* risk of default, and as Corzine would later regret, perception matters more than reality.

Having the right mental model, or map, proves essential for strategic risk management, the set of principles, processes, teams, and tools that allow firms to manage strategic risks, which are those uncertainties, events, and exposures that create threats to—or opportunities to expand—their core competitive advantages. The core principles that support successful SRM create the contours of good mental maps. Principles undergird process, the structural arrangements and organizational systems that guide SRM teams as they employ tools to identify, monitor, manage, and respond to strategic risks. Principles come first, processes second, people and actions last. The view from thirty thousand feet informs the one at ten thousand feet, which then drives action on the ground.

Mental Maps

Peter Senge defined mental models as "deeply ingrained assumptions, generalizations, or even pictures or images that influence how we understand the world and how we take action."[10] We all have mental models that we build from experience, and we use those models constantly as we make decisions. Models help us make big and little decisions. For example, your assumptions and images about how fast freeways clog or parking lots fill determines when you leave for work and what route you take. Once at work, assumptions about internal or external job candidates, often accompanied by vivid memories of successful or failed hires, inform your decisions about how to fill job openings. Every decision you make about the future incorporates some assumptions. You rely on mental maps for much of what you do.

Mental maps arise from experience. You faced substantial uncertainty about commuting on your first day because you didn't have any baseline for how quickly the parking lot filled. Over time, experience allowed you to turn that uncertainty into risk; the parking situation went from a mere guess to a known average with predictable variation. Today, your mental map does a great job of mitigating the downside risk of arriving late for work.

Mental maps, based on averages and anticipatable variation, help us deal with risk, but they can lead us astray when we face uncertainty. Your mental map may tell you that hiring internal candidates leads to better outcomes, given a history of past hires that supports that judgment. But when you need to hire for a position entailing brand-new skills, your default assumptions can lead to very bad outcomes. If the new position requires skills or knowledge that no internal candidate has, then your map of hiring from within points you in the wrong direction. You'll hire someone without the right skills and hope they can do the job. In this case, hope is not a good strategy.

Thomas Chermack relates a wonderful story that highlights the pitfalls that come from seeking guidance from the wrong mental map. The story concerns the early Spanish explorers sailing to the west coast of North America.[11] The explorers had two goals: first, to increase the wealth of the Spanish Crown by finding gold and laying claim to land; and second, to serve God by preaching the Word and converting natives to the Christian faith. The first ships reached what we now call the southern tip of the Baja California Peninsula as early as 1533.[12] The explorers had cartographic skills and started drawing maps for future voyages that accounted for the inland waterway up the Baja.

By 1635, other explorers had had sailed far enough north to enter the Straits of Juan de Fuca and the upper Puget Sound. These cartographers also saw an inland waterway as far as the eye could see, and their maps reflected this reality. When the official mapmakers back in Spain connected the southern Baja Peninsula with the northern Puget Sound, the entire west coast, what they called California, appeared as an island. Figure 3.1 reproduces the Herman Moll map, a famous depiction of California as an island. This inaccurate map survived for another century, despite reports of a west coast firmly connected to the mainland. The map finally changed in 1747, when the Spanish king issued a royal edict that California was part of the mainland. It's a humorous tale of geographic mishaps, but who really cares?

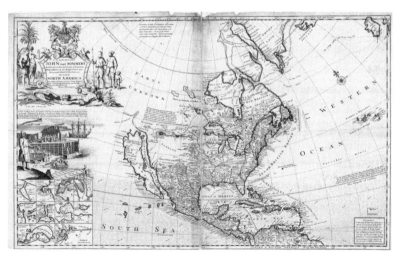

Figure 3.1 Herman Map of North America, 1712

The Spanish missionaries spreading the word of God cared. Groups of missionaries landed in Monterey Bay and prepared for their journey inland. Believing they would eventually reach the coast on the other side of the island, they brought boats with them to cross the inside passage. The boats had to be disassembled and packed by mules across California. Eventually, the missionaries hit the Sierra Nevada mountain range, with its twelve thousand-foot peaks, and after that the parched Nevada desert. They needed lots of equipment, but never a boat. The additional weight and logistical demands of dismantling and transporting boats slowed their progress and resulted in unneeded hardships, failures, disappointments, and deaths. Bad mental maps led to poor strategy and almost impossible execution.

The idea of California as an island arose from a hallmark of uncertainty absorption: the people making the consolidated map of the North American west coast weren't the same ones who charted each section. The executive mapmakers knew they could rely on individual cartographers aboard the ships to create an accurate description of the local territory they saw. The failure came in the process of integrating those individual maps into a larger picture that captured the underlying reality of the new land. Those local mapmakers presented very accurate local maps but failed to communicate that their maps relied on brief and limited encounters with the entirety of the landmass. They absorbed that uncertainty and encouraged an assumption that connected Puget Sound and the Gulf of California through an inland sea.

The failure at MF Global revealed several bad mental maps that guided both Jon Corzine and the board. Corzine had loved trading since his earliest days at Goldman, and at MF he simply employed his Goldman playbook: accumulate a large position in a security to maximize returns. At Goldman, unlike at MF, he could rely on the large diversified asset base of the firm to cover margin calls and volatility, but MF Global had 1% of the market cap of Goldman.[13] MF Global had no safety net to absorb fluctuations in bond pricing and few cash reserves to cover margin calls.

The MF board relied on its own faulty maps. They bet the future of a thousand-plus-employee firm on the skill and dexterity of one trader, based on hopes about the power and skill of one individual to save a company. They also proved quite willing to believe that the long-term liquidity and profitability problems at MF could be solved with a single short-term windfall. The lived experience of most companies, financial or industrial, teaches that these less-than-rational hopes and beliefs almost always prove chimerical. Finally, the board failed to appreciate the massive inherent risk in the RTM purchase mechanism. If a crisis arose, and it did, MF could not unwind its position fast enough to remain solvent.

Given the importance of mental maps in guiding strategy and strategic risk management, we'll spend the rest of the chapter describing the right mental maps to make SRM an effective effort. Successful SRM maps build on four critical pillars that stand as compass points to define and give direction: first, focus on unknowns; second, clarify risk capacity as well as appetite; third, embed SRM with other risk management tools; and fourth, integrate SRM into the strategic decision-making process.

Compass Point 1: Focus on Unknowns, both Known and Unknown

The SRM process identifies and assesses strategic risks so that they can be monitored and managed, either mitigated or exploited. SRM provides a holistic view of key uncertainties that inform strategy, and its primary job lies in finding and framing those uncertainties. Searching out uncertainty is the first principle of the SRM mental map, and to accomplish that task, teams must focus on unknowns.

Donald Rumsfeld, George W. Bush's secretary of defense, differentiated between the known and unknown. He explained: "There are known knowns; there are things we know we know. We also know there are known unknowns; that is to say we know there are some things we do not know. But there are also unknown unknowns—the ones we don't know we don't know. And if one looks throughout the history of our country and other free countries, it is the latter category that tend to be the difficult ones."[14] We'd complete his matrix by adding a fourth category: unknown knowns, things we don't know that we know.

Risk management programs, writ large, collectively deal with and manage different quadrants in the Rumsfeld matrix. Traditional risk management, from insurance and hedges to safety, security, and compliance programs, fit in the first quadrant: known knowns. Management knows that each activity matters and provides protection against real hazards to the organization, and each activity focuses on a known, calculable, and defined peril. These risks invite well-developed management strategies, from risk transfer to active mitigation and management. MF Global had well-developed systems to manage most of its known known risks, from credit to interest rate risk. After the scandal in 2008, it implemented systems to monitor and mitigate sales process risk, to deter rogue trading.

Enterprise risk management, the amalgamation and consideration of risks that span business units or functions, solves the problem of the second quadrant, that of unknown knowns. The full extent, reach, and correlation of these risks may remain unknown to individual managers, although their impact can be aggregated, predicted, and estimated centrally. The relentless grind of day-to-day work keeps managers focused on their sphere of responsibility. Without the active intervention of ERM, few have the time or incentive to consider how his or her actions create or mitigate risk for their compatriots throughout the organization. MF Global developed a state-of-the-art ERM program that alerted the board to excessive risk taking that threatened the viability of the entire enterprise.

The remaining quadrants, known unknowns and unknown unknowns, arguably bound the domain of strategic risk management. Keep in mind that SRM deals primarily with environmental uncertainty, not specific risk categories. Management might be aware of the origins and sources of some of those uncertainties, such as advances in artificial intelligence and machine learning or shifting societal values. However, the fuzzy and unsettled nature of these uncertainties, combined with continuous turbulence in most markets, means that the real impact on an individual company's strategic advantages cannot be calculated or predicted with any degree of precision. At the extreme, for example, when encountering the pivots and revolutions in political systems, neither executive management teams nor gurus can know even the roughest contours until they begin to appear.

Corzine falsely assumed that a known unknown, how a third-party guarantor would react to perceived risk, was actually a known known. He believed that the margin minders at LCH saw the world as he did and would base their margin calls on the actual, underlying risk. He failed to incorporate the importance of perceived versus actual risk as a source of uncertainty. LCH, and many other traders, based their assessments on the uncertainty surrounding the fate of Greece. In 2009, officials revealed a financial black hole in Greece's government budgets and an impending deficit equaling 12% of the country's gross domestic product.

The first Greek debt crisis followed, and the country's fate hung in the balance until 2010, when Germany's Angela Merkel, leader of the European Union's most stable economy, provided last-resort guarantees on Greek bonds. In 2011, just as MF had expanded its portfolio of sovereign debt, Greece announced a budget deficit of more than 13% of GDP.[15] And so began the second Greek crisis. Throughout the summer, a perceived threat of default increased, which raised interest rates on all European sovereign debt instruments, due to a broader perception of heightened default risk. LCH responded by ratcheting up its margin requirements on MF's purchases.

Unknown unknowns represent a particularly virulent form of strategic risk. By definition, they are "UROs" (unidentified risk objects) and remain hidden from detection, absent specific efforts to seek them out. Careful scrutiny of initial signs and signals of unusual threats and systematic monitoring when the first tendrils of trouble break the surface is essential. To paraphrase the legendary Jedi master Obi-Wan Kenobi of *Star Wars* fame, when managers or risk professionals feel a great disturbance in the Force, it's time to pay close attention.

LCH's actions may have surprised Corzine, although we are hard pressed to classify them as unknown unknowns. It's more likely that he had failed to embrace political strategist Lee Atwater's refrain that "perception is reality." In chapters 5 and 6, we'll describe how companies can effectively deal with these vexing uncertainties and get their heads around thinking seriously about unknown unknowns. For now, we emphasize that focusing on what's unknown and uncertain, not what's known and risky, represents the first bedrock principle of SRM.

Compass Point 2: Clarify Risk Capacity and Risk Appetite

If focus on the uncertain and unknown is the foundational principle of an SRM mental map, the next compass point is a close second. MF Global had a risk appetite statement, a description of how much risk the firm would be willing to take, that had been developed well before Corzine began speculating in Eurobonds. Unfortunately, this calculation proved of little value when he confronted the board with an ultimatum: expand the company's risk limitations or he would leave and take a lot of potential profit with him. What MF's board lacked, in addition to some sorely needed intestinal fortitude, was a proper recognition of the firm's risk capacity.

Risk appetite and capacity, foundational ERM tools, often create significant confusion for managers. Novices view the terms as synonymous; however, each captures a different effect on strategic risk. Think of poker and the speculative gains and losses possible. Risk appetite tells a player how much to bet on any given hand, while risk capacity describes the total amount of loss that would drive her from the table. Professional players make sure that their appetite never exceeds their capacity, no matter how lucky they feel or the length of their current streak. If our player fails to know her risk capacity, she'll make poor decisions about risk appetite, taking on more than she can handle in any one bet.

In a strategic sense, risk capacity articulates the central elements of competitive advantage. A loss of advantage "capacity" would gut the strategy. On the other hand, reinforced advantage can cement and enhance the firm's strategic position. Executives should associate risk capacity with the first strategy question: Why do we win with customers? Competitive value resides in the answer, a deep understanding of why customers do business with the firm at all. In turn, the sources of that created value (which is strategy's second question, about how value is created) represent the "chips" available for play, and this also clarifies what strategic uncertainties might jeopardize or jump-start competitive advantage.

Competitive advantages built around differentiation depend on assets and processes that increase customers' willingness to pay for the firm's product or service offerings. Uncertainties that invite customers to rethink their willingness to pay, from scandals and failures that damage brands to innovations that redefine the job to be done, threaten or strengthen competitive advantage. Cost leadership follows the same logic. Sources of advantage, whether in raw materials, supply chains, proprietary technologies, or other means of competitive dominance, sketch the contours of risk capacity. For low-cost or differentiation determination, the questions are simple: What changes render ineffective or turbocharge the assets and processes that generate value for our customers? How much shock could our means of advantage withstand before it disappears? What changes would sustainably extend our advantage?

Risk appetite is a subset of capacity and should specify the amount a company is willing to invest in any single project or initiative. Risk appetite helps leaders develop a strategic risk profile—the optimal balance between risk and return and, in turn, how much to invest in mitigating threats or pursuing opportunities. A clear notion of risk appetite, often contained in a formal statement, nurtures a healthy appreciation of and respect for incorporating risk in decision making.

Jon Corzine, like many other executives we've worked with, disliked the idea of a risk appetite statement, viewing it as a fetter that inhibited the range of options available to respond to a changing environment. Our experience suggests otherwise. Risk appetite statements help managers to prioritize among competing needs and opportunities and to make smarter choices around both strategy and implementation. It enables and underpins, rather than disables and undermines, sound strategic bets in the face of scarce resources. When risk appetite flows from risk capacity, boards and executive teams have a holistic perspective that informs decisions about responding to strategic threats and pursuing advantage-extending opportunities.

We've described the conceptual and qualitative foundations for both risk appetite and capacity. When firms build on this foundation, they can establish relevant quantitative anchors to guide decision making. SRM logic invites executive teams to identify measurable expressions of each of the PEST forces to indicate the emergence and progression of strategic uncertainty. Measures of assets, equity, or earnings at risk provide hard numeric guidance to determine appropriate responses to strategic uncertainties.[16] These measures help managers calibrate threats and opportunities, which then suggest resource allocation choices to mitigate or exploit uncertainties. The ability to clarify and quantify risk appetite and capacity is of such importance that we've included a second appendix at the back of the book to provide a short primer on the process of developing these important documents.

Compass Point 3: Embed with ERM and Other Risk Tools

This compass point offers executives good news, in that progressing to SRM doesn't mean jettisoning either TRM or ERM. In particular, mature ERM programs furnish many of the basic organizational elements, job titles, and positions that enable SRM. All of the energy, money, political capital, and time spent to adopt COSO I or II or to comply with Dodd-Frank requirements reduces the additional increments necessary for SRM. Practically speaking, TRM builds the base and ERM provides critical support architecture and mind-sets that allow SRM to flourish. SRM and ERM complement each other in two important ways. First, ERM provides an organization-wide capability for thinking about risk, while SRM attends to uncertainties. Second, ERM helps companies preserve existing value, while SRM aids in the search for creating new value.

Strategy, in commonplace terms, describes at least three different situations: important or long-term-oriented activities or decisions, issues that concern the entire organization, and the creation and maintenance of a competitive advantage. ERM represented a quantum leap in intensity and sophistication because it offered leaders the ability to manage risk cross-organizationally. If TRM focused on the first notion of strategy, ERM provided a window to see and manage the second. Infrastructure suited to that purpose wasn't installed without cost, and in most organizations, outside of the shared services world, there are very few operational systems that can effectively integrate silos.

This matters for competitive advantage, the third definition of strategy, because the best competitive advantages have causal roots spread throughout the firm. Strategy authority Michael Porter argued almost twenty-five years ago that competitive advantages housed in a single function create less overall value and prove more difficult to sustain than advantages spanning several functions. His prime example was Southwest Airlines in 1996.[17] Southwest's low-cost platform spans several functions, from operations (only one type of aircraft and an open seating policy), through marketing (they didn't and still don't subscribe to aggregators such as Expedia to sell tickets), and on to human resources and culture (nonunion labor and staff focused on creating a fun experience for passengers). Aggressive fuel hedging, which we classify as successful TRM execution, has also played a major role in the airline's financial performance, historically.

Over the past twenty-plus years we've seen the large legacy carriers (for instance, Continental, Delta, and United, before consolidation) all attempt low-fare pricing. None of them gained traction because each sought to replicate some functional element of Southwest's strategy, such as open seating, and failed to engage in the silo-busting, cross-functional, activity-inducing change needed to truly compete. Southwest remains the nation's premier discount airline because its competitive advantage spans the organization. ERM lays out a template to help strategy makers think and measure organization-wide.

SRM adoption leverages ERM architectural investments that promote breadth of competitive advantage. That's a prime source of complementarity. TRM and ERM provide important threat protection tools. SRM, because it considers future uncertainties, offers marginal additional protection. Instead, it opens a window in competitive advantage by capitalizing on change and forging links between uncertainty and value creation.

Figure 3.2 illustrates a productive, synergistic relationship. TRM and ERM concentrate efforts on value preservation, while SRM opens the door to value creation. On the left side of the chart are the various organizational mandates assumed by TRM/ERM: ensure compliance with existing rules and regulations, design systems to avoid risks and hazards when possible, and adequately mitigate or transfer known risks through insurance, hedges, or other financial instruments. The right-hand side outlines a different set of mechanisms and processes that arise through a shift toward SRM. Each of these elements allows an organization to frame, consider, and respond to new strategic uncertainties in their environment.

Embedding SRM in an existing risk management framework and leveraging complementarity doesn't necessitate redundancy or overlap. As companies adopted ERM principles and built out programs, they usually housed ERM in audit, accounting, or finance, or they hired outside consultants, often the large accounting firms, to help design and implement freestanding systems. The norms of accounting and finance meant a strong preoccupation with risks that could be predicted and estimated.

	ERM: Value Preservation			SRM: Value Creation			
	Compliance	Avoidance	Insurance	Slack	Information	Debate	Anticipate
Definition/ Description	Meet regulatory obligations	Eliminate risk categories	Mitigate/ Eliminate downside	Provide resource cushion	Higher quality information for decisions	Robust debate, new perspectives	Proactively consider opportunities
Value through	Not Compound Loss	Avoid loss events	Reduce impact of loss events	Quickly deploy slack	Depth/ accuracy/ completeness of decisions	Breadth of perspectives/ alternatives in decisions	Exploit opportunities/ first mover advantages

Figure 3.2: How ERM and SRM create value

Competitive advantage, and changes in the external environment, run perpendicular to the logical demands of accounting and finance. They require exploratory research, creative thinking, and experimentation to understand complex interactions and unpredictable outcomes—known unknowns and unknown unknowns. To that point, integrating SRM with ERM does not automatically mean a home in the usual neighborhoods, where its tools and mind-set won't be optimized. As you'll read in detail in chapter 4, we advocate an executive risk management function that works with but is separate from audit, accounting, finance, and legal. The thirty thousand–foot principle of a close, embedded working relationship informs and guides processes and actions at the ten thousand–foot level.

Compass Point 4: Integrate SRM into the Strategy Complex

As compass point 3 enables and energizes the *RM* component of SRM, the last principle does this for the strategic, *S*, aspect. Here, we lay out at a high level how SRM and the organization's existing strategic planning function complement each other. Let's begin by defining strategic planning. According to the Strategy Management Group, it is a process and activities "used to set priorities, focus energy and resources, strengthen operations, ensure that employees and other stakeholders are working toward common goals, establish agreement around intended outcomes/results, and assess and adjust the organization's direction in response to a changing environment."[18] That's quite a laundry list!

When we look closely, we can see that, at its core, strategic planning is the process, working through responsible individuals and groups, that ensures that resources are allocated in a systematic way to support and bring to fruition the organization's most important goals, one of which is the development and maintenance of a competitive advantage. Strategic planning, as a resource allocation process, then, helps firms answer and implement strategy's second question: How will we create and deliver unique value? Strategic planning takes those goals as given and concerns itself with translating them into market-facing activities, typically over a three- to five-year time horizon. On some periodic basis, the board and the C-suite reassess the environment, determine new high-level objectives, and communicate them to the professionals in strategic planning, who then translate those goals into concrete, time-delimited action plans and budgets.

Over the next three years or so, strategic planners allocate resources and monitor performance against the agreed-upon targets and goals. As the cycle draws to a close, they provide progress assessments to the executive team, who then begin the goal-setting cycle again. As that cycle nears completion, strategic planning may engage in a formal process of environmental scanning to note important changes in the market, industry, or general environment. To complete the picture, all of these strategy-setting activities are exposed to annual budget process skirmishes and quarterly business unit performance reviews, which can create side-door impacts and adjustments to plans.

We accept that our description captures a stylized reality, and we note three important limitations of the typical strategic planning process. First, it presumes, but does not guarantee, that the goals and objectives that drive the plan will create and sustain a real competitive advantage. Unless senior leaders have a clear and concise vision of competitive advantage through crisp answers to the four questions raised in chapter 2, strategic planning degrades into nothing more than resource planning. It basically becomes a schedule and calendar for incremental capital spending. Strategic planners implement, but don't craft, strategy.

Second, if, the team in strategic planning scans the environment for changes, they do so on a regular schedule, every three to five years. This presumes that critical shifts in the environment will either conform to the strategic planning cycle and appear at regular, three-to-five-year intervals or, if they appear, they will not become significant until they can be incorporated into the strategic planning horizon and process. In short, market conditions must dictate planning timing, cadence, and execution, not the other way around.

Finally, because goal setting may or may not be linked to competitive advantage, any subsequent environmental analysis may or may not identity those shifts in the PEST forces that actually matter for competitive advantage and generate strategic risk. Even if external changes and shifts conform to the strategic planning calendar, strategic planning personnel, in a staff role, often lack direct connections with line executives and managers that allow them to communicate potential strategic risks to those affected. They communicate upward and face the pressure to absorb the inherent uncertainty and ambiguity in emerging strategic risks. Uncertainty disappears as information moves up the organization, and again as it moves down a different channel to relevant business units.

SRM provides the antidote to each of these three problems. The first problem concerns resource planning versus planning for competitive advantage. The mission of SRM, its raison d'être, is to identify and assess uncertainty that impacts competitive advantage. SRM complements traditional strategic planning because it requires a clear and clearly communicated vision of competitive advantage to do its own work. The clarity and open communication around strategy spills over to other functions, including strategic planning, and allows those functions to do their jobs better. SRM becomes the steward of competitive advantage, making sure that all those broad goals and high-level objectives support and sustain competitive advantage, the answer to the four critical questions of strategy. SRM in the hands of the C-suite ensures that someone has clear responsibility for competitive advantage.

Second, SRM professionals engage in constant environmental scanning, with a clear focus on external changes that create risk or opportunity for competitive advantage. They aren't limited to a three-to-five-year glance at the environment. In chapters 5 and 6, we'll introduce a set of tools for use in systematically scanning the environment for nascent strategic risks. These tools seek to identify and consider those uncertainties that eventually threaten or enable competitive advantage. They promote continual environmental scanning and an organizational response, even—and especially—when strategic risks don't conform to bureaucratic norms and strategic planning cycles.

Finally, SRM seamlessly embeds with strategic planning, as well as with leaders in business units and functions, in ways that foster regular and open communication. The tools of SRM allow managers to quickly and concisely identify the core uncertainties that drive strategic risks. Communication happens horizontally between SRM experts and line managers, and that helps eliminate the natural tendency for uncertainty absorption when information moves vertically. SRM at least avoids the double filter of moving information up to bosses and then back down to other units. Indeed, SRM facilitates more rapid and more regular communication that blunts the hierarchy's natural propensity for uncertainty absorption.

Conclusion

Aristotle taught, millennia ago, that events result from multiple causes, and the story of MF Global fits this profile. Aristotle noted proximal causes, or those immediate triggers that bring about final consequences. The crisis in liquidity brought about by the London Clearing House's margin calls brought down MF Global. That's the proximal cause. Events also have distal causes, indirect actions and longer-term effects that bring about subsequent events. The distal, and deep, cause of failure at MF Global was a set of faulty mental maps. Some were held by individuals such as Corzine, and others were held among individuals such as the board of directors. Those maps led to poor strategic choices. MF could never become a mini Goldman; it lacked the capital to do so. Bad maps exacerbated the strategy–execution gap, and MF Global's risk tools proved powerless to stop the train from hurtling down the wrong track.

In this chapter, we've focused on mental maps and, to mix metaphors, the view from thirty thousand feet. Our collective experience has taught us that if firms, boards, and executive teams fail to employ the right mental models, then what happens at the ten thousand–foot or ground levels will be much less effective. The four compass points that we've outline here show that SRM is not the enemy of the search for competitive advantage, of current efforts in risk management, including ERM, or of well-designed strategic planning. In chapter 4, we move from high-level mental maps and take up the programmatic integration of SRM into existing efforts around ERM and strategic planning—the view from ten thousand feet. We begin the chapter by looking at another high-profile failure of risk management to call out bad strategy and prevent its implementation. The company in question? Wells Fargo and Company.

CHAPTER 4

SRM at Ten Thousand Feet: Organizational Structure, Processes, and Roles

This chapter takes up the second element of strategic risk management, the set of processes that facilitate the work of SRM teams. SRM represents a dynamic capability for organizations, a function and process that makes other processes better and helps them adapt to changing markets and environments. We outline why SRM sits in the executive suite, and we describe the processes and roles of an effective chief risk officer.

· · · · ·

Few images in the financial services industry are more iconic than the stagecoach and galloping horses of Wells Fargo and Company. Over its almost 170-year history, Wells Fargo evolved from a reliable and safe banking, delivery, and transportation company that connected America's old states with California into one of the nation's largest financial institutions. Wells Fargo gained a reputation for dependability and trust, and the bank expanded with, and wove itself into, the American economy of the twentieth century.

Analysts and regulators lauded Wells Fargo for its clever strategic fore-sight during the 2008 financial sector meltdown. The bank participated in subprime and other exotic mortgage products such as Alt-A, but it never allowed these risky assets a substantial place on the balance sheet. CEO John Stumpf explained, "With no documentation, no income verification, and at the [then existing interest] rate . . . there was no return built in for risk."[1] The bank followed a low-risk strategy with regard to the market for exotic financial instruments and largely stayed out. Instead, its strategic energy focused on existing customers, and the bank made its money by deepening its relationship with customers through cross-selling products and expanding its share of wallet.[2]

A conservative, main street image proved to be a strong strategic asset. Warren Buffett, the Oracle of Omaha, noted, "You make money on custom-ers by having a helluva spread on assets and not doing anything really dumb. And that's what they [Wells Fargo] do."[3] By 2015, Wells was the nation's most valuable bank, and mutual fund giant Morningstar named Stumpf its CEO of the year, recognizing how he "guided the bank through a difficult period in the industry and shunned activities that put profits ahead of customers."[4]

Putting customers ahead of profits defined the company's image until September 8, 2016, when three federal agencies announced that Wells had agreed to pay a $185 million fine for surreptitiously opening more than 2 million phantom accounts for its retail customers.[5] Given the goal of aggressive, "cross-sell" growth—meaning as many product sales to individual customers as possible—executives in Wells Fargo's Community Banking division had, since 2011, relied on old-fashioned carrot-and-stick incentives—bonuses and the threat of being demoted or fired—to motivate employees.[6] "Trust" is mentioned in the bank's thirty-seven-page mission statement twenty-four times, but concerns about ethics did not even play the role of speed bump to slow the fraudulent behavior.[7]

Bank tellers and loan officers opened hordes of new accounts, sometimes forging signatures to complete the necessary paperwork. In many cases, they would transfer a small amount of money from an existing account into the new one to validate the transaction. The result? Credit for cross-selling. The *Los Angeles Times* described another tactic: "Employees opened dupli-cate accounts, sometimes without customers' knowledge . . . Workers also used a bank database to identify customers who had been pre-approved for credit cards—then ordered the plastic without asking them." According to a former Wells Fargo personal banker, "They'd just tell the customers: 'You're getting a credit card.'"[8]

Customer accounts fraud stemmed from the most mundane of operating risks: sales process and incentives. Eventually, the risk spread throughout the Community Banking division and beyond. Unchecked incentives and relentless pressure to cross-sell led to problems in the auto lending portfolio (false insurance policies) and in the wealth and investment advisory group (selling for commission instead of to meet customer needs). It took five years for the threat to fully materialize. Wells Fargo's inattention to the sales risk problem was, as Buffett might say, a "dumb thing."

Such a dumb thing seems inexplicable, given that Wells Fargo had a recognized competence in risk management. The company had decentralized the corporate risk function around 2005 in order to more effectively monitor and respond to its complex operating environment. This decentralized system helped to keep Wells Fargo out of deep water during the financial crisis. Later, the bank established formal channels to escalate the most significant individual risks to an enterprise risk management committee composed of senior business unit leaders and various C-suite representatives.

In turn, the committee had a clear and direct reporting relationship to the risk committee of the board of directors. Wells Fargo hired Michael Loughlin, in 2010, as its full-time chief risk officer, in the wake of the financial sector meltdown. Underscoring the seriousness of the effort, McKinsey and Company was hired in 2013 to conduct an extensive review and made recommendations to strengthen the corporate risk program. In 2015, the CRO established a sales practices oversight unit within the corporate risk function, whose goal was to monitor sales risk at the Community Banking division. From the outside, Wells Fargo appeared to be highly competent in ERM.[9]

From the inside, however, ERM was an engine leaking oil. Underneath the veneer of a well-established ERM program festered a cluster of interrelated problems. Critical operating processes and structural reporting relationships left the CRO and other risk managers out of key decisions. They could advise and inform line managers but had no authority to stop questionable practices. Community Banking chief Carrie Tolstedt, had, by all accounts, little regard for risk management, and she shunted risk managers to the sidelines of the division. Further exacerbating the problem, risk professionals with their advice could not overcome the positional and personal relationship between Tolstedt and Stumpf. Until very late in the scandal, Tolstedt was able to manage the message in a way that prevented risk realities from surfacing at the board level. Unfortunately, Stumpf turned out to be the wrong field commander for ERM, given his unswerving commitment to cross-selling as the primary growth engine, his reputation for not wanting to hear bad news, and his visible support of Tolstedt and other leaders of the Community Banking arm.

Data was available to track the impact of the bank's sales process risk—proxies such as the rolling funding rate, the termination percentage for sales integrity violations, and customer-level product sales. But Wells Fargo failed in its appraisal of these data, in the aggregate, and failed to take seriously the looming impropriety. Thresholds and tolerances for the risk were set too high to put the brakes on aggressive growth. Investigators later found some discussion of the potential reputational risk the company could face from incentives gone awry, but the ERM committee didn't envision an extreme worst-case scenario that even approached a federal cease and desist order that would halt the ability to expand.[10]

To his credit, Loughlin is on record exercising a measure of creative SRM thinking. In an exchange with Matthew Raphaelson, former Community Bank executive vice president, he suggested taking a revenue-based approach to sales (which would provide a potential new upside and higher quality) instead of emphasizing individual sales professional cross-sell unit metrics (which engenders actual downside risk and is low quality). This is precisely the type of contribution that SRM should make, but, in the case of Wells Fargo, the suggestion never saw the light of day. Ultimately, the risk assessment of the growth strategy considered that cross-selling might not reach target rates. Regrettably, that evaluation also failed to account for a complete backfire and the resulting jeopardy of fictitious accounts.

Stumpf and some of the executives who surrounded him employed flawed mental maps, which led them to a set of informal processes that discounted the need for, and messages from, the CRO and other risk managers. They sincerely believed that Wells Fargo was an ethical and trustworthy organization, which justified shutting risk managers out of strategy and implementation decisions, both structurally and politically. After all, the bank worked hard to inculcate in its "team members" the company's mission and values, and surely these people, steeped in and deeply committed to that mission, would refuse to engage in unethical or untrustworthy behavior. Put simply, good people can push boundaries without crossing the line, or so these leaders thought. When directed and pressured by their managers, however, thousands of Wells Fargo team members proved quite willing to cross several lines.

Aggressive sales practices led to bad behavior, which gave rise to another clearly identified problem, the normalization of deviance, in which "people within the organization become so much accustomed to a deviant behavior that they don't consider it as deviant, despite the fact that they far exceed their own rules for [propriety]."[11] People at all levels of the bank crossed ethical (and legal) lines, but leaders clung to the idea that their behaviors still matched the mission and vision.

Scandals that began in the Community Bank division spawned separate investigations by the Federal Reserve Bank of San Francisco and by the bank's independent directors. As of early 2019, Wells Fargo has paid nearly $3 billion in fines, restitution, and settlements ordered by the Consumer Financial Protection Bureau, the Office of the Comptroller of the Currency, the Securities and Exchange Commission, the city and county of Los Angeles, and each of the fifty states in which the bank operates. Stumpf resigned in disgrace and forfeited $41 million in compensation. Three other senior executives, including Carrie Tolstedt, were dismissed as well. During the two years following September 16, 2016, the share price of Wells Fargo increased 22% while the Dow Jones Index appreciated 44%.[12]

When executives employ correct mental maps, they can structure SRM in ways that integrate strategy and risk. If executives get the processes and structures right, the political problems will fade and the firm can realize the full value of SRM programs. SRM can fulfill the promise of risk management, identified more than a half century ago by economist Dr. Robert Rennie: "To the extent that the risk manager can improve his techniques for measuring risk and to the extent that he can reduce uncertainty, he can extend the growth horizons of the firm. Such a role for the risk manager will be more difficult to perform . . . but it is a function vital to the decision-making process of the modern corporation."[13] We take up the question of structure first and then discuss the processes the allow SRM to flourish.

The Right Structural Fit for SRM

Structure is perhaps the most malleable element of any organization. We've sat with executives at lunch and literally redrawn their organizational chart on a napkin. Changing structure with ease, though, belies the perils of redrawing key relationships without serious thought and consideration. Charlton Ogburn captured the essence of these perils when he wrote about his service in the U.S. Army during World War II: "We trained hard, but it seemed that every time we were beginning to form up into teams we would be reorganized. . . . I was to learn later in life that, perhaps because we are so good at organizing, we tend . . . to meet any new situation by reorganizing; and a wonderful method it can be for creating the illusion of progress while producing confusion, inefficiency and demoralization."[14]

We would add *ineffectiveness* to that list of negative outcomes. A properly structured *anything*, but particularly a SRM program, demands that leaders ask and answer two fundamental questions. First they must ask "What type of activity are we trying to structure?" Based on the answer, the second question is "Where, in terms of level and function, should we put the program or position so it can function most effectively?" We can't answer question 2 until we answer question 1, so let's begin with the type of activity that SRM represents.

SRM as a Dynamic Capability

Dynamic capability, an imposing-sounding term, came into vogue for strategists at the end of the past millennium and in the first decade of the new one. When strategy began as a field of study and practice, in the late 1970s, it borrowed heavily from industrial economics. The work of Michael Porter and others argued that good strategy amounted to finding the right industry in which to compete.[15] By the early 1990s, strategists began to see that a firm's unique resources and capabilities, its idiosyncratic assets and processes, mattered for competitive advantage. Companies have two types of capabilities. The first, operating capabilities, describe the routines and processes that get the day-to-day work of the organization done. Operating capabilities reside in every function, from accounting procedures for month-end closings and expense report reimbursements to sales routines about customer relationship management and executing contracts and agreements.

Dynamic capabilities, on the other hand, enable the firm "to integrate, build, and reconfigure internal and external competences to address rapidly changing environments."[16] In practical terms, they usually span functions and help operating capabilities respond to changes in the market or to continuously improve. Programs such as lean manufacturing, Kaizen, or Six Sigma can be illustrative of dynamic capabilities. Kaizen doesn't produce products; it improves the processes that produce products. Disney's ability to create and manage new brands such as Disney Home Video, or ESPN's expansion into documentary films and restaurants, provide tangible examples of dynamic capabilities.

SRM represents a dynamic capability. It doesn't decide what a firm's competitive strategy ought to be; it helps that strategy respond to uncertainties in ways that preserve or extend competitive advantage. SRM builds organizational ambidexterity, or the ability to engage risk as simultaneously downside and upside propositions, and it fosters resilience, the ability to thrive though change, in both operating and executive units. Like other dynamic capabilities, such as Six Sigma or brand development, SRM works best when it occupies its own, relatively independent home in the organization. In what follows, we'll outline how firms can set up an independent SRM function but still integrate it with other risk functions and with the strategy complex of formulation, planning, and implementation.

Where Does SRM Fit on the Organization Chart?

An appreciation of the role of SRM as a dynamic capability designed to help senior managers thrive through uncertainty provides the answer to the question of where an SRM program and other risk management functions belong. We begin by thinking about progressive levels of mangers, from those at the bottom of the hierarchy, who focus on narrowly defined activities, to the team at the top responsible for decisions about long-term viability. Our illustration uses a common, everyday risk factor: the weather.

Consider the impact of weather on the business of insuring personal dwellings, using the example of the multinational company Allianz SE, which generates more than €50 billion ($57 billion) in annual premiums from homeowners across the globe.[17] The Allianz agent who sells a new policy on a home in Spain, for example, doesn't pay much attention to the weather, except to know that inclement weather might delay her commute to meet the homeowner and get the paperwork signed. Maybe the weather provides a conversation starter, but that's about it. One level up in the process, the policy underwriter cares more about the weather, particularly if the house sits in a higher-risk zone, perhaps in a floodplain or near a heavily wooded area.

At the top of the organization, the senior team responsible for the Allianz homeowners unit's profit and loss has a very different view of the weather. Their views on atmospheric and environmental conditions over the medium term, such as the frequency and severity of wind, water, and fire exposures, will factor into actuarial projections, pricing decisions, and financial risk management strategies such as reinsurance. Ultimately, the long-run implications of weather and climate change matter to members of the Allianz Board of Management and its Supervisory Board. The uncertainty regarding climate change, the impact of which may take decades or more to fully understand, will influence whether Allianz remains in the homeowners insurance market at all.

Figure 4.1 generalizes this logic.[18] Individual contributors, functional specialists, and unit managers implement strategy. Their work generates the revenues and costs that in large part determine short-term profitability. These implementers generally focus on the current budget cycle and may

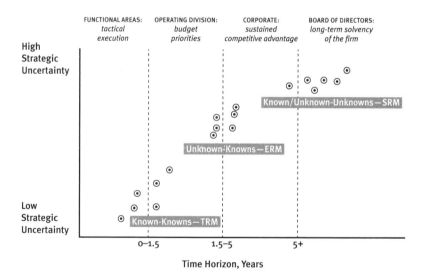

Figure 4.1 *The Strategic Uncertainty Frontier. Adapted from* The Strategy Paradox, *Michael Raynor, 2007*

have an eighteen-month horizon when implementing a major new initiative. Just as the Allianz agent knows the probability of rain today, those at the bottom of the hierarchy live in a world of known knowns. This is the level where traditional risk management, insurance, hedges, safety programs, and compliance fits. TRM belongs where its time horizon and uncertainty frontier match that of its organizational counterparts.

Middle managers deal with issues that are eighteen months to three or five years out. This group thinks about consecutive budget cycles and has responsibility for implementing multiyear strategic plans. For the head of the homeowners line of business at Allianz, quarterly and annual targets certainly matter. But what keeps her up as night? It's how to sustain consistent business unit performance beyond the immediate accounting period and how to make contributions to the greater organizational good. We're now in an arena where the scope of risk is wider and more complex, and where competitive advantage faces threats. ERM programs and staff sit naturally at this level of the organization, and they should deal with counterparts who share the same operating time frame and whose work spans multiple units or functions.

Moving along the horizon, you see that SRM fits squarely in the C-suite. SRM performs a critical task for senior executives and directors: it helps them make sense of and plan for events and exposures currently unknown, with unclear and unpredictable outcomes. These unknowns determine the long-term viability of current competitive advantages and inform change options designed to maintain or extend that advantage. In the case of Allianz, competitive advantage depends on a combination of great customer service delivered by local agents—differentiation—and actuarially smart pricing by the responsible business unit leaders. These competencies may matter little in the long run, however, if the firm competes in an industry sector that is facing structural decline.

To sum up, when we know what job each risk management activity performs, we know the appropriate level of the hierarchy from which each should operate, and with which managers they should interact. TRM fits with other managers who deal with known knowns at the line operating level. ERM focuses on unknown knowns, risk aggregation across multiple units in the hierarchy, and how those risks scale as they combine. Middle managers, division heads, and business unit leaders focus on these same issues of multifunctional and multi-unit coordination under conditions of moderate uncertainty. SRM is best positioned in the C-suite because its job to be done—the identification and assessment of highly uncertain events and exposures—aligns with the executive agenda.

Ideally, a firm's entire risk management apparatus should operate under the direction of a C-level executive, the chief risk officer. Our recommendation should not be seen as just a call for another "CxO" position, or for the creation of another functional silo, or for a power grab by any one member of the executive suite. Companies need a CRO to coordinate all risk management activities—TRM, ERM, and SRM. TRM and ERM offer structure and processes that complement and reinforce the work of the SRM group. Central to our purposes, the CRO ensures that the risk management functions have adequate human and financial capital inputs to do their work. An empowered CRO ensures that the team's output becomes input to the strategy formulation and implementation process.

We've seen a number of companies create a virtual Potemkin village for the office of the CRO, with the appropriate titles and mandates but without the authority or political standing to do more than advise and inform when difficult calls must be made. Risk management at Wells Fargo filled this bill. It checked many of the right boxes but failed to deliver when put to the test. So getting the structure right matters, but getting the processes right matters just as much, if not more.

The Right Processes and Role:
The Chief Risk Officer

James Lam has the distinction of becoming industry CRO number 001 when General Electric Capital created the role, in 1993. At that time, the financial services unit brought in just over one of every three revenue dollars for the General Electric conglomerate.[19] Lam oversaw financial risks at GE Capital, and his hiring represented the company's response to the regulatory activism that had resulted in the passage of the Sarbanes-Oxley Act and to federal legislation addressing the lack of sufficient financial controls, which had led to the scandals at Enron, WorldCom, and Tyco International.[20] Lam's role was to assess and manage the risks that could jeopardize the financial viability of both his division and the larger entity.

A decade later, the COSO 2004 framework ensconced the CRO in the corporate hierarchy and the position expanded from financial risk oversight to leading and coordinating all risk management activities. In this light, the CRO's portfolio is focused on three tasks: identify, evaluate, and report material internal and external risks to the board and the senior management team.[21] The 2008 financial crisis spurred more regulation and a new risk management architecture. Section 165(h) of the Dodd-Frank Wall Street Reform and Consumer Protection Act later mandated that financial institutions with $50 billion in assets must have a chief risk officer, a stand-alone risk committee, an enterprise risk management program, and an independent director with risk management expertise.[22]

On the positive side, these and other regulations created a secure and expanded role for the CRO, moving the position beyond financial risks to include business cycle, customer preference, cybersecurity, macroeconomic and political, operational, supply chain, and of course strategic risks. On the negative side, the regulatory drive created a significant set of reporting requirements and the office of the CRO, in most companies, became identified—and preoccupied—with compliance and reporting. As we saw with MF Global in chapter 3 and Wells Fargo here, many organizations set up an office of the CRO but failed to grant it sufficient organizational standing to act independently. We suggest three elements that will help the CRO to function effectively: empowerment, integration, and strategy.

The Empowered Chief Risk Officer

Formal authority and informal power aren't the only keys to creating an efficient and effective office of the CRO, but they are the two most important ones. As a member of the C-suite, the CRO must have the formal authority that grants them control over their own budget and human capital development and deployment. The CRO also needs hard-line reporting relationships, upward to the board and laterally to key executives, especially to the general counsel, the chief financial officer, and the chief strategy officer. These clear lines of accountability move the CRO beyond a role of "advise and inform" to "assess and direct."

Ultimate authority over, and responsibility for, all risk management activities in the firm—TRM, ERM, and SRM—should be held by the CRO. A formal charter approved by the board will buttresses the importance of the CRO's work, and it legitimates the pesky and often intrusive work of risk management in the operating parts of the organization. Many line managers still envision dealing with risk as a disconnected bolt-on to their core work. They fail to realize that their core work both begets and absorbs risk. A formal charter can move risk management from the side of their plate to the center, where it commands sufficient attention.

While the CRO assists those working in TRM and ERM, the role proves critical for SRM. An effective charter document should mandate that strategic risk identification, assessment, reporting, and management all belong in the wheelhouse of the CRO. Ideally, it should define strategic risks as we have: as any exposure, event, occurrence, or situation, and the associated uncertainty, that fundamentally threatens or enables a company's competitive advantage or its viability as a going concern. Finally, a well-crafted document specifies that a consideration of these risks (events, exposures, and uncertainties) will be included in the strategic planning process.

Thomas Stanton, a risk management specialist at Johns Hopkins University, served as a member of the Financial Crisis Inquiry Commission that deconstructed the great meltdown of 2008. Writing of those who successfully navigated the crisis compared to those who did not, Stanton noted:

> Successful firms such as JPMorgan Chase, Goldman Sachs, Wells Fargo [as of 2008], and Toronto Dominion managed risk in different ways. What they had in common was a *respect for the risk function* and the importance of managing risk–return tradeoffs on a firm-wide basis. Unsuccessful firms frequently dismissed (Freddie Mac), sidetracked (Lehman), isolated (AIG), layered their risk officers far down in the firm (Countrywide), or otherwise disregarded them (Fannie Mae). At many firms . . . risk management was a compliance exercise rather than a rigorous undertaking (emphasis added).[23]

Formal authority, as we've described it, provides a bulwark and shield that prevents the risk function, including SRM, from operating on the periphery of the organizational plate and helps it to maintain centrality. What CROs need, however, is a two-edged sword to cut through resistance and get their work done. One edge is their formal authority to impact individuals or groups and to punish them for noncompliance or reward them for positive work. CROs typically have little reward power other than trivial, symbolic awards (think "Best Division for Risk Management"). They may have extensive coercive power, due to the regulatory mandates that make up much of their work; however, coercive power often breeds resentment that results in sidelining behaviors on the part of line managers, as Stanton noted.

Informal, personal power provides CROs with a sharp edge that cuts through bureaucratic red tape and endears them to, rather than enrages, colleagues and coworkers.[24] It is the broad-based, deep knowledge of risk and organizational finance required to speak and understand the language of corporate strategy. The best CROs have to hold their own in technical discussions about risk, strategy, and economic performance. Personal power comes not just from expertise but also from admiration. Effective CROs—the ones with real influence—bring valuable interpersonal skills to their work.

Admiration, or referent power, arises when others see in the power holder traits or characteristics that they like, or if they aspire to be like that person. Put simply, "If I like, respect, and admire you, you can exercise power over me because I want to please you."[25] Traits like charisma or overall gregariousness can create referent power, but a much stronger power base comes from character and demeanor. Powerful CROs "shoot straight," know their stuff, and make their case frankly, honestly, and with respect. They engage in cognitive conflict around issues, behaviors, and plans but avoid affective, personal, conflict.[26] They know line managers will often disagree with what they recommend—usually they call for prudence and put constraints on action—and they handle disagreement without becoming disagreeable. Organizations that respect the risk function will enable a personally empowered CRO. Integrating the CRO and his or her work with others in the C-suite, particularly with the CSO, is the next process to operationalize.

The Integrated Chief Risk Officer

Integration of SRM, ERM, and TRM with the CRO, and with the CSO, sets the table for the organization to realize and leverage the complementarities we outlined in chapter 3. TRM and ERM enhance the overall value of SRM, as these functions pave the way forward. First, these two processes raise awareness of the interrelatedness of risk and core work throughout the organization. When aligned with the appropriate management levels (illustrated in figure 4.1), TRM and ERM help managers understand the intimate relationships between known risks and business responsibilities at all levels. Understanding known risks is a prerequisite for contemplating the nature and potential impact of the unknown, uncertain nature and effects of strategic risks.

Second, when properly situated and managed, TRM and ERM create communication pathways and protocols for information to move up, down, and across the organization. For example, compliance measurement and reporting systems establish structural conduits and operational cadences for sharing risk information. ERM, with its cross-functional committees, task forces, and initiatives, deepens those pathways and establishes its own systems and logic. SRM can slipstream onto these processes and into these communication rhythms with fewer startup costs or political resistance. Great strategic risk management requires great TRM and ERM programs.

Synchronization among the risk functions will foster organizational draft instead of drag through SRM. Further, integration between the offices of the CRO and the CSO can put that draft to productive use and embed SRM in the firm's strategy complex—strategy making and implementation carried out though strategic and resource planning processes. Tight alignment enhances both functions, building from a deep understanding of the common interests shared by the SRM team, led by the CRO, and the strategy complex, administered by the CSO.

Those common interests may be buried below the surface, however. The strategy complex of an organization, particularly as embodied in executives like Jon Corzine or Carrie Tolstedt or in the office of a CSO, may come to view risk management exclusively as a governor and a constraining force. In turn, risk management will appear to be at odds with revenue and profit growth and, by extension, to be an enemy of shareholders. In the extreme, we have worked with many companies in which the CRO became the "CNO"—the chief naysayer.

Such a view, in fact, proves contrary to shareholder interests. Fiduciary responsibility provides a correct doctrinal model of how firms, in the capacity of an authorized agent, best serve their principals, namely, the shareholders.[27] A fiduciary has a good faith obligation to undertake actions that create the best outcome for the principals, as those principals have defined them. Shareholders desire maximum returns, and managers have a fiduciary duty to work to obtain them and to enrich their principals. Growth strategies help to fulfill this duty of good faith.

Fiduciaries have an additional obligation, however: the duty of care. They must act in ways that avoid exposing the interests of their principals to unreasonable risks or irrational uncertainty, without the consent of those principals. Risk management, when done well, plays this role in properly attenuating and calibrating growth strategies. Analytical work that produces outcomes such as quantification of risk capacity (how much a firm can afford to lose) and formal decisions around risk appetite (how much exposure the firm will accept at any one time) help management teams establish financial guardrails that keep growth from careering out of control.

CROs and their teams share a fiduciary duty with CSOs and their teams. When they collaborate, cooperate, and integrate their work, they contribute effectively to the performance of management's fiduciary duty. This is one area of common interest, but not the only one. The CRO and the SRM team should seek to inform and improve the strategy process, an outcome consistent with the responsibilities of the CSO.

The Strategic Chief Risk Officer

We've argued for empowering the CRO, aligning the three functional areas of risk management, and recognizing the integration opportunities between CROs and CSOs. As we continue to hover at a ten thousand–foot view of SRM, we develop a clear understanding of how this CRO–CSO relationship can best be positioned. Whether it's a relationship between specific individuals, staffed departments, or broadly constituted "offices," both sides face the strategy complex with their respective interests firmly in mind. SRM provides the synchronization mechanism that enables these people and processes to come together and conceptualize, formalize, and operationalize strategy for maximum effectiveness. Essentially, SRM is a two-sided coin, backed by risk and strategy professionals, that funds strategic thinking, planning, decision making, and execution. And both sides have big stakes in developing for the firm strategy that wins for shareholders.

Consider strategy's four questions from chapter 1 as a way to frame CRO–CSO interests around strategic thinking. As leaders initially ask these questions, the SRM team should not focus on erecting roadblocks. Rather than adopting a position of "How can we stop strategy from becoming too aggressive?,'' SRM should deeply probe uncertainties: How will long-term forces and exposures in the environment impact strategy? Which of those will threaten current advantages—or strengthen them? What new potential advantages might exist in future worlds? Table 4.1 captures these common interests between CRO and CSO and calibrates their perspectives, which we will amplify.

Where should we compete? CSOs seek to uncover markets that their firms can efficiently enter and exploit. Paradoxically, they also demand resource allocations—from capital investments to achieve scale to marketing efforts to build the brand—that raise the costs of entry. Entry decisions must make sense within a specified competitive context, defined by current technologies, customer demands, supply chains, and other elements. SRM addresses potential changes to that competitive context. For example, will political revolutions in the developing world endanger supply sources of critical inputs? How might the classification of a supply source as a conflict zone affect the firm's ability to obtain and use precious metals inputs? What happens to the CSO's dedicated investments when the context changes?

Why will we win with customers? Firms win by offering something different than their competitors, by operating at a lower cost basis, or

Perspectives	Downside Risks of Strategy "What's the worst that could happen?"	Upside Risks of Strategy "What's the best that could happen?"	Downside Risks of Strategy "What will keep it from working?"	Upside Risks of Strategy "What do we need to make it work?"
Office of the Chief Risk Officer	Inability to identify and mitigate downside • Brand damage • New correlations • Known/unknown unknowns	Correctly perceive and realize opportunity • Brand extension • New correlations • Known/unknown unknowns	Gaps and delays in risk data • Inadequate modeling • Decision-making biases • Failure to communicate • Unknowns become knowns	Knowledge of opportunity evolution/timing • Brand creation • New correlations • Unknowns become knowns
Office of the Chief Strategy Officer	Competitive parity—no advantage • Suboptimal choice • Opportunity costs • Unacceptable return on investment	Quantum shift in competitive advantage • Optimal choices • Exercise strategic options • Solid return on investment	Ease of replication • Faulty execution • Market timing • Lack of resources • Poor competitive intelligence	Create barriers to imitation • Capital investments • Knowledge and learning • Excellent market knowledge

Table 4.1: The Complementary Roles of the Chief Risk Officer and the Chief Strategy Officer

through a combination of both. Strategic investments in differentiation assume predictable customer preferences, and those in cost reduction build on durable technological regimes. But, over the longer term, that stability crumbles. Most firms can plan for gradual evolution in preferences or technologies, but high-velocity environments, disruptive innovations, and outright revolutions leave them exposed. CROs and SRM teams can contribute to wise strategic investments by helping decision makers predict the evolutionary path of preferences and technology. They also provide early warning about potential revolutions and the implications for current competitive advantages.

How will we win with customers? The SRM process helps CSOs consider changes in the mix of resources and capabilities that create new differentiation or low-cost positions, which in turn change the "how we win" calculus. A generation ago, scant attention was paid to where a company sourced its precious substances. When the "blood" or conflict diamond movement took off around the turn of the millennium, such ignorance changed relatively quickly. What initially seemed to be a limited retail market phenomenon about wedding rings and jewelry grew to include all minerals exported from conflict-torn countries. In the 1990s, ownership of mines in these countries made sense, to guarantee stable supplies, but in a conflict-metals world, ownership became a strategic liability. Tools and techniques we introduce in chapter 6 equip SRM teams to provide CSOs with the ability to sense and respond to such potential threats on the horizon and to adjust decision making accordingly.

Why can't competitors copy our competitive advantage? Sustainable competitive advantages are only as strong as the barriers that impede their replication and the competencies that dictate the speed of adjustment to the threats of rivals. Sustaining advantage, or seeing it erode, happens over time. When strategy is first conceived, strategy makers aren't looking a decade into the future to gauge how robust barriers to imitation will be. However, they usually fail to update their vision as the years roll by, which leads to the loss of competitive advantage. This can be similar to an explosive device with a long fuse—years of sizzling buildup, and then competitive advantage is destroyed in a powerful outburst as barriers crumble. SRM and the CRO should be looking ten to fifteen years out, all the time. That allows them to help defuse potential threats to sustainability long before the point of no return.

Dialogue between the CRO and CSO around the four questions is a progressive exercise to grapple with uncertainty. It is targeted at developing viable strategic options for the firm and informing choices about those options. That dialogue leverages the individual power of unique CRO and CSO perspectives into an integrated whole. As options begin to emerge from the SRM-driven conversation, two additional questions surface that draw attention to the risks to and of strategy.

What will keep the strategy from working? A CRO considering the risks to a strategic choice will, by training and experience, have a professional inclination to emphasize the rigor of the analytics that support the choice. Gaps in or unavailability of data, insufficient or misdirected modeling, and overly optimistic probabilistic risk assessments (a well-known cognitive bias) all are factors that may lead to failure in the CRO's estimation. On the other hand, CSOs tend to be more concerned about the operational risks of implementing choices. Faulty launch plans, poor execution, ill-advised market timing, lack of ongoing resources to support the choice, and poor competitive intelligence are deficiencies that can derail a CSO's progress.

What's the worst that could happen? In the eyes of the CSO, the significant risks of a strategy include ease of replication, lack of incremental or sustained competitive advantage, opportunity costs relative to other choices, or unacceptable return on investment. Each situation presents significant risk to financial performance commitments and the investments upon which they are predicated. The CRO should focus on the firm's ability to mitigate projected downside effects at their most uncertain extreme, including possible brand or reputational damage, unexpected risk correlations that generate serious exposures, or the appearance of unknown unknowns from the Rumsfeld matrix.

The depth of discourse between the CRO and CSO, the willingness to collaborate, and the quality of the relationship are the critical components of SRM success. Their interests, perspectives, and abilities, when brought together—sometimes in agreement, other times in conflict—embed SRM in the strategy complex in a way that yields value far beyond compliance. Indeed, talented CROs will model this type of common-interest relationship building with others in the C-suite—with CFOs, to reduce financial volatility; with general counsels, to adjust to regulatory change; with COOs and chief information officers, to ensure digital risk management resilience; and with CEOs, to weigh in directly on strategic options. When these relationships function well, SRM becomes a true dynamic capability, a set of "unique and difficult-to-replicate skills, processes, procedures, organizational structures, decision rules and disciplines which undergird enterprise-level sensing, seizing and reconfiguring capabilities."[28] SRM makes every organizational unit it touches perform better, both *in* time and, especially, *over* time.

Conclusion

In this chapter, we moved from principles to processes, from thirty thousand to ten thousand feet. Chapter 3 dealt with mind-sets and the strategic synergies available when SRM aligns with downstream risk management processes (namely, TRM and ERM) and strategic planning. Here, we addressed organizational structure, operating processes, and key relationships under the guidance of the SRM champion, the CRO. The CRO has a unique opportunity to embed SRM into the DNA of the organization as a true dynamic capability, one that represents a new way to manage a certain class of risks that help executives craft strategies. SRM must have the firm foundation created by engaging the outlooks and perspectives presented in chapter 3. Similarly, SRM has very little chance of success if senior leaders fail to create a real CRO empowered by formal charter and informal ability to forge collaboration and cooperation with others in the C-suite and to create and execute a risk-informed strategy.

From thirty thousand and ten thousand feet, we now move to ground level in the next two chapters. Chapter 5 deals with who should staff the unique SRM function, where they may uncover strategic threats and opportunities, and how to frame these in a way that other organizational units can understand and that facilitates the effective monitoring and management of those strategic risks over the decade or more from first notice to bona fide risk.

CHAPTER 5

SRM at Ground Level: Why, Who and Where, and How?

This chapter takes up the next elements in developing a strategic risk management program: teams and tools. We focus on the team in this chapter: why every organization needs a dedicated SRM team, who should be on that team, where they should look for strategic risk, and how they can frame those risks in ways that others in the organization can quickly understand. We begin with Intel's misadventures in the smartphone market and explain how an SRM team might have helped.

. . . . .

William Shockley went West, from New Jersey to Mountain View, California, in 1955, to start a company manufacturing his own invention—one for which he would share the 1956 Nobel Prize in Physics. Shockley and two other Bell Labs scientists had created the first transistor, and Shockley left the East Coast for sunny California because he, unlike his coinventors, believed in and wanted to exploit the economic potential of the semiconductor. Shockley Semiconductor attracted a solid group of young engineers who began work on commercializing the silicon-based device; however, Shockley's minions would find that working for the Nobel laureate proved difficult. "He was a brilliant, pivotal and controversial figure, stimulating to work *with* but often difficult to work *for* (emphasis added)."[1]

Within two years, eight of his top engineers had had their fill of Shockley's autocratic leadership, and the "traitorous eight" left to form their own firm, Fairchild Semiconductor. The engineers produced great innovations and products, but the Fairchild Camera and Instrument Corporation, its New York investor and namesake, never understood the business or its potential. Fairchild failed to reinvest profits in advancing semiconductor manufacturing, instead using the cash for a series of failed acquisitions. In 1968, a frustrated Robert Noyce, company president, and Gordon Moore, head of research and development, formed their own company, NM Electronics. The pair soon purchased the rights to a new name, Integrated Electronics, or Intel.[2]

Intel engineers, under Moore's direction, pushed the envelope of semiconductor development. In 1969, the company brought its first chip to market. It was a powerful semiconductor with a new design feature, a small silicon gate that integrated the chip's memory circuits with other important hardware. The company bought an old manufacturing plant from Union Carbide and began producing chips.[3] Eager for business that would build on Moore's expertise, knowledge, and reputation in the industry, Intel took a contract from Japanese calculator maker Busicom to produce a chip for a mathematical calculator.

The result was a four-chip set, the 4004, that could perform multiple tasks. Indeed, this tiny four-bit chip packed as much calculating power as the room of vacuum tubes that ran the world's first computer back in 1947.[4] Intel introduced an advanced eight-bit version of the initial design, the 8008 processor, in 1972. The 8008 was the first of multiple generations of processors that combined massive computing power and small size to run an emerging class of machines—microcomputers, commonly known as personal computers, or PCs.

Intel built its strategy around one of Moore's key insights: about every two years, the number of transistors on a silicon wafer roughly doubled, with no commensurate increase in production cost. Each generation cut computing costs in half. The 8008 followed this pattern, containing 3,500 transistors, compared to the 2,300 on the 4004, an increase of 50% in just one year. This regularity become enshrined as Moore's Law.[5]

Intel applied Moore's Law through a set of parallel development processes known as the Tick-Tock model. "Tick" engineers, led by COO Andy

Grove, focused on manufacturing and process innovations that maintained, or lowered, the cost element of Moore's Law through the relentless pursuit of economies of scale, increasingly precise equipment, and control processes that reduced defect rates. "Tock" engineers, under Moore's direction, worked to double the number of transistors on each chip without increasing its footprint. Tick-Tock required huge amounts of capital. In 1980, the company invested $252 million in Tick-Tock capital expenditures and R&D, which was 29% of revenue. By 2005, that figure had increased forty-three times, to $11 billion ($5.8 billion in capital expenditure and $5.1 billion in R&D), still 28% percent of revenue and about five times the average spent on R&D across the U.S. economy.[6]

Intel grew rapidly, and it earned the huge margins that underwrote Tick-Tock by combining high-volume sales with high margins. Successive generations of chips doubled processing power while manufacturing efficiencies controlled costs. It proved to be an extraordinary one-two punch that competitors couldn't replicate. Indeed, Intel's only competition appeared because computer manufacturers required second-source agreements for such a critical part. These agreements forced Intel to share its chip designs with other semiconductor firms.

Intel changed that in 1986, with its fifth-generation processor, the 80386. The 386 contained 275,000 transistors and featured a clock speed 2.5 times faster than its predecessor. Impressively, it employed a thirty-two-bit architecture, which by itself doubled the processing power of the new machine.[7] Intel decided to exploit this leap and end the industry practice of multiple-source agreements. Compaq Computer, with 3% of the PC market, agreed to sole-source the 386 chip from Intel and gained an immediate advantage in the end-user PC market. Intel subsequently forced other manufacturers to adopt a similar purchasing agreement. The sole-source policy would not survive a legal challenge, but for five years Intel enjoyed a monopolist's margins on 386 sales. The company maintained those margins in the early 1990s through ever more powerful chips and by branding their chips as "Intel Inside." The company continued to enjoy both high volumes and high margins, which drove Tick-Tock and shareholder returns well into the new century.

The market for semiconductors changed dramatically in 2007, with the introduction of Apple's iPhone. The emergence of mobile devices accelerated the decline in PC sales, the bedrock of Intel's revenue, which had been declining since 2005 as tablet computers gained traction. Apple's original iPhone used not Intel's chips but Samsung's ARM11 processor. Intel could have, and probably should have, dominated the smartphone market. In 2005, Steve Jobs had approached Intel's new CEO, Paul Otellini, about a new project. Apple intended to enter the cellular phone market with its own device, then under development. The phone required a chip just powerful enough to run the phone's core applications, but the processor had to operate at very low power in order to enhance the life of each battery charge.

As Otellini considered Jobs's offer, he knew that Intel could produce a low-power chip, but the timeline meant that Intel would be selling a stripped-down version of its high-end chips at a price point that would not command the margins needed to fuel Tick-Tock. These chips could only succeed for Intel if they generated huge volumes to overcome the anemic margins. Otellini and his team looked at Apple's earlier Newton and at the intense competition in the cellular phone handset market, a market Apple had not yet entered. He saw substantial uncertainty around the phone and, by extension, around Intel's success. Otellini passed on the opportunity.

The rest, as they say, is history. iPhone sales exploded. Apple sold 1.4 million units in 2007 and 11.63 million in 2008, a growth rate of 830%.[8] Intel not only missed out on selling chips for mobile devices but also saw its PC business shrink over the next several years. By 2013, most analysts saw the PC as a commodity and predicted continued decline for the devices in the face of smartphones and tablets. Intel's server business remained strong, as mobile devices drove internet connectivity and traffic, and as of 2019 the company continues to pursue the emerging market for the so-called internet of things, a market filled with more uncertainty and slower growth than pundits expected. Intel is still the largest semiconductor company globally, but Otellini's failure to read the smartphone tea leaves cost his company, and its shareholders at the time, dearly.

Otellini claimed a lack of any sense of potential market size. He noted, in a 2013 interview:

> The thing you have to remember is that this was before the iPhone was introduced and *no one knew* what the iPhone would do . . . At the end of the day, there was a chip that they were interested in that they wanted to pay a certain

price for . . . and that price was below our *forecasted cost.* I couldn't see it. It wasn't one of these things you can make up on volume. And in hindsight, the forecasted cost was wrong and the volume was 100x *what anyone thought* (emphasis added).[9]

Creating the SRM Team

Otellini desperately needed SRM, a team and tools to help him assess and model the manifestation of the strategic risk the iPhone represented. SRM would not have provided a point forecast for either internal costs or market size; however, the teams and tools we outline in this chapter and the next would have given Otellini an order-of-magnitude estimate of market size and the potential trajectory of the new product. Before describing an SRM dream team, we first explain why organizations need a dedicated team at all.

The organization chart we present in figure 5.1 shows a robust and well-designed risk function, one that builds on the foundational principles we outlined in chapter 3 and brings to life the processes and roles we described in chapter 4. The CRO serves as a member of the C-suite executive team and interfaces on a regular basis with the CSO, the CFO, and general counsel in areas of joint concern or responsibility. The risk function covers three broad areas of responsibility: compliance (CROs have either solid-line reporting responsibility or dotted-line responsibility, shared with the CFO and general counsel); "tactical" risk (operating, financial, currency, safety, and security—including cybersecurity—risk, and ERM); and strategic risk.

Compliance personnel look backwards to make sure that the organization has followed all relevant rules and regulations that lie within their specific domain, as with Title IX officers for universities or Dodd-Frank reporting for financial institutions. Talented compliance officers act as the organization's experts in known rules. They spend the bulk to their time asking and reporting the answers to the question "Did we follow the rules?" They spend far less time, if any, asking or reporting about "Will we follow the rules in the future?" If they have time for the latter question, their time horizon tends to be short term, as they figure out how to make sure the organization does not stray from in-place rules and regulations.

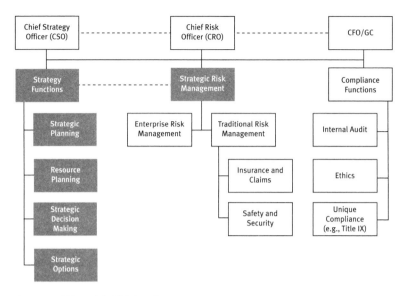

Figure 5.1   SRM and the Risk Function

Tactical risk managers focus on current risks, events, and exposures that can be predicted, rigorously modeled, and managed, minimized, or mitigated through traditional insurance, organizational processes, or programs. Important work? Certainly. Tactical risk managers have a much broader portfolio of interests than their compliance siblings; cybersecurity or safety arguably considers a larger scale and has a broader scope than does Title IX. They still live in the world of known knowns, and their focus lies squarely on today. The past provides a useful benchmark for assessing today's risks. Managing tactical risks may involve short-term (one quarter) or medium-term (up to eight quarters) initiatives to better manage risk, but anything longer term falls into the fuzzy future. Our experience teaches us that the ERM team, as a component of the tactical risk management function, has a fairly broad portfolio, as they consider risks that span departments, functions, or products. Although they live in the known-unknowns quadrant, their to-do list and programmatic solutions rarely look further than eight quarters. The main focus for ERM professionals and their tactical risk management associates is on the here and now.

The strategic risk team, in contrast, has a wide-ranging portfolio of concerns, and their focus may begin—and we emphasize *may*—eight quarters out, but SRM teams should focus on and frame issues of importance that are between twelve and forty quarters in the future. Such a long time horizon means that the SRM team embraces volatility, uncertainty, complexity, and ambiguity, because potential strategic risks will change and morph as they mature over time. The mind-sets and skill sets of SRM specialists differ markedly from those of compliance and tactical risk managers.

The notion of "I-shaped" versus "T-shaped" people captures the differences between the strategic and tactical risk management teams.[10] *Is* are specialists, with deep knowledge and expertise in a narrow functional area (*I* is in fact the narrowest letter in the English alphabet). Intel is a company filled with I-shaped people, whether they are engineers, salespeople, or financial analysts. What Otellini needed, however, were T-shaped people, who have an area of deep experience (the vertical element of the *T*) but who also have broader knowledge and interests that span areas and domains (the top of the *T*). *Ts* see more, and see more differently, than *Is*. Members of the SRM team need deep expertise in strategy and competitive advantage (the vertical element) along with broad knowledge in some other field, anything from art history to zoology, which helps them to look across environments and see things others miss. The job description for the SRM team begins with "Be a T-shaped person."

The best SRM teams operate under a charter from the board and at the direction of the CRO, but SRM teams must search for more than people who can live within a corporate constitution. They should avoid the limitations and narrow focus of the I-shaped technical specialists working in other dedicated risk functions. Nonetheless, SRM teammates can't just simply be broad, akin to a human em dash (—), because breadth alone provides no depth or historical, long-term perspective. The most desirable T-shaped people possess two other characteristics to contribute to an SRM team, one technical and one social.

Individual Characteristics: Curious Polymaths

Smart high school students, the ones taking lots of advanced, college-level courses, embody the ideal candidates, in terms of the breadth bar at the top of the *T*. They usually have a broad knowledge of what's currently popular, a knack for spotting the next big trend, and lack the tethers of assumptions, biases, and filters that come with age. These folks often disdain compliance and don't observe known guardrails, for better or worse. Perhaps that's why they pay so much for auto insurance. It's also a strong indicator of a future orientation and a fascination with the multifaceted possibilities that reside there.

What they gain in terms of the breadth bar, though, they lack in the vertical component. This void is scant knowledge of frameworks, models, and theories that allow signal to pierce through the noise of ambiguous and complex events. Life experience is low on the scale, as well; they lack the advantage of age, which helps cut at the joints between the timely/temporary and the timeless/permanent. Our preferred candidates, like the vertical line of the *T*, lie perpendicular to the enthusiasm and naïveté of teenagers. They are professionally trained adults with enough time in the saddle to know the difference between transitory fashion swings and lasting paradigm shifts, people who realize the value and the limits of customs, norms, and rules.

How does one combine these orthogonal characteristics? Look for curious polymaths. Polymaths have deep knowledge gained through a combination of formal training and informal experience. Critically, their knowledge and interests can span many unrelated areas. Undergraduate degree holders in the arts and sciences are a logical starting point to locate the kind of polymaths that make great *T*s and strategic risk analysts. Polymaths are individuals who ask questions about one domain of activity from the perspective of another domain. For example, how can we make computing more mobile? They arrive at answers by combining and synthesizing elements from different perspective to generate insightful solutions.

Polymaths have broad knowledge that creates top of the *T*, which they supplement with a genuine and abiding curiosity. Curiosity propels the search for deep causal drivers and understanding of new and foreign frontiers. It fuels the analysis and work that uncovers the deep structure of problems, how elements and mechanisms create cause and effect. It engenders a respect for the dynamic nature of cause and effect relationships and invites polymaths to think *over* time as well as *in* time. Curious people respect history. They understand Winston Churchill's claim that "the longer you can look back, the farther you can look forward."[11] They ask the complementary questions "How did we get here?" and "Where are we headed next?"

An MBA or similar advanced training helps our curious polymaths develop the *I* they'll need to succeed, which is a thorough understanding of strategy. SRM team members require extensive knowledge about the economic fundamentals of the business, the sources of the company's competitive advantage, and the relentlessly changing nature of competitive markets. MBAs, by design, gain a comprehensive working knowledge of each of the core functional areas of firms. Beyond the basics, many programs offer extended work in strategy. This additional study may incorporate both the "general's view," which synthesizes those functions into a big picture, and familiarity with drivers of unique, embedded customer value.

Group Characteristics: Respectful Hockey Players

SRM is a team sport for two reasons. First, the field of potential strategic risks is far too wide for a single individual to cover in any meaningful way. It must encompass a true 360-degree organizational perspective—the totality of its operations, value chain, customer engagement, competitor behaviors, technological evolutions and revolutions, governmental policy pivots and shifts, and long-term changes in social values and mores. Second, and driven by the reality of uncertainty absorption, a robust process of moving from observed reality to inferences about potential risks requires rigorous use of analytical frameworks and greatly benefits from multiple inputs. Team judgments trump individual ones in the complex work of determining strategic risks.

High-performing SRM teams field curious polymaths who work and play well with others. "Playing well" means not only collaborative interaction but also the willingness and ability to figuratively shove or throw an occasional elbow in the interest of breaking through barriers, as is the case in contact sports. Hockey provides a great example of how effective teams play together. Every day in practice, players beat on each other. Being kind, going slow, or sparing a teammate a hard check when called for makes for a pleasant experience, but it leads to more losses than wins. Great teams push themselves because they recognize that the inherent talent of each member (a prerequisite to be on the team) can fully express itself through active resistance.

Talents and ideas produce fruit in a setting of assertive inquiry. A. G. Lafley, the legendary Procter & Gamble CEO who doubled revenues during his watch, instilled a decision culture of assertive inquiry at P&G.[12] Assertive inquiry exists between the extremes of argumentative individual decision making ("I'm right, so get on board!") and acquiescent group processes ("I don't know, what do you all think?"). Assertive inquiry combines these polar opposites into a productive stance: "I've done a lot of work here and I think I'm right, but my perspective is limited and so I might be wrong." Teams with this mentality avoid the lash of arrogant individualism and the laziness of nonrigorous group processes. Assertive inquiry exhibits the hockey team mentality: individual excellence may render a strong decision, but it only becomes wise through the hands-on participation of the group.

Uncertainty absorption persists because of an enduring truth about organizational process, and SRM will be no exception. It is that laziness about getting the right people on the team, and lack of attention to creating the right culture results in quick and superficial insights. Uncertainty is then reduced though a cheap process of simplification and silent acquiescence. If strategic risks matter as much as we claim, and they do, then, as Jim Collins observed, "getting the right people on [the right] bus" precedes and enables later success. Questions of *who* must come before questions of *what*.[13] Now that we've dealt with the *who* question, we'll turn our attention to *where* the SRM team should look to find strategic risks.

Looking for Strategic Risks

Coimbatore Krishnarao (C. K.) Prahalad was "able to change the strategy landscape," as he puts it, and reshape the way companies thought about winning in their markets. His thinking around strategic intent and core competencies taught managers that companies possess more than just plant, equipment, and financial capital. Human intelligence and accumulated organizational learning prove equally powerful in creating and sustaining a winning position. Prahalad was a curious polymath. When he was asked, shortly before his death, how he changed a field of study, Prahalad answered that he centered his attention on weak signals. He explained: "Each weak signal was a contradictory phenomenon that was not happening across the board. You could very easily say, 'Dismiss it, this is an outlier, so we don't have to worry about it.' But the outliers and weak signals were the places to find a different way to think about the problem."[14]

Weak Signals

Our SRM team, a group of curious polymaths, scans a firm's PEST environments looking for weak signals that contain trace vibrations of potential futures. This includes dialoguing with various specialists within the organization as well as observing indicators in other industries for potential relevance. There are three main types of phenomena: those that contradict current logic, theory, or best practices; those that represent rare or extreme outliers; and those that appear and reappear intermittently over time.

Contradictory phenomena get discounted because they don't fit into or align with existing models of the way the markets work. Managers conveniently explain them away as the proverbial exception that proves the rule. Think back to the opening case in chapter 1. Neither cable TV nor ESPN fit into the existing broadcast network paradigm and television business model of the 1970s. Logic held that cable, with its traditional focus on rural Americans, would never generate enough eyeballs to attract big advertising dollars. ESPN should fail because it sought to satisfy a narrow audience but success in television came through, and was measured by, mass appeal.

What were the weak signals in this case? First, there existed unmet demand among rural Americans that could not be satisfied by current offerings; hence the introduction of cable. Second, unmet demand invites new business models because existing models leave those customers underserved. For cable, that model became subscriptions, under which customers paid for a previously free but now markedly better product. Even today, 60% of ESPN's revenue comes from subscriber fees.[15] Third, potential customers lived in rural America, but once the value of ESPN and cable's targeted offerings became apparent, the medium could easily encroach on the networks' prime territory: cities. Those weak signals turned into reality; as of 2017, the Big Three (ABC, CBS, and NBC) faced 136 cable competitors and their market share had fallen from almost 100% in 1980 to just over 25%.[16]

Theory-contradicting weak signals foreshadow strategic risks because they suggest that "fixed star" assumptions supporting current competitive advantages may no longer be as fixed as their purveyors presume. These weak signals suggest caution in continuing to invest in activities that might, in the future, lose their uniqueness to customers. They also indicate that additional, perhaps nontraditional, competitors may enter the market and respond in unanticipated ways that flow from different assumptions. Contradictory phenomena imply an increasingly malleable competitive landscape, and the key to success is forming revised assumptions about the nature and sustainability of current competitive advantages.

Outliers, extreme events, get ignored because they are rare and difficult for analysts to understand. Disney's purchase of twenty-seven thousand acres in Florida—a parcel 170 times the size of Disneyland—defied easy comprehension. Prescient analysts would have noted a strong signal that the sheer size of the property and a grandiose vision for Walt Disney World would consume management's attention for the foreseeable future. The direct impact of the purchase would likely shift internal resources toward theme parks and real estate management. The scale and scope of Disney World would require the development of previously unnecessary internal capabilities around large-scale real estate development and property management.

Other, weaker signals became meaningful over time. Walt Disney's unexpected death in 1966 exposed a lack of succession planning. Leadership under Roy Disney and his successors featured a preoccupation with cost containment, which meant that emerging real estate expertise came at the expense of the studio's existing capabilities, particularly in animated films. Sheer purchase size made the dynamics of development difficult to predict. Permitting processes, design and planning, and the actual construction of the park created a cadence that left huge tracts of land undeveloped. When Walt Disney World opened, in October 1971, it consumed a mere 107 acres, and Epcot, in 1982, added only another three hundred. Thus, 1.5% of the land generated revenue but 100% sat on the balance sheet as an untapped source of potential cash flow.

Outliers herald strategic risk because they spotlight stresses on organizational environments or systems. Competitive advantage builds from a stable configuration of internal and interconnected processes, resources, and capabilities, behaving somewhat like an inflated balloon. Outlier events put pressure on one part of the balloon, which causes all the other parts to move and respond. How the system reconfigures itself may threaten the core—recall how Disney's animation capabilities were gutted—or create opportunities for the expansion and extension of competitive advantages.

Intermittent phenomena get ignored because they appear, disappear, and then reappear under a different guise that, to casual observers, looks like something brand new. Fourteen years before Apple brought its iPhone to market, it introduced the Newton, a device touted as the first personal digital assistant. The small machine hoped to untether people from their desktop computers, and in that sense it represented the first mobile device. However, the Newton failed miserably, primarily because its handwriting recognition software proved unable to handle more than basic tasks.[17]

The Newton failed, but within three years the PalmPilot appeared. The first Pilots had all the features of the Newton, and its engineers had successfully cracked the code on handwriting recognition. Palm grew from nothing in 1996 to $720 million in sales by the turn of the millennium.[18] In 1999, Research in Motion introduced the BlackBerry, a handheld phone that allowed users to send e-mails and browse the internet. Cellular phones added computerlike features, and in June 2007, the first-generation iPhone was released and gave birth to the smartphone industry. The route from desktop to mobile took almost a decade and a half and featured a number of false starts and restarts.

Intermittent events, like the appearance of the Newton and then the PalmPilot, presage the emergence of strategic risks as they signal underlying shifts in design, economics, or technological attempts to satisfy nascent customer demands. A wise SRM team at Intel would have taken note of the Newton's attempt to create a new technological platform and, by the time the PalmPilot came on the market, would have identified mobile computing as a viable but immature market. What looked like an early fad would now appear as real strategic risk, full of opportunity and threat.

Could a high-performing SRM team have seen the risk in 1993 instead of in 1999? The Newton represented a very weak signal, but to see it as a source of strategic risk requires another analytical focus: the search for the deep structure that underlies an event or phenomenon. Deep structure, including a search for causal drivers and the ability to project growth trajectories, represents the second element SRM teams should look for.

Deep Structure and PEST

Table 5.1 sifts the three weak signals we have discussed (ESPN, Disney, and the Newton) through the PEST filters introduced earlier. We highlight the role of these forces in setting the stage for each strategic risk.

POLITICAL

Analysts could have foreseen the potential opportunity and threat of cable TV, though maybe not ESPN directly, as early as 1972, when the Nixon administration initiated deregulation of the industry. Those regulatory changes allowed, among other things, the more than 2,800 local cable systems to import "distant signals" from nonlocal stations for distribution to their viewers.[19] This change set the stage for cable "superstations" such as TBS, CNN, and eventually ESPN. Bill Rasmussen's seedling venture would fall into fertile soil, as ESPN appeared at a time when the political orientations allowed it to flourish.

Macro-Level Forces				
	Political	Economic	Social	Technological
The advent of ESPN	United States begins deregulating cable (1972) to allow more programming	The decline of the age of mass market goods and the rise of segmentation	Sports, both participation and programming, becoming more central to American life	Satellite transmission technology brings content to geographically dispersed cable providers
Disney's Florida land purchase	Local and state regulatory agencies grant Disney development rights	The reality that development causes land to appreciate in value over time	Increasing willingness of individuals and families to travel to destination resorts	Technological challenges involved in water management, power provision, and construction
Apple's Newton and mobile computing	Laissez-faire policy regimes toward electronic innovation and new technology	Moore's Law—the cost of complex computing operations falls at a predictable rate	Growing demographic of computer literate/ electronically "native" people. Preferences for miniaturization	Moore's Law— increasing technical capabilities in chipsets fuels more complex computing

Figure 5.1: A PEST Analysis of Three Weak Signals

ECONOMIC

Land is a physical asset that costs a lot to develop, and the realities of draining swampland, redirecting water, building a power grid, and laying roads all require tremendous amounts of capital. These necessities precede the equally intensive, commercially valuable work of attraction, hotel, and restaurant construction. It takes a long time and large amounts of capital investment to develop large tracts, and the value added by development drives up the market price of that land. Two decades after its purchase, the market value of Disney's Florida property acted like blood in the water that attracted takeover sharks.

SOCIAL

The social force helps to explain the failure of Apple's Newton and the eventual success of the Palm, BlackBerry, and iPhone. One perspective saw the Newton as just another failed toy for technophiles and the rich. From another perspective, however, it represented a first foray into an increasingly important demographic: people "native" to technological gadgets, for whom mobile computers create tremendous value. Newton hoped to, but could not, satisfy a clear consumer preference for mobility and miniaturization in electronic devices, a preference that the Sony Walkman had shown to be quite robust in the late 1980s. Palm and BlackBerry solved the key technological problems, both exposing and exploiting the latent demand for untethered computing.

TECHNOLOGICAL

Technology proves to be a critical tectonic plate for strategic risks. Emerging use of satellite transmission for cable signals gave ESPN access to a national market from the beginning. The technical hurdles of transforming central Florida into a magic kingdom called into question the wisdom of the scale of Walt's Florida purchase. Newton leveraged Moore's Law to drive miniaturization in hardware, but the insurmountable challenge came from the crudeness of handwriting recognition software.

The PEST model adds depth to the search for weak signals, discerning between merely "weak" phenomena and events that "signal" paradigm shifts and the emergence of strategic risks. Table 5.1 illustrates how each PEST factor contributed to the appearance of strategic uncertainty. Smart SRM teams look for connections among elements in assessing the strength of weak signals. Once the team has identified contradictory events, outliers, or recurrent events that presage strategic risks, they need a mechanism to frame those risks that facilitates easy communication and implies a monitoring strategy.

Framing Strategic Risks

John Bugalla developed a prototype of the Strategic Uncertainty Decision Map more than a decade ago to help his clients understand the nature of enterprise-level risks, those that span multiple subunits. Version 2.0 of this tool, presented in figure 5.2, helps SRM teams frame strategic risks in ways that allow others to grasp their essential nature, causes, and potential impact. As we will explain, the tool works on the reality that weak signals take time to mature and blossom into full-blown strategic risks.

Although the map looks like the targets used by archers or sharpshooters, the analyst does not aim for the center when using it. That is the point at which uncertainty transforms into risk and the ownership of emerging risks passes to management teams to develop specific response plans. Risk analysts plot each weak signal in a space defined by the core PEST drivers and the estimated time to impact. A rich and useful map will contain multiple potential strategic uncertainties, initially weak signals that become stronger over time, in each quadrant and time horizon.

The axes have no titles, as they exist to separate the four PEST engines of uncertainty. Placement of the risks in locations marked by the four

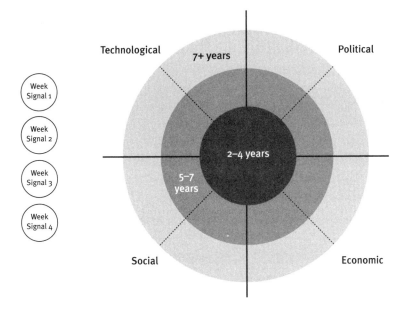

Figure 5.2   The Strategic Uncertainty Map

quadrants is the first task and proceeds according the underlying forces moving each weak signal. Signals driven by a single PEST force lie directly along the dotted axis. Risks arising equally from two PEST forces are plotted on the solid axis that separates those two forces. (Note that if the forces were political and social, the target is simply redrawn to create an adjacency.) The location might move over time, but the PEST forces provide a baseline to track evolutionary progress or revolutionary pivots.

Next, situating risks temporally differentiates the strategic uncertainty map from traditional risk management tools. It enables analysts to capture the three-dimensional maturity of strategic risk: over time, from weak and uncertain signal to strong, and differentiated between likely risk or opportunity. A simple rule of thumb controls the placement of signals into the time horizon—the weaker the signal, the greater the uncertainty and the longer the runway until a threat or opportunity emerges. The first appearance of a new signal sends it to the outer band. A second occurrence of an intermittent signal captures initial maturation and the signal moves inward. When fully expressed risks reach the inner circle, ownership of the emerging risk transfers to specific line managers, who develop response plans.

Understanding the Mobile Computing Market with the Strategic Uncertainty Map

Newton, as the first weak signal, lands on the map somewhere in the space linking technological and social forces. Technologically, the Newton represented an incremental advance along the hardware dimension of miniaturization but a longer leap in terms of software, handwriting recognition, and embryonic capabilities for wireless synching between two devices. Socially, the personal digital assistant hoped to exploit a long-term preference toward miniaturization and fuzzy demand for particular digital solutions for tasks such as calendaring, scheduling, and note taking.

The Newton device in 1993 occupies a place in the outer time band. Developers had yet to solve the core software and synching problems, which would allow it to reach a larger market. A smart SRM team could calibrate a time estimate through research on the projected trajectory of handwriting recognition. Clues were likely available, such as through academic conferences on the topic or by encouraging research centers and individual experts to join the conversation about the topic. Our team seeks answers to key questions, such as how long did it take to get to where we are? Is development speeding up or staying on the current pace? How steep are the hills just ahead?

Having identified a one-off weak signal, the team would have continued to monitor for others. It came in the form of the PalmPilot, in 1996 and 1997. Palm solved the core handwriting recognition and wireless connectivity challenges. These advances combined to turn the Palm into a mass market device. By 1998, Palm was selling a million units a year, and 2 million a year later.[20] A market existed for mobile computing devices, and more functionality meant a larger market. In early 2002, Palm licensed its operating system and software to all comers, and the company incorporated a low-power ARM-based central processing unit as the brain of its devices.[21]

Palm solved the most vexing technical problems and proved that a profitable mobile device market did exist. BlackBerry's first phone, in 1999, complete with e-mail and web browsing, buttressed such a view. BlackBerry entered an already crowded cellular phone market, but the extent of mobile connectivity it offered created sufficient space to flourish. BlackBerry hit 1 million subscribers within a year (about 70% of what the iPhone later did), and another 3 million by 2005.[22] Clear evidence existed that a product offering customers additional features could generate substantial volume quickly.

By mid-2002, fully five years before the launch of the iPhone and three years before Jobs approached Otellini, a properly constructed strategic uncertainty map would have shown that the weak signal of the Newton had transformed into a strategic risk and opportunity labeled "mobile computing devices." Palm and BlackBerry both exposed the latent demand and market potential of such a device by reaching 1 million units annually within two years of launch. (Apple sold 1.4 million iPhones in its first year, more than double Palm's sales velocity.) The team also would have linked the evolution of mobile devices to low-power central processing units, precisely the kind of processor Jobs asked Intel to produce just three years later.

SRM team members own the responsibility to track weak signals until they give birth to strategic risks. By 2002 or 2003, the SRM group would have informed Intel's C-suite and board that mobile computing risk should be incorporated into the planning and activities of the appropriate Tick-Tock engineering groups. A well-developed strategic uncertainty map sets the stage for order-of-magnitude estimates about potential volumes and sales velocity and for teams actively working on cost-effective chips at the 2005 decision point.

We've omitted discussion of the size of the small circles on the map that become strategic risks. They begin life as weak signals. As those signals mature and strengthen over time, analysts classify strategic risks and opportunities and estimate the speed of movement toward the center. Two questions arise: What does the size of the circle represent, and what determines the size of the circle? The answers are found in the potential impact of an identified strategic risk. In and of itself, the strategic uncertainty map provides little guidance on sizing. The tools we outline in chapter 6 address this issue.

Conclusion

This chapter answered four "ground-level" questions: Why have a dedicated SRM team? Who should be on that team? Where should they look for strategic risks? How should one frame those risks in ways that others can easily grasp and understand. Firms need dedicated SRM teams because strategic risks aren't like tactical ones. Curious polymaths possess considerable skills to search for strategic risks, but they need to play a full-contact game and use the methods of assertive inquiry as they do their work. Looking for, assessing, and evaluating weak signals in the marketplace or the larger social environment are the rules of this game. We finished with the *how* question and introduced the Strategic Uncertainty Decision Map as a tool that helps the SRM team frame potential strategic risks.

The eventual success of the Newton as it morphed into the iPhone illustrates the power of, and need for, careful analysis a decade or more in advance. Apple capitalized on the strategic uncertainty that the Newton tried to exploit, and they won big. Intel lost not only the first generation of smartphones but also ensuing ones. We've argued here that an SRM team would have helped Paul Otellini see that the volume potential of smartphones would more than make up for the thin margins their chips would earn. Chapter 6 moves from the SRM team and the Strategic Uncertainty Decision Map tool as a framing device and introduces three new tools to evaluate the potential impact of strategic risks and to develop management plans for them.

CHAPTER 6

SRM at Ground Level: What Tools to Analyze and Manage Strategic Risks

This chapter presents three core tools for the strategic risk management team to use. The first, scenario planning, helps leaders understand how weak signals might evolve and become strategic risks. The second, wargaming, allows them to examine a particular manifestation of a future scenario and see how they, and other important stakeholders, might respond. With knowledge of possible and probable responses, teams employ the third tool, the Risk Ownership Map, to actively manage strategic risks.

. . . . .

Ole Kirk Christiansen founded the LEGO company in 1932 to market his high-quality wooden toys. The word *LEGO* is a mash-up of two Danish words, *leg* and *godt*, which translate to "play well," and the company's mission is to inspire and develop the builders of tomorrow.[1] Its product and financial fortunes changed dramatically in 1958, when LEGO phased out wooden toys and took a risk on a new, patented plastic brick. This distinctive interlocking cube allowed children, and adults, virtually unlimited potential for building and play. LEGO bricks underpin every fabulous LEGO creation, from simple little houses to complex representations of the world's great cities. In 1999, *Fortune* magazine cited the LEGO brick as one of the best products of the twentieth century.[2]

Ole's company prospered for most of the twentieth century, but as the new millennium dawned, LEGO sailed into two strong VUCA headwinds. With the expiration of the company's patent, LEGO faced increasingly sophisticated competitors with very similar products, such as China's BanBao, Canadian firm Mega Bloks, Tyco Super Blocks, and K'Nex engineering sets. Its core customer, five- to nine-year-old boys, also began to change. The rising generation seemed to prefer story-driven, action-packed video games and entertainment on the emerging internet instead of do-it-yourself construction sets.

Internally, LEGO became complacent. With over six decades of unrivaled success, LEGO designers and executives, based in tiny Billund, Denmark, felt they well knew what their customers wanted and would buy. For the most part, if the company produced a toy, it would sell. And LEGO produced lots of toys. From 1994 to 1998, the company tripled its rate of new product introduction. Notably, as the twenty-first century began, most of those toys failed to sell.[3] Revenue peaked in 2000, at DKK 8,379 million ($1,243 million), dipped to a low point of DKK 6,295 million ($933 million) in 2004, and was still lagging behind its 2000 peak in 2005. Equally troubling were the operating and net profit losses in 2003 and 2004, which had turned slightly positive in 2005 only through major expense reductions.[4] Bankruptcy appeared on the horizon—a once inconceivable prospect for the founding Kristiansen family.[5]

LEGO began the long climb back to profitability under the guidance of a former McKinsey consultant, CEO Jørgen Vig Knudstorp, and CFO Jesper Ovesen, a numbers-loving transplant from Danske Bank. Together they created a multiyear "shared vision" renewal plan. First, stabilize the company and eliminate unprofitable lines. Throughout 2003 and 2004, LEGO de-risked its business by eliminating many poorly selling products and refocusing its sales efforts on working with retail partners. In 2005 and 2006, the company initiated its second goal, to build a defensible core of profitable platform products. LEGO returned to its core value proposition, a system of interlocking products—not just bricks—that created a system of play with endless possibilities for its core customers. To do this, LEGO had to reacquaint itself with those core customers, young boys and adult fans, who held continuing loyalty to the company.

By 2006, Knudstorp and Ovesen felt ready to begin the third element of their shared vision: revitalize the brand and grow the company.[6] With stable, growing earnings, the company took on additional risks associated with new products and geographic expansion. This third element would rely on equal parts design and development creativity, supported by operational and financial discipline. LEGO needed a risk management group that could help provide that discipline. While the company had a strong commitment to ERM, the unit largely reacted to change and focused on minimizing losses. It had little to offer about strategy or growth. Ovesen looked for the right leader for the ERM group, and in late 2006 decided upon Hans Læssøe.[7]

Læssøe encountered risk management processes centered on risk assessment and the mitigation of financial, operating, and force majeure risks. Each category had a different set of activities attached to it. For example, financial risks were subject to hedging techniques established by the board of directors, business unit plans specified operational risks, and insurable risks aligned with the annual commercial insurance-buying market cycle. According to the 2006 LEGO Group annual report, four specific risks—market development, brand development, outsourcing, and innovation—were elevated to the attention of the board of directors.

Læssøe, a twenty-five-year company veteran, would soon change all that. He had served as a corporate strategic controller with zero years of risk management experience. In his own words, he was "an ignorant practitioner" with a willingness to learn and a penchant for data-driven decision making.[8] Over the next half decade, Læssøe and his team would provide an example of the power of SRM to influence strategy making and execution and would contribute to the LEGO Group turnaround. On their watch, strategic risk management discipline allowed creativity to turn into profitability.

Læssøe and his group's successful efforts stand in stark contrast to the saga of Wells Fargo. Wells Fargo turned a blind eye to a problematic internal sales process, allowing it to metastasize into a strategic calamity. On the other hand, the LEGO Group grappled with a lack of alignment between sales and strategy, including input sourcing, production timing, and global logistical support. Læssøe's team created unique sales scenarios for each market, built operating and financial models, and employed sophisticated Monte Carlo simulations to uncover the drivers and ramifications of misalignments.[9] With the data in hand, the SRM team helped LEGO executives move beyond gut instinct as a guide to strategy.

Making use of an existing business planning process known as "prepare for uncertainty," Læssøe launched Active Risk and Opportunity Planning (AROP), which shifted risk management from a reactive, loss-avoiding role to a proactive tool to help executives answer strategic questions about the future. The team led scenario planning sessions with the company's consumer insight group to conceive plausible rather than predictive insights about potential futures. These took the form of global, macroeconomic strategic scenarios intended to stress-test risk and resilience in light of the current market and product portfolio that the LEGO Group confronted. When faced with data unavailability, Læssøe fabricated an internal "process expert network" of project managers to make use of their structured expert judgment and drive executive discussion.[10]

Willingness to proactively search for new opportunities and to rigorously analyze what the future might be like in those markets gave the LEGO Group additional perspective to determine where and how the company could expand in a cutthroat toy market. SRM analysis and financial modeling helped executives to expand in both Asia and the United States at the onset of the Great Recession.

With the SRM team producing actionable insights, the company experienced phenomenal growth. In the ten-year period from 2005 to 2015, revenue increased 408%, from DKK 7,050 million ($1,058 million) to DKK 35,780 million ($5,370 million), and net profit grew 1,720%, from DKK 505 million ($75 million) to DKK 9,174 million ($1,377 million), far outpacing a toy market that was yielding low-single-digit growth over the same time frame. The LEGO Group's profits quadrupled in the compressed window of 2008 to 2010, a time when many manufacturing companies struggled to break even.[11]

At LEGO, several critical factors converged to create an ideal environment for SRM to flourish: a tightly held private company in turnaround mode, a highly analytical CEO, a strong champion in the CFO, an embedded ERM foundation upon which to build, virtually unrestricted access to resources, uniquely talented leadership, and a dedicated staff to spearhead SRM adoption. As the chief day-to-day practitioner, Læssøe took full advantage of his operational span of influence and made good use of many tools and principles to forge an SRM function that added value.

Philosophically, Læssøe changed LEGO's approach to risk. "We had already taken the risks and decided on our strategy, but only started doing something about them afterwards." LEGO needed a "naturally integrated" approach to risk management that considered the impact of uncertainty on the LEGO global business model. To do so, Læssøe changed the mindset and focus from the past and the rearview mirror to the future and the front windshield.[12]

Læssøe intuitively understood the importance of risk management as an exercise in organizational ambidexterity, fully encompassing both downside risk and upside value propositions.[13] He went to management with the idea that SRM "enables us to focus on opportunities and take bigger chances because we have defined risk tolerances."[14] Læssøe moved LEGO toward fulfilling a prediction of Robert Rennie, which we cited earlier: "To the extent that the risk manager can improve his techniques for measuring risk and to the extent that he can reduce uncertainty, he can extend the growth horizons of the firm."[15]

Læssøe summarized his view of the role of SRM in this way: "Risk management is not just about the top layer of a group. It should be part of what you do as a company every day. You want to see a natural approach to risk management where people ask about uncertainties, rather than only focusing on sales or profit targets."[16] These deeds did not go unnoticed, and Læssøe's contributions led to multiple commendations, including a Corporation of the Year innovation award from *Operational Risk & Regulation*, in 2011.

Hans Læssøe and his risk leadership sets the stage for this chapter. LEGO represents one of the few examples of truly successful SRM and illustrates several important elements of what we have called for in earlier chapters. Consistent with our call for ERM and SRM to work in tandem, Læssøe built the company's SRM practice on a strong existing ERM platform that could leverage the skills, expertise, and access to resources that ERM provided to move risk management to a forward-looking, opportunity-seeking approach. Although LEGO had no chief strategy officer, as the de facto chief risk officer, Læssøe integrated his efforts with the executives and line managers who crafted and implemented strategy. Relevant to the discussion that follows, he grounded SRM in a set of strong, data-driven analytical tools. The next section describes three strategy devices that your company can put in an SRM tool kit: scenario planning, wargaming, and the Risk Ownership Map.

The Tools of SRM

Scenario planning, wargaming, and the Risk Ownership Map build upon the core premises of this book. Uncertainty, or the inability to create probabilities and point forecasts, characterizes strategic risk and requires analytical tools fit for purpose to assess, evaluate, and plan for strategic risk. These devices aren't designed to bring critical uncertainties to resolution. Rather, they inform the SRM analysts and decision makers who explore potential development trajectories and implications for possible futures. In turn, risk-informed decision making enables the type of effective SRM that narrows the strategy–execution gap.

Let's begin with a straw man example to illustrate the need for different tools, using the stock-in-trade risk management heat map. Heat maps are two-dimensional rectangles in which the probability of a risk exposure or event and its potential financial impact define the axes. A typical map, as shown in figure 6.1, marks the axes by qualitative measures (low, medium, high), although some maps use actual probability or dollar ranges. The shift from light to medium to dark grey demarcate increasing degrees of risk and suggest appropriate management responses. The three colors of the traffic semaphore, green, yellow, and red, demarcate increasing degrees of risk and suggest the appropriate management response. Decision makers can

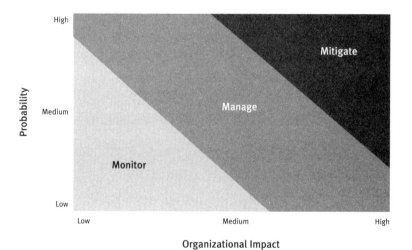

Figure 6.1   A traditional heat map

observe, at a glance, a rudimentary risk profile of the organization, illustrated by individual risk relativities. From here, managers can assign ownership of individual risks to organizational actors and develop response strategies.

Our notion of SRM fits with the map's impact axis. Where we part ways is in our focus on the impact to competitive advantage, not specific end-of-pipe financial measures. Our SRM instruments assess the potential scale and scope of that impact and yield ranges and order-of-magnitude projections. The larger problem, for us, rests with the probability axis. As we've argued throughout this book, uncertainty drives strategic risk, and uncertainty belies a point probability forecast. Uncertainty doesn't really lend itself to even the broad categorization of "more probable" and "less probable" until time passes, weak signals mature, and uncertainty begins to resolve and reveal a clear trajectory.

So the heat map provides, at best, a snapshot in time, but SRM requires a video. Heat maps are useful when risks can be categorized in the known known or even the unknown known quadrants of the Rumsfeld matrix. We believe that strategists and executives need a different set of tools to deal with the uncertainty that characterizes strategic risk. Each tool we present here provides insight into how uncertainty may evolve, rather than where it might end up.

Scenario Planning

Herman Kahn, a RAND Corporation military analyst, studied the conditions that might lead to a nuclear war in the decade following World War II. "Thinking the unthinkable" was Kahn's job description, a job that made him the model for Dr. Strangelove in Stanley Kubrick's 1964 dark comedy.[17] Thinking the unthinkable required a new way to model the future, one that accounted for, embraced, and even celebrated the inherent uncertainty and reality of multiple possible outcomes. Kahn's systematic approach created different scenarios to outline the perimeter of potential futures. Today, scenario planning provides a powerful tool for people hoping to understand what the future might look like.

Scenario planning provides leaders with a structured process to generate stories and images that enliven four potentially radically different futures. Scenario planning is kryptonite to the natural tendency toward uncertainty absorption. Extreme outcomes are its explicit aims, and its structure overcomes the natural bureaucratic tendency toward incremental, conservative forecasts (such as *best case*, *worst case*, and *expected case*). Scenario planning accentuates extreme outcomes because the exercise seeks to define the outer edges of what's possible. Decision makers need to consider the implications of these almost fantastical scenarios before dialing back to more realistic assessments. Scenario planning entails four steps.

STEP 1: DETERMINE THE QUESTION AND THE TIME FRAME

Scenario planning's output targets the board and senior executives, those responsible for the longest time horizon and having the most flexible view of strategy. Scenario time frames should match the board's strategy horizon, usually seven to ten years. Thinking a decade out moves the team far beyond point forecasts drawn from current demand or production technologies. Good questions that satisfy Goldilocks's demands begin the process; these have sufficient breadth to invite a wide-angle investigation of the future but are not so broad that analysts are forced to boil the ocean to get an answer. Inquiry is based on product classes or fundamental cost drivers, not individual products or inputs. Scenarios incorporate product and factor market considerations but avoid the complexity of industries or sectors.

We don't know what questions Hans Læssøe and his team asked about the Chinese and U.S. markets that prompted expansion, but they seem to have been good ones. We also believe that it's easier to learn from failure than from success, so we'll return to the case we used in chapter 5, Intel's decision to forego the smartphone market, to illustrate how scenario planning works. What questions should Intel have asked, and when should they have asked them, in order to make a better decision? How could they have spotted the bread crumbs we identified in chapter 5 and seen the iPhone's potential? Poor questions would be "What is the future of the Newton, or the Palm?" This is too narrow. Likewise, "What is the future of mobile electronics?" is too broad, covering too many sectors. A more constructive question is "What is the future of mobile computing?" This query gets beyond individual products and deals directly with the job to be done: computing on the go. It also puts a marker on what would have been, in 1993 or 1996, the trend toward miniaturization and mobility.

We, as the Intel SRM team, would have begun creating scenarios in late 1996 or early 1997, when the first Palms gained traction in the market. As noted in chapter 5, Newton was sufficiently novel and constituted a signal about a potential future strategic risk. However, the gadget never took off, which appended "weak" to the signal. Apple continued production until Steve Jobs returned to the helm and canceled the product in 1998.[18] The appearance of the Palm and its early success validated the concept of mobile computing, and by the time the BlackBerry appeared, the future was beginning to converge.

STEP 2: IDENTIFY THE KEY UNCERTAINTIES

By definition, the future is uncertain. Not all uncertainty is the same, and some uncertainty matters more than others. There are always key or critical uncertainties acting as barriers to stymie progress toward a clear and definable future. When these material and long-term uncertainties resolve, planners can then think in terms of risks—a set of payoffs and attendant probabilities that affords both consumers and producers the wherewithal to make investment decisions. Tangible investments give birth to one future as they simultaneously kill off alternatives. Demand for certain product and service classes grows while demand for others shrinks.

Analysts find these critical uncertainties resident in the PEST forces. Deep policy shifts such as from regulation to unfettered markets, the turn from fashionable to foundational among consumers, alternative business models that alter production and related costs, or quantum leaps in technological progress (as described in Moore's Law) are representative of these key uncertainties. Even among the PEST forces, differences in the criticality of the drivers will vary. At times, technology and social changes matter more, while at other times political and economic forces dominate.

Scenario planning works best when two uncertainties stand out. In an ideal world, they are independent, or orthogonal, in the language of the model. However, because the PEST elements interrelate with each other to create a unified system, complete independence proves illusory. In its design, the PEST model yields twelve potential two-force configurations, and removing duplicates culls that number to six: political-economic, political-social, political-technological, economic-social, economic-technological, and social-technological. Planners need to carefully choose which pair will play the greatest role.

Mobile device marketability depended on resolving technical challenges, but consumer preference and latent demand for miniaturization already existed in the electronics sector. By 1996, Palm had solved the core technical challenge of an effective user interface, and the advent of the World Wide Web would eliminate most connectivity challenges. For us, two uncertainties seem key. One could take the preference for miniaturization as given, but would a small, mobile computer be a complement to or a substitute for the then-dominant platform of desktop computing? Sony's Walkman proved the appeal of mobile music, but no one ditched their home stereo or CD player. Walkmans were just a complement. Would a mobile computing device be any different?

Similarly, advances in cellular technology (1993) and the rise of the internet (1995–1996) implied better connectivity, but would that connectivity prove expensive or cheap for a mass audience? America Online, the earliest version of mass internet connectivity, required dial-up fees, but it also carried the opportunity cost of tying up one's only phone connection while one was on line. In 1993, mobile hardware still represented an expensive investment, one exacerbated by gaps in the accompanying cellular networks. The rise of the Web enhanced the value of connectivity and the appeal of mobile devices, so the key question in the mid-1990s, for us, would have been how accessible and how expensive internet access would be. With these as our dimensions, or axes, we move on to the next step.

STEP 3: LABEL THE AXES AND CREATE THE SCENARIOS

Each axis represents a continuum, and, consistent with the goals of scenario planning, the endpoints need to capture extreme potential outcomes. Scenario builders should avoid bland-sounding labels such as *pessimistic*, *optimistic*, *more*, or *less* and instead use graphic descriptions like *Mariana Trench* or *Moonshot*. End points define the peaks of what's ultimately possible, not the muddy valleys of the currently probable. Being outlandish here is a virtue, because expansive boundaries leave plenty of room for imaginative thinking. Catchy and provocative labels resist uncertainty absorption and the dominance of midrange thinking.

Scenario cartographers draw their maps by placing the uncertainty continua perpendicular to and bisecting each other. This arrangement creates four quadrants corresponding to the available combinations of the critical uncertainties. One quadrant will be "low-low" and one "high-high," based on the ends of each continuum. These two represent opposite worlds, an interesting diagonal that lends itself to consistent responses. Low-low typically represents an extension of the status quo, as uncertainties resolve in ways little different from current arrangements. While it is attractive to market incumbents because it features little need for new investment, the low-low outcome has a low prima facie probability of 25%.

If the low-low quadrant favors current competitors, then the high-high future opens opportunities for new entry, through either entrepreneurial startups or corporate diversification, by firms with the resources and capabilities to perform the job to be done in a radically different future. High-high, like its opposite, has a 25% chance of coming to fruition.

The off-diagonal quadrants foreshadow complex futures, ones without the clarity of little or radical change. These quadrants contain high-low blends, and decision makers need to attend to the nuances of each configuration in terms of market sizes, segments, production possibilities, and regulatory regimes. A blended, complex world represents the most likely outcome, with a 50% probability of some high-low combination.

The next task involves naming each scenario. Good scenarios employ provocative titles that emphasize the potential inherent in each one. Again, the goal is to create extreme cases that move normally staid strategic planners to view the future differently. Catchy sound bites work best, and richly descriptive words like *heaven* and *hell*, *paradise* and *purgatory*, invite decision makers to push the boundaries of their own thinking about what's possible. The final element of the map is a rich picture of each scenario that describes a discrete future in terms of elements of interest, such as product categories, cost drivers, or the nature and shape of consumer demand.

Figure 6.2 presents a simple scenario map for mobile computing, as it might have looked in 1996 and 1997. Our logic suggested that we frame the future in terms of how customers would use a mobile device (as a substitute or complement to a desktop machine) and of the ubiquity of connectivity, based on final consumer cost. Different futures are laid out in the four scenarios, and our map would have provided Intel planners with a high-level take on two product categories: large desktop machines (then the dominant form of computing) and small mobile devices. Catchy scenario titles help engage decision makers in the next phase.

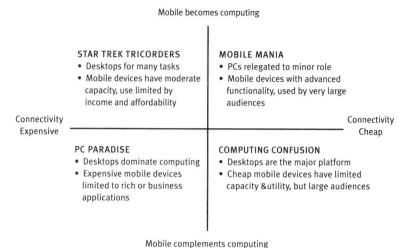

Mobile becomes computing

STAR TREK TRICORDERS	MOBILE MANIA
• Desktops for many tasks	• PCs relegated to minor role
• Mobile devices have moderate capacity, use limited by income and affordability	• Mobile devices with advanced functionality, used by very large audiences

Connectivity Expensive ———————————————————————— Connectivity Cheap

PC PARADISE	COMPUTING CONFUSION
• Desktops dominate computing	• Desktops are the major platform
• Expensive mobile devices limited to rich or business applications	• Cheap mobile devices have limited capacity &utility, but large audiences

Mobile complements computing

Figure 6.2   Potential scenarios in mobile computing, ca 1996-8

STEP 4: IDENTIFY TRIGGERS AND POTENTIAL INVESTMENTS

With four different futures now in view, the final element of scenario planning involves identifying signs and signals that indicate which version of the future will become reality and determining initial investments to prepare for an uncertain future. For example, how could Intel planners know whether mobile devices would become complements or substitutes for desktop machines? What early investments would pay dividends regardless of the final future of mobile devices?

Overall sales of specific products like the Newton or Palm provide one identification metric. After a certain point, the tech enthusiast market becomes saturated and more mainstream users, albeit still early adopters, convert to the platform. Development of an ecosystem also signals clarity about the future. When software vendors begin developing applications such as a mobile version of Microsoft Office, or cellular connectivity tools emerge that allow users to perform more sophisticated tasks, then analysts foresee a future in which mobile substitutes for the PC. Once the team defines these key identifiers, they design appropriate deep data collection and monitoring protocols to spot early convergence toward one particular future.

Planners and decision makers need to think in terms of platform investments—spending that provides the company with knowledge and skills that are valuable across multiple futures. Investments at this early stage should not be limited to products or services valuable in one future only but should focus on gaining knowledge, setting standards, generating processes, or shaping regulation around the core uncertainty drivers that apply across all the potential futures. It may prove impossible to make investments that cover all four futures, but good investments will often cover at least two, and often three, future states.

In terms of mobile computing, the ability of users to connect with other devices matters in all four futures. What varies is the ubiquity and cost of connectivity. In the mid-1990s, planners should be suggesting that Intel supplement its deep knowledge about wired connectivity and the server business with information about the current state and trajectory of cellular and wireless connectivity. This would answer questions like "What types of chipsets would work best for these new mobile platforms?"

The company might also join industry associations or lobbying groups and send engineers to academic and trade conferences to get in the flow of cellular and wireless ecosystem developments. These investments provide Intel with insight into how the connectivity market might evolve and afford a seat at the tables where regulatory and technical standards are being established. As the future leans toward a particular connectivity paradigm, Intel engineers are better positioned to more rapidly develop products and services for a changing world.

Scenario planning presents possible competitive environment outcomes, but it offers limited guidance for specific internal responses to environmental changes. There are several ways to move forward. Hans Læssøe has developed a matrix named the PAPA model (Prepare, Act, Park, Adapt), which prioritizes strategic responses and actions.[19] Wargaming, the next model in our SRM tool kit, also gives decision makers a way to simulate expected and possible responses.

Wargaming

Economist and game theorist Thomas Schelling spent the summer of 1957 at RAND, as the Cold War continued to ramp up. Inspired by the RAND scholars he found playing limited, tactical wargames, Schelling came up with a different approach that focused more on overall strategy to reflect the type of risks he saw as most critical. Called Red vs. Blue, his contest thrust participants into a highly competitive arena designed to tease out the likelihood of tactical conflict escalating to strategic nuclear war.[20]

Fortunately, nuclear war is an off-the-table consideration for most business decisions. We'll describe how SRM teams can use the machinery of Red vs. Blue games to assist decision makers in comprehending the action and investment trajectories in the futures suggested by scenario planning. Wargaming offers planners the ability to see how different actors will naturally respond as they apply their current assumptions, logic, and values to a changed environment. The tool surfaces unavoidable tensions and conflicts in those responses, as well as ones arising from poor communications and faulty assumptions. In short, wargaming allows teams to make mistakes in battle and to learn, without spilling real blood.

To conduct a Red vs. Blue game, analysts need four elements: A red team, a blue team, a control team, and an opening "crisis." Each team begins with a set of goals and objectives that define a win for that team and outcomes that would constitute a clear loss. Each team has between five and seven members, but no one has a preassigned role (such as secretary of state or director of marketing) that would bias or limit their perspective. Each team member should be fully involved in all decision making; the goal is to maximize team members' engagement and input into decisions and their commitment to implementing those decisions. The teams may be direct competitors or they may simply be different stakeholders in an industry value chain. Red and blue team members come from the organization, and the control team may as well, or leaders might engage consultants to design and run the game as the control team.

Effective wargames last two to four days, with ample time for a number of decision rounds, followed by an extensive debriefing to capture learning. The control team begins the game by presenting both teams with a concrete triggering event, perhaps a major crisis or a small event capable of mushrooming into something major. Schelling, trying to prevent nuclear war, used trigger events that involved some type of Soviet aggression or provocation against a U.S. ally. For an Intel wargame team in 1993, the trigger might have been what turned out to be the PalmPilot, or in 2000 it might have been the BlackBerry, which was currently storming the market.

The red and blue teams don't just react to the trigger willy-nilly. They must follow a set protocol. Each team first has to decide and define what just happened, what type of threat the trigger represents, and how they think the other team will respond over some designated time period. For Schelling and military games, this might be hours or days, but for a business wargame, the time frame might be several quarters. Each team develops an action plan that outlines three types of responses: what will they do immediately on their own, what will they do at some time in the future, and what actions would be contingent upon what their opponent does. Each team takes a half day to debate, discuss, and develop a fairly robust action plan, which they submit to the control team.

The control team considers the actions of red and blue and creates a new situation that moves the game to the next round. Control evaluates independent actions and projects consequences as well as contingent actions. Control then presents red and blue with the next stage situation, which includes the outcomes of red's and blue's actions but may also include additional triggers or elements. In our example, control may introduce a new wrinkle in connectivity capabilities, platforms, or products, just to stir up the game. Red and blue then formulate their next set of decisions. Rinse and repeat for as many rounds as desired, usually three (for a two-day retreat) or five (for a four-day retreat).

The game's outcome matters little, the actual learning a lot. The control team finishes the simulation with a half- to full-day debrief. Individuals and teams need to document what they learned. What went as expected? What surprised them, either about their own actions or those of the other team? Where did they make mistakes? What would they do differently? The debrief concludes with an action plan designed to foster three outcomes: the elimination of mistakes, particularly those caused by faulty shared assumptions or values; the strengthening of what worked or what the organization needs to keep doing; and a plan for adding skills, knowledge, or outlooks that would have led to better outcomes.

The value of a wargame lies in the ability of teams to make and learn from mistakes without having to spill blood, corporate dollars, market share points, or head count. A well-designed game gets decision makers to react naturally and then see how those actions play out over time. A set of ongoing wargames tracking the rise of mobile computing from the Newton through the BlackBerry, and including the iPod and iPad, would have left Paul Otellini with a clear sense of his company's true cost, and the available margin, for the low-power chip Steve Jobs wanted. He also should have had a better idea about the size of the potential market, its growth trajectory, and the expected impact on Intel's core PC chips. Put simply, the tools of

SRM could have prevented point forecasts that were, as Otellini claimed, one hundred times in error. Intel might have been the industry standout in mobile, just as it dominated the desktop.

Leaders should engage in wargames each time a weak signal becomes stronger or converges toward a predictable trajectory. As signals mature, interest shifts away from the original PEST drivers and causes and toward expected functional or business units impacts. The final tool in our kit, the Risk Ownership Map, guides the SRM team and senior leaders to make this transition and begin active response planning.

The Risk Ownership Map

Wargames help executive teams understand how their organization might respond to a concrete future. Schelling found that the participants in his wargames learned important lessons in these new worlds, chief among them was to prepare for potential futures. After the SRM team leads organization leaders through a series of wargames, which should expose flaws in their current response patterns, the Risk Ownership Map becomes an attractive tool to plan for a better future. Figure 6.3 displays the map.

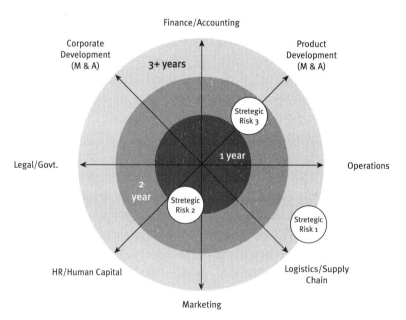

Figure 6.3 The Risk Ownership Map

This map has three key elements: lines that delineate internal centers of ownership, accountability, and responsibility for strategic risks; bands that indicate the "time to impact," or when the organization estimates it must actually respond to strategic risks; and circles representing the risks themselves. It is composed of operational departments, shared services, and corporate functions to afford decision makers a full range of response options to protect or enhance firm performance.

The lines indicate which organizational units will assume ownership for emerging strategic risks. As the SRM team transfers responsibility to one or more of these owners, two important shifts occur. Organizational responses move from monitoring risks to gain understanding to actively managing them to mitigate threats or exploit opportunities. Ownership transfer also signifies a change in focus. Attention turns from the causes and creators of strategic risks, the movement of PEST forces, and shifts to the consequences and curators of risks, impacts on organizational functioning, and competitive advantage, all with real financial consequences. Risks in the outer circles might feature joint ownership between the SRM team, strategic planning, and operating units. As responses mature, ownership is passed to line executives exclusively.

Bands on the map capture the lively movement of risks as the organization anticipates and prepares for impact. The SRM team, which has been managing and monitoring each risk from its early inception as a weak signal, shares what it has learned about risk evolution and trajectory in the form of key risk indicators—measures that allow owners to track how quickly probability becomes actual exposure. Movement toward ground zero may not follow a rigid calendar sequence. The map should be reviewed often by the board's risk committee. These periodic check-ins allow for new assessments of risk velocity and trajectory, so that senior leaders and operating mangers can adjust actions, budgets, and plans accordingly.

Black circles represent the individual risks. What our map shows is where responsibility and accountability for each risk rests. Figure 6.3 shows one risk having multiple owners because a thoughtful response might require multiple actions from different organizational units. What our map can't show is that each circle needs to specify the resources and investments needed to mount an adequate response and formulate key performance indicators and timelines that measure project success.

Actual transfer of risk from the SRM team to the balance of the organization represents a critical transition. Handoffs include more than just passing responsibility to the line executive leading the day-to-day effort. There should be a clearly identified risk owner at each level of management, from the board through the C-suite and on to the ultimate owner. Since the key players should have been involved in scenario generation and previous wargames, the transfer process should meet with minimal surprise.

The Risk Ownership Map forges an explicit link between those making strategy and those executing it. Response plans have been informed by the perhaps years-long process of weak signal monitoring, and strategies have been formulated as the risk emerged and refined as it matured. Line executives involved with execution (notwithstanding role turnover) were players in the wargames and might have had a hand in strategy formulation. Execution becomes an instinctive follow-on activity. Those formulating and executing employ a common playbook.

What we've described as a handoff isn't a hard event but more a stage in an ongoing process. Senior leaders and the board can use the map to provide ample oversight of risk management activities, and a critical part of that oversight process includes communication. The board's risk committee establishes an appropriate cadence for accountability reporting and adjustment. This ensures that members of the C-suite receive timely updates on the actions, progress, and successes of owners in preparing for risk impact. A disconnect between those making and implementing strategy creates and widens the gap between the two. The Risk Ownership Map gives organizations a formal method to make sure the two groups remain connected.

Elements of the Risk Ownership Map that drive implementation, budgets, action plans, key performance and risk indicators, and timelines contribute to resolving a final source of the strategy–execution gap: lack of sufficient resources for implementation. Transfer of ownership away from the SRM team triggers an early and frank discussion about resource requirements, in hard assets or soft human capital, to ensure adequate responses. SRM processes that have monitored signals and communicated strategic risk potential over a period of years create institutional credibility that sets the stage for an honest dialogue about those resource demands. It makes little sense to see weak signals evolve, note their potential impact, and then fail respond appropriately as weak signals manifest as strategic risks.

Conclusion

Hindsight bias offers us twenty-twenty vision. Looking back, we can trace in detail the path that led from the Newton to the iPhone. Our story doesn't rely on a false claim of prescience or state that we could have detected what others couldn't. We do believe a trail of bread crumbs existed from 1993 through 2005, however small and intermittent, at least until the introduction of the BlackBerry, in 1999. BlackBerry's rapid growth implied that connectivity via cellular networks and wireless internet could be had at a price point that would attract many mainstream users. By the turn of the millennium, our scenario map devolves to two potential futures: a world where large numbers of people supplemented their desktop life with a mobile device or one where mobile displaced PCs.

Resolution of the uncertainty—whether mobile would be a complement to or substitute for desktop computers—took longer. The weakest signal of interest here came at the birth of Salesforce in 1999. Salesforce was founded on the premise of software as a service, a model in which users never download or store software on a hard drive; they access it and its functionality over the Web.[21] Although it would take fifteen years to morph into cloud computing, the viability of Salesforce and other companies tilted the future in favor of mobile as a substitute for life on a deskbound PC.

The LEGO Group cracked the code and developed an SRM program that contributed to strategic success. Some have touted the company as the European version of Apple or Google, a truly great company. Intel is also great company but had a markedly different risk management story during a critical industry-transforming period in its history. Paul Otellini's assessment of the strategic risk of the Newton, and consequently his decision to pass on Steve Jobs's offer, seems unsupported by any SRM engagement, tools, or thinking (or by ERM, for that matter). Alternatively, if such insight was available, we can reasonably conclude that it was either shelved or dismissed, to the detriment of all stakeholders.

We've shown here how a tool of SRM, scenario planning, could have been utilized by Intel to frame different futures. In chapter 7, we bring together all four tools in an analysis of the total economic transformation implied by the rise of self-driving cars.

CHAPTER 7

"The Future Ain't What it Used to Be!"

In this chapter, we apply the tools of strategic risk management to a current (as of 2019) strategic challenge: the long-term, tectonic changes in the automobile industry. We'll employ our SRM tools to peer into the competitive future for three companies affected by the rise of self-driving (autonomous) vehicles (Canon), by ride hailing and ridesharing (State Farm Insurance), and by electric vehicles (the Coca-Cola Company).

. . . . .

Lawrence Peter Berra (1925–2015) attended a movie with his friend Jack Maguire one afternoon when both were teenagers. The movie featured a short piece on India, and Maguire noticed that Lawrence resembled a yoga guru in the film, and, as friends do, he tagged his friend "Yogi." The nickname stuck, and the man we know as Yogi Berra would go on to play nineteen years with the New York Yankees, winning three American League Most Valuable Player awards and ten World Series titles. He was a feared hitter in clutch situations and contributed to the dynastic success the Yankees enjoyed in the late 1940s and the 1950s. After retirement, he managed both the Yankees and the Mets, leading each to the World Series.

His lasting fame, however, came from his mouth, not his bat. As a catcher, Berra talked incessantly to throw batters off their game. He once told slugger Hank Aaron, during a World Series game, to "hit with the label up on the bat." An exasperated Aaron responded, "I came up here to hit, not to read." Berra's wordplay eventually led to a set of "Yogi-isms," famous turns of phrase that made their way into everyday speech and quotation books. Some of his most famous lines are "It's déjà vu all over again," "It ain't over till it's over," and "When you come to a fork in the road, take it." The title of this chapter comes from our favorite Yogi-ism, which fits with a VUCA world: "The future ain't what it used to be."[1]

We live in a VUCA world, one that is volatile, uncertain, complex, and ambiguous. As we look at the world, we see a future filled with more, not less, VUCA. The future certainly ain't what it used to be. Our argument throughout the book has been that SRM provides boards, C-suite executives, and managers at every level a set of tools to not only survive but also thrive in a VUCA world. In this chapter, we take a very current and fundamental set of changes afoot in the automobile industry that typify a VUCA world and explore how the tools of SRM can help companies respond to the threats and opportunities these changes represent.

The Automobile in the Twenty-First Century

Automobiles have changed the face, nature, and trajectory of society more than perhaps any invention since Johannes Gutenberg created the movable-type printing press. The automobile transformed a useless by-product of kerosene production in the mid- to late nineteenth century—gasoline—into a major energy source in the twentieth.[2] It gave rise to the assembly line, which drove down the cost of producing manufactured goods while driving up wages. Affordable cars, and workers that could afford them, spawned the growth of suburbs and required massive public investments in roads and freeways, private parking garages, and the iconic shopping mall. The automobile became a status symbol and a source of identity for millions of aficionados.

This short list offers a mere glimpse of the breadth and depth of the automobile industry in societies around the globe. To this, we could add downside issues with air quality and with geopolitical uncertainty over oil prices and supplies. As we enter the third decade of the twenty-first century, the auto industry stands on the precipice of major, disruptive transformation, one likely to again reshape life and societies. Three independent but interrelated changes seem primed to propel the industry over the cliff and into new, uncharted territory. In terms of the PEST framework essential to SRM, one change is technological, one is a combination of technological and social elements, and the third is economic.

Change number one, the development of autonomous, or self-driving, vehicles, arose from the natural momentum of technological progress, driven in no small measure by Moore's Law. Growth of ridesharing services, the second change, was spawned by advances in software and wireless connectivity and offers a powerful business model to meet people's transportation-related jobs to be done. The rise of the electric vehicle, change three, has returned an old technology to prominence. Its deployment now waits for cost competitiveness between battery- and gasoline-powered cars and trucks.

Each change represents a very real threat but also a tremendous opportunity for companies throughout the economy. Figure 7.1 shows the potential impact of autonomous vehicles. The inner circle contains industries disrupted first, and the outer band captures some of the ripple effects on the

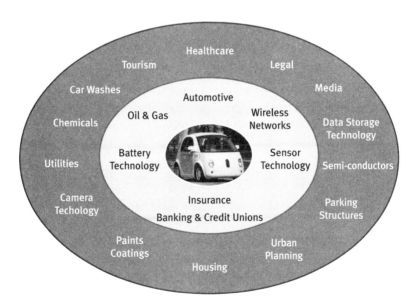

Figure 7.1 The impact of changes in the automobile (Short and Long Term)

larger economy. We can easily identify the strategic risks facing Chevron, Exxon, Ford, General Motors, Lyft, and Uber. However, in this chapter, we focus on the impact of each of these tectonic changes on three companies that might not immediately come to mind: Canon and the strategic risk of self-driving cars, State Farm Insurance and the spread of ridesharing, and the Coca-Cola Company and the retreat from petroleum. We'll briefly walk through three of our four tools to illustrate their value. We won't speculate on what a Risk Ownership Map might look like, because signals in the markets have not matured into strategic risks as we go to press.

Self-Driving Cars and Canon

Remote control cars have existed since the 1960s, but what we today consider autonomous vehicle technology originated when the U.S. Defense Advanced Research Projects Administration (DARPA) funded a series of competitions during the first decade of the twenty-first century to create an autonomous vehicle for military use. The Grand Challenge of 2004 offered a cash prize of $1 million to the team whose vehicle could successfully navigate a 142-mile course through California's Mojave Desert. No team claimed the prize, and the top vehicle traveled a whopping 7.5 miles. Nonetheless, according to DARPA project lead Lieutenant Colonel Scott Wadle, "That first competition created a community of innovators, engineers, students, programmers, off-road racers, backyard mechanics, inventors and dreamers who came together to make history by trying to solve a tough technical problem. . . . The fresh thinking they brought was the spark that has triggered major advances in the development of autonomous robotic ground vehicle technology in the years since."[3]

Teams and technologies improved. In the next Grand Challenge, a year later, fifteen vehicles traversed the 132-mile course. In 2007, DARPA upped the stakes with the Urban Challenge. The winning vehicle had to navigate a complex course that featured everyday hazards such as traffic and pedestrians and had to obey rules such as speed limits and allowable turns. Six teams saw success. Carnegie Mellon University's Tartan team took home the $2 million prize and made Pittsburgh a developmental hub as a result.[4]

Fully autonomous operation requires that a vehicle accurately sense the road and its associated conditions with the same precision as humans. Our senses of sight and sound allow us to perceive objects clearly and to establish their speed, distance, and direction. Sensing technology represents a huge hurdle for self-driving vehicles, and, in a moment of déjà vu that recalls the VHS/Beta war, engineers employ two different systems: light detection and ranging (LiDAR) and radio detection and ranging (radar). As the names imply, LiDAR detects light and radar detects radio waves. The LiDAR unit on the car emits a series of laser pulses, up to 150,000 per second, that bounce off of obstacles; the time delays in bounce-back allow sophisticated software to map objects—their nature, speed, distance, and direction.[5]

Radar uses radio wave pulses to do the same thing. Each system has advantages and drawbacks. LiDAR's advantage comes in its detailed data and the pictures it generates, but it doesn't work well in poor weather conditions and has real problems with recognition at distances less than thirty meters. Radar, on the other hand, is far less expensive and works well in all weather conditions but can't distinguish shapes very well. Two small cars close together, for example, may appear to radar as one large, long vehicle.

Engineers employ a classic tactic, whether using LiDAR or radar, which is a redundant system of cameras. Cameras supplement LiDAR by providing sensing and imaging data at short distances and in all weather conditions. They assist radar by providing superior recognition of objects. Cameras also provide a redundant source of images, should LiDAR or radar fail or suffer glitches.

The company that would become Canon Inc. opened its doors in Tokyo, in 1933, as the Precision Optical Instruments Laboratory. Its first 35-millimeter camera, the Kwanon, appeared in 1934. With global ambitions, the company trademarked "Canon" in 1935 and changed its name in 1947. Canon opened its first U.S. division in 1965, selling both cameras and its latest innovation, a black-and-white plain paper copy machine that employed the company's excellent image capture technology. Canon did very well in the copier market, and it continued to innovate aggressively. By 1980, Canon's sales matched those of market leader Xerox. By 1990, the firm sold about $1 billion more in copiers each year than Xerox.[6]

High-quality Canon cameras had always generated strong sales around the world. In the 1970s and 1980s, Canon entered the professional market for camera bodies and lenses and established a market-leading position in the era of silver halide film. The company successfully navigated the digital photography revolution, and in 2017, Canon commanded almost 50% of the digital single-lens reflex (DSLR) market.[7] Sony, by contrast, sells fewer than one in seven DSLR cameras. Importantly, Sony owns another market:

it provides the bulk of the digital cameras for Apple's iPhone and smartphones from other makers. In 2016, the market for DSLR cameras shrank by 35% while smartphone sales increased by 5%.[8]

Canon, and most other DSLR manufacturers, stumbled in producing cameras for the masses via the smartphone industry. Autonomous vehicles, and the need for camera-based redundancy, offer a second chance for companies who lost in the last round of innovation. For Canon, self-driving cars represent a strategic risk, a rare opportunity to redeem itself from a strikeout in the smartphone market. How might SRM help Canon understand and exploit this strategic risk?

STRATEGIC UNCERTAINTY MAP

A map for self-driving cars would calibrate the time until risk maturity based on the level of autonomy the vehicle employs. The Society for Automotive Engineers created a rubric with five discrete levels of autonomy: driver assist (cruise control), partial automation (lane control), highly automated (limited vehicle control), fully automated/driver override (default vehicle control), and fully automated (complete vehicle control). Cars on the road today incorporate levels 1 and 2, so these are now tactical, not strategic risks.

Some vehicles employ level 3, like Tesla's autopilot feature; however, recurring problems with the technology have limited its application. Autopilot, requiring a number of cameras and sensors, may be two to five years out, straddling the first and second bands on the target. Several states now allow testing of level 4 cars, and some limited testing of level 5. Challenges facing levels 4 and 5 have little to do with sensors. The problem lies in limitations in artificial intelligence and machine learning, which means that self-driving cars can't yet make human-caliber driving decisions. Research continues, but test cars still have problems solving basic tasks like left-hand turns, and they show no ability to deal with the unexpected or truly surprising traffic events that give humans fits. We'd put fully autonomous vehicles at seven or more years out.

The strategic uncertainty map indicates a clear risk in the technology quadrant and weak signals in other important quadrants. In the United States, as of 2019, the political quadrant reveals a patchwork of state laws that allow various forms of testing and offer different definitions of important terms like *driver*.[9] These strengthening signals deserve close monitoring, as does action by the U.S. Department of Transportation, which adopted rules in 2018 to speed innovation and testing of level 4 and 5 vehicles. Social tolerance for, and embrace of, self-driving technology remains unknown, as do the economic advantages of self-driving vehicles, particularly of fully autonomous vehicles.

SCENARIO PLANNING

The strategic uncertainty map reveals an opportunity in the emerging market for level 3 cars (autopilot) and potential opportunities in levels 4 and 5. Here we see a moderate threat to Canon if a close competitor such as Nikon captures the vehicle market and uses the resulting scale and profits to erode Canon's margins in the DSLR market. We envision great opportunities for Canon to enter the vehicle market, where currently no player has substantial market share.

Based on the PEST forces, a scenario would build on one dimension that captures the likelihood that high-quality camera technology becomes a required redundancy. Such a requirement would come from government or through an industry association mandate, and we could, for example, draw a Stringent vs. Lax Regulation dimension. The other dimension we see as most relevant arises from the economic value of self-driving cars. If these vehicles provide real economic gains—greater fuel economy, reduced commuting times, no real need for private vehicle ownership and its attendant costs—then we'd expect a future with ubiquitous autonomous vehicles. If the economic gains prove minor, self-driving cars may be limited to fleets or hobbyists. The second dimension becomes Broad vs. Narrow Adoption.

Canon might face a very favorable future (DSLR Dream) with stringent regulation and broad adoption, a very unfavorable one (Minor Muddled Mess) of low regulation and narrow adoption, a pleasant scenario (Tidy Profits) of high regulation and narrow adoption, or a highly competitive future (the Wild West) of low regulation and broad adoption. Platform investments directed to understanding the complex relationships among images, LiDAR- or radar-generated shapes, software algorithms, and the state of the art around machine learning appear prudent at this stage. Other investments depend on the result of wargames.

WARGAMING

Our autonomous vehicle wargame begins with a concrete version of a discrete scenario and invites internal decision makers to adopt one of three roles: the Canon executive team, a competitor in the marketplace, or another key stakeholder such as a supplier, partner, or regulator. For the first wargame, we choose the Wild West scenario.

Assume that it's 2023. The U.S. federal government, the European Union, and the Japanese and Chinese governments all adopt their own self-driving sensor standards. Rather than specify particular technologies, these regulations cite desired outcomes in terms of image quality, speeds, and other critical factors. Different camera technologies might fill that bill.

Several manufacturers have begun development of autonomous vehicles with capabilities for levels 3 through 5. Early market data indicates buyers preferring differentiation in price points and features. It is, in short, a wild and competitive environment for both vehicles and camera/sensor systems. The questions for each team, say Canon and Sony, follow from chapter 6. What unilateral and immediate actions would they take? What unilateral actions over time? What actions depend on what the other team does? What resources and capabilities are necessary to make their decisions work? In the initial round, the answer to the resources question is vitally important. What about acquisitions to speed development? Or "crash" investment and building resources internally? Whether made or bought, how would the value of those resources vary with the strategic moves of their competitor?

The wargame invites Canon to think through the details of the Wild West. It also would allow them to backcast and consider making investments today to prepare for such a world. Those investments might include acquisitions, changes to R&D spending, or partnerships with software companies like Waymo or Apple or with automakers such as Toyota or Nissan. We don't know which scenario will prevail, but the company could gather different teams and wargame the other scenarios. The joint output from multiple games would provide valuable information about potential strategic actions that span all four possible outcomes.

Ridesharing, Autonomous Vehicles, and State Farm Insurance

With the DARPA Urban Challenge, 2007 was the pivotal year when self-driving cars moved from the realm of superhero fantasy (the Batmobile) to potential reality. In 2008, we saw the birth of ridesharing, which brought to market a logic and related logistics that call into question the assumptions of personal vehicle ownership. That year, Travis Kalanick and Garrett Camp, two twentysomething, freshly minted millionaires who had sold their own startups, met in Paris at the LeWeb conference, a futuristic tech gathering. Legend has it that they hatched the idea for Uber—using a smartphone app to hail a ride—one night as they waited for a taxi that never came. Camp continued work on the idea for an UberCab and later recruited Kalanick as "chief incubator."[10]

UberCab launched in May of 2010 and, following a cease and desist order from the City of San Francisco for using the word *cab* (a regulated business in the city), changed its name to Uber. The ease of hailing a ride from a phone fueled the company's phenomenal growth. Uber has experienced its share of controversy and challenge, but in 2019 the company completed an initial public offering with a day 1 valuation of almost $70 billion.[11]

Back to 2008. The company that would become Lyft had just received its first round of funding from angel investor and eBay senior executive Sean Aggarwal. Logan Green had started Zimride a year before to help college students find carpool rides to get home for holidays.[12] Green and his partner, John Zimmer, plowed sixty dollars of that first investment into frog and beaver costumes that they wore to campuses to drum up business. They used Facebook to connect riders with carpools, a service that expanded to corporate clients in 2010.

Facing slow growth and a small total market, they cast about for more services to offer and came up with Lyft, a true peer-to-peer ridesharing service. In 2010, both taxis and Uber relied on commercial drivers. Lyft, instead, offered a ride with a "friend." By 2013, it become clear that Lyft was the growth opportunity that Green, Zimmer, and their investors had been looking for. Lyft and Uber began to compete, and still do, for riders and drivers in the cities where they operate. Lyft brings in a little more than 10% of Uber's revenue, and its 2019 initial public offering valued the firm at $26.5 billion, just over one-third of Uber's valuation.[13]

Uber and Lyft popularized ridesharing services, but the impact has gone beyond a simple peer-to-peer platform. A number of firms now offer home delivery of anything from restaurant food to groceries, packages, or other small freight. Using the same model, users can rent scooters or bikes (Bird or Lime) for recreation or for very short trips (zero to one mile). Uber and Lyft can meet medium-range transportation needs (from one to fifty miles), and new services like Turo feature carsharing, essentially private vehicle rentals, for longer trips (more than fifty miles) or for extended time periods.

George Jacob "G. J." Mecherle started State Farm, in 1922, to sell auto insurance to farmers near his hometown of Bloomington, Illinois, offering them better rates than companies whose premiums also had to cover more expensive urban motorists. The company sold only auto insurance and in 1944 had one million policies in force.[14] The "good neighbor" (according to State Farm's famous jingle, written by Barry Manilow) has long been the nation's largest auto policy writer, and in 2017 it wrote just under $42 billion worth of policies, covering 18% of the U.S. personal auto market.

Importantly, $42 billion represented 65% of the company's property and casualty revenue, almost eight times its life insurance revenue, and sixty times its revenue from health insurance.[15] State Farm does not disclose the number of auto policies it writes, but we can safely assume that a substantial majority of its 81 million U.S. policyholders get their auto insurance through one of the company's sixty-five thousand employees and nineteen thousand independent agents. For State Farm, auto insurance is the eight hundred–pound gorilla.

Insurance risk for Uber and Lyft drivers arises when they stop using their car for personal use and begin livery, or commercial, use. At that point, an individual's personal coverage stops and the rideshare company covers the driver. Rideshare companies, who are not insurance experts by any means, created basic and cheap policies to cover drivers, and State Farm now writes policies to fill gaps in that coverage. When a driver engages the app, State Farm's rider continues their personal policy. The driver now has two policies in force, and State Farm and the ridesharing company will fight out who ends up paying any claims. Gap coverage provides State Farm with a chance to earn extra premiums for limited exposure.

State Farm survived, and profited from, the advent of ridesharing. The problem now is that ridesharing and increasingly ubiquitous delivery options raise the question of vehicle ownership. Competition continues to drive down the price of these services and to replace the need for, and expense of, automobile ownership for a significant segment of the population—the 55% who live in cities.[16] What happens to State Farm's $42 billion in revenues if auto ownership declines by double digits? The question gets more urgent if we couple ridesharing with levels 3 through 5 of self-driving cars, which promise increased safety and fewer accidents. Loss payouts would shrink, which is a positive for State Farm, but premiums on these cars might fall from dollars a month to pennies. How could the tools of SRM help State Farm? Let's see.

THE STRATEGIC UNCERTAINTY MAP

The strategic risk to State Farm materializes from the confluence of two events, each of which should be tracked on the strategic uncertainty map. The self-driving vehicle risk looks much like our analysis for Canon: serious movement to levels 4 and 5 remains seven-plus years in the future. That said, a State Farm SRM team would keep abreast of developments on both technological and regulatory fronts. Progress might not follow a linear trajectory. Once engineers and regulators reach key milestones, progress might take off.

We'd put the second set of weak signals, a movement away from ownership, on the line dividing the social and economic PEST forces. Automobile ownership has both an economic component (in dollars and in opportunity cost of ownership) and a social component (self-identification and status), and the team should look for weak signals in each area. Rising scooter renters such as Bird and Lime extend the effective range of ridesharing for very short trips, raising both the relative dollar and opportunity costs of owning a vehicle. Long-distance or long-term ridesharing (rentals) such as Turo also make owning an auto a more expensive proposition. Our SRM team should monitor growth rates, profitability, and competitive entry in these segments.

On the social side, iGeneration (or Generation Z) digital natives represent the best gauge of how individual identity and social status of auto ownership may change. This is the "love group" of users for ridesharing and delivery and is well worth watching. As this group ages, we'd expect them to buy fewer cars, especially if they are living in urban environments. Given the demographics of this postmillennial generation, we'd consider social changes to be weak but strengthening signals, with a serious threat five to seven years out.

SCENARIO PLANNING

Given the dual nature of the strategic risk, we'd create scenarios around the ultimate penetration and use of each element. Will self-driving cars remain relevant and dominate the auto market of the more distant future, fifteen to twenty years out, or will they be owned by fleet services and techno-nerds? Will auto ownership remain at current levels and ridesharing remain a complementary form of transportation, or will the number of title holders plummet—say, by half or more? These dimensions give us a high-high quadrant (Insurer's Nightmare), in which self-driving cars and ridesharing become the dominant form of transportation; a low-low one (Cafeteria of Offerings), in which ridesharing and self-driving machines complement private owners driving their own cars; and two high-low quadrants. Squeezed Margins captures a world in which safe, self-driving cars combine with a low prevalence of ridesharing (high private ownership), and Shrinking Market features pervasive ridesharing and a strong majority of human-operated vehicles.

Given the state of technological progress, we'd see the Cafeteria of Options as unlikely over the very long term. Technical and regulatory delays, coupled with minimal economic gains for ridesharing, or social backlash against ridesharing or self-driving cars, could extend the lifetime of a Cafeteria of Options (more gap coverage type policies) well into the future. Each of the other scenarios entails true strategic risks: the possible destruction of State Farm's auto business or its growth and development of a new competitive advantage. Investments that seek to understand the drivers and trajectory of self-driving cars and ridesharing make obvious sense. Much like the Canon case, wargames would provide insight into more specific actions.

WARGAMING

We'd kick off a Red vs. Blue game in the worst possible world for State Farm, the Insurer's Nightmare, featuring a shrinking market and razor-thin margins. The blue team represents State Farm and the red a large competitor like GEICO or Progressive. We'll assume that it's 2025. A clear pattern emerges: about 40% of the iGen demographic will eschew vehicle ownership. Level 4 self-driving cars look to become the norm, and the actual passenger-carrying miles driven by level 5, fully autonomous vehicles, grows exponentially. Both vehicle ownership and human driving prepare for a precipitous drop, perhaps on the order of 50% to 60%.

The questions for blue and red follow the pattern we saw for Canon. What unilateral and immediate actions would they take? What unilateral actions would they take over time? What actions would depend on what the other team does? What resources and capabilities would they need to make their decisions work? Two viable strategic options stand out in this doomsday scenario: exit or dominance. Business as usual won't work, as the declining number of policyholders won't support State Farm's large network of in-house and independent agents, and eroding margins will exacerbate the cash drain of huge investments in advertising and marketing.

The real decision facing State Farm and its competitors might be "Go big or go home." Would State Farm see its decision as unilateral or as calibrated to moves GEICO or Progressive might make? The deepest question turns on State Farm's strategy and shared values: How important is the auto insurance business to the company? If the answer is anything less than "This is who we are," then exit becomes a serious option. Living the Insurer's Nightmare entails serious adjustments to the scale and scope of State Farm's operations, and the goal goes beyond market share leadership to industry dominance. In this horrific world, only a handful of insurers might survive, and being the largest one would bestow significant competitive advantages in a small market.

Self-Driving Cars, Electric Cars, and Coca-Cola

Karl Friedrich Benz (1844–1929) developed the first complete internal combustion automobile in 1885.[17] Five years later, William Morris, a chemist living in Des Moines, Iowa, debuted a six-passenger electric carriage.[18] Cars powered by electricity, gasoline, and steam coexisted and competed for dominance in the early days of the industry. By 1900, electricity powered about one in three cars on the road. Electric vehicles offered owners an easy-to-start, quiet car that didn't emit coal smoke or noxious gasoline fumes.

In spite of these advantages, however, two factors doomed electric cars: range and cost. Electric cars worked well in cities but couldn't travel more than a few miles on a charge, and so anything beyond a short commute was out of the question. In addition, as late as 1912, an electric car sold for $1,750, almost three times the $650 cost of a gasoline-powered one. Electric cars faded from the scene by 1935.

Economic, social, and political changes in the 1970s resurrected the electric vehicle project. The price of gasoline spiked in 1973, due to an embargo by Arab members of the Organization of Petroleum Exporting Companies, and those prices never returned to their pre-embargo level. Socially, the automobile had become a source of pollution, and toxic air quality led policy makers to search for alternatives. In 1976, Congress enacted legislation supporting research into alternative energy vehicles, including electric.

In 1990, clean air and emission rules became more stringent, which added incentive to research into electric vehicles.

Tesla, the most well-known electric vehicle maker today, entered the market in 2006, a half decade after Toyota introduced its popular hybrid, the Prius, in 2000. The Prius became an identity car among celebrities and others wanting to publicly display their environmental bona fides around clean air, but its price premium kept it out of the mass market. Producers of hybrids or all-electric vehicles continued to proliferate. By the end of 2018, U.S. highways carried a million electric vehicles, and drivers could recharge at one of more than twenty thousand stations nationwide.[19]

While those twenty thousand charging stations—a number certain to increase—enable cross-country trips, the bulk of driving occurs in commutes and short trips (less than twenty-five miles) in the area of people's homes. The beauty of an electric vehicle is its ability to recharge at home every night, lowering total cost and avoiding the need for stops for gas. Apparent strategic risk, both threat and opportunity, lies in reduced gasoline consumption, and Big Oil sees threats to its entire value chain, from upstream exploration (due to a reduced need for new reserves) to downstream retailing (a result of fewer gallons consumed).

Given the potential for massive disruption in the energy sector, then, why focus on carbonated soft drinks? Because when drivers of electric cars don't stop for gas, they'll skip the Coke, cookie, or a bag of chips that so often accompany fuel purchases. In 2017, convenience stores generated about 19% of revenues for U.S. soft drink makers. Loss of the convenience store channel could devastate the Coca-Cola Company and its rivals.[20]

Atlanta pharmacist John S. Pemberton created Coca-Cola in 1886, just a year after Benz brought his automobile to market. Pemberton marketed his drink, laced with then-legal cocaine, as a tonic for common ailments and sold it through local soda fountains. Sales reached almost four hundred thousand gallons per year by the beginning of the twentieth century. Coke sold concentrated syrup to independent bottlers around the country, along with an exclusive license to produce and market the beverage. This business model allowed for rapid expansion, and the classic Coca-Cola bottle could be found everywhere; the company even followed U.S. troops around the globe, in 1943, when Dwight D. Eisenhower helped set up ten bottling plants around the world.[21]

The Coca-Cola Company, and soft drink manufacturers in general, experienced explosive growth through the twentieth century, with annual per-person consumption peaking near the end of the century at fifty-three gallons, or 565 twelve-ounce cans. That's a can and a half for every person in the United States, every day. The red Coca-Cola logo became an American and global icon, and the company provided investors with healthy returns.

Coke is no stranger to strategic risk—concerns about the health impacts of soda consumption have grown in the new millennium. By 2017, per-person consumption had fallen to just over thirty-nine gallons—still more than a twelve-ounce can per day but a decline of more than 25%.[22] As soda sales tumbled, Coke diversified its product portfolio. It bought or brought to market bottled water (Dasani), juices (Minute Maid and Odwalla), sports drinks (Powerade), tea (Honest Tea), and coffee (Costa). In spite of these additions, revenues fell from a peak of $48 billion in 2012 to $35.4 billion in 2017, a decline of 27%.

Coke responded the health-based strategic risks by focusing on value added rather than total volume to stanch the flow. It raised prices on its flagship brands of Coke and Diet Coke as well as on other beverages. The long-term strategic risk from electric vehicles might erase another 20% of Coke's volume, and it might lead to a greater decline in overall revenue, because convenience stores sell single-size beverages at the highest per-ounce price. How might the tools of SRM help the company's senior leadership plan for the reduction or elimination of a key sales channel?

STRATEGIC UNCERTAINTY MAP

The recent decline in Coke's revenue traces to its strategic exposure in PEST's social force: shifting global preferences toward more healthy diets and a reticence to imbibe empty calories. The electric vehicle strategic risk lies solidly in the economic quadrant, along the dotted line; the cost of buying an electronic vehicle limits widespread adoption. Tesla hopes to ramp up production of its Model 3, to come down the learning curve and profitably sell the vehicle at $35,000, a price point attractive to middle-class buyers. As of 2019, Model 3s sell for more than $50,000 and the company seems unable to earn profits at the lower price point. SRM analysts should monitor the price of a Tesla Model 3 and of planned electric models from Ford, General Motors (GM), and others. When that price holds at something like $35,000, then sales rates should improve and the strategic threat should mature.

The movement toward electric vehicles should occur slowly, however. Unlike a century ago, when electric and gasoline cars dueled for market share, most people already own a car, and so an electric vehicle becomes a replacement car. In the post–financial crisis world today, drivers tend to replace their cars every six to eight years.[23] Put simply, if electric vehicles sales somehow climbed to 50% of all new cars sold, it still would take about seven years for them to constitute half the market. Thus, we'd put the risk to the convenience store channel at a decade out.

Our belief is that a decline in convenience store sales should mimic overall Coca-Cola revenue declines. The channel won't collapse in a spectacular implosion. Rather, sales will most likely decline at a steady but increasing pace, maybe 2% to 3% per year above health-related downward sales pressure at the beginning, accelerating to 5% as convenience stores sell less fuel. Our map suggests a good future for Coke. Yes, the channel will shrink, but not overnight, and the company has ample time to plan a response.

SCENARIO PLANNING

The market share of electric vehicles represents one obvious dimension of interest for this strategic risk. Will gasoline engines suffer the same fate in the twenty-first century that electric ones did in the twentieth? Will electricity kill gasoline or will the two coexist, each serving unique customer needs? We label this dimension Electricity Dominates and Sustainable Gasoline (forgive the potential oxymoron). It will define the ultimate channel size. Emphasis on health and the negative aura around sugary drinks will continue to determine both the product mix and sales volume of offerings by Coke, so we label the other dimension Soda Is Satan and So-Delicious.

We end up with a high-high world, Electricity Dominates and Soda Is Satan, in which Coke loses a key channel amid ever-falling sales (All Natural); a low-low world, Sustainable Gasoline and So-Delicious, that reflects something close to the status quo (Sustainable Niche); and two high-low futures: Alternative Channels (Electricity Dominates and So-Delicious) and Alternative Products (Sustainable Gasoline and Soda Is Satan). The best case sees sales of Coca-Cola falling to some stable level, the worst sees a world in which soda is the exception rather than the rule; the two mixed worlds identify threats to the business and opportunities for growth.

What types of investment make sense under all scenarios? We see one area as extremely useful: continued efforts to understand and influence the perception of Coca-Cola products in the marketplace. Monitoring the tobacco companies and their move into e-cigarettes can provide guidance into how definitions of *healthy* evolve, and the role for "sin," or indulgence, products in that world.

WARGAMING

Who is the opponent in the wargame here? Which stakeholder does Coke most want to understand and use as a guide to its own behavior? Canon had a choice of opponents, and competitors represented the logical choice for State Farm. We see the most valuable blue team opponent for Coke (obviously the red team) in a wargame as a large convenience store chain, such as Marathon Petroleum's Speedway or the Canadian firm Alimentation Couche-Tard. Coke and convenience stores exist in a symbiotic relationship—what's good for one tends to be good for the other—and how this system coevolves in the face of electric vehicles matters. Aligned action will fare better than each company acting solely in its own interest.

We'd begin with one of the high-low worlds and then move to the other, and we may not even consider high-high and low-low, because the key strategic choices for Coke relate to where people will buy in the future (distribution channels), or, if the channels remain, it's all about what people will buy (product mix). Wargames segregate each one as an independent force before combining their effects. For example, if grocery sales replace convenience store sales, but with the same product mix, how does Coca-Cola win or create more shelf space in your local grocery store? That's a different, but perhaps complementary, challenge than optimizing product mix within a set amount of shelf space.

Conclusion

We conclude by returning to figure 7.1. Our discussion has been on the implications of changes in the auto industry, using three companies and industries that don't come readily to mind: cameras, insurers, and soda manufacturers. The societal changes of autonomous vehicles, ridesharing, and electric cars will ripple throughout the economy and reframe our lives, just as the automobile did a century ago. What will housing developments look like with no garages? Or condo complexes, malls, and downtown areas with 40% to 50% fewer parking stalls? What happens to companies that make the paint for roadways as the lines on the road become critical elements in the sensing ecosystem? How might a radical reduction in the number of auto accidents change the emergency health-care system? Each of these industries, and all of us, live in a world that is VUCA—and stands to become more VUCA over time.

A VUCA world generates strategic risks. In this chapter, we've only scratched the surface of the ways in which today's competitive advantages will need to change to avoid evaporating or missing chances for expansion and renewal. It's too early to even consider which groups in each company will end up owning and managing the strategic risks. Our tools provide real insight to equip SRM teams, CROs, and their senior leaders to flexibly respond to emerging futures. We believe that our analysis can help Canon, State Farm, and Coca-Cola make more informed, more timely, and ultimately better decisions about strategic actions and investments to survive and thrive in whichever new world materializes.

For these three old-line companies, and all others, Yogi Berra provided more insight than humor. It's true that the future ain't what it used to be. Because of that, and because of increasing VUCA, it will be essential that SRM contributes value over time, and we now turn our attention to this important topic.

CHAPTER 8

SRM for the Long Term: Culture, Communication, Ethics, and Integrity

This chapter describes two critical elements for making strategic risk management a sustainable and value-creating business process: alignment with organizational culture, and communication systems that integrate SRM into the core work of the strategy complex and the organization. The 7-S model, pioneered by McKinsey and Company, provides a useful framework for thinking about alignment, and we introduce our final tool, the Strategic Risk Reporting Matrix, to help SRM teams communicate with the board and other C-level executives. Organizational integrity is the final key element that must be in place for SRM programs to work.

· · · · ·

September 7, 1979, had been a picturesque, sunny late summer Connecticut day, the temperature in the upper seventies, with a slight breeze blowing. The forecast called for a cool night, a low of about fifty degrees, but no storms to threaten what should be a calm, beautiful weekend.[1] Inside a mobile production trailer in Bristol, however, calm did not describe the scene. At seven o'clock that evening, Bill Rasmussen's new baby, ESPN, would take to the airwaves, with hosts George Grande and Lee Leonard giving birth to the network. Whether it would survive was anyone's guess. An estimated thirty thousand viewers tuned in that night to see if all sports, all the time could hold their interest.

Grande and Leonard, decked out in orange jackets to represent the team colors of financial underwriter Getty Oil, ad-libbed most of that first thirty-minute segment. After all, when they moved beyond the usual two minutes of scores that fans were accustomed to, Grande and Leonard sailed into uncharted waters. As the weeks and months went by, ESPN's on-air talent navigated this new world by innovating. They took risks like providing detailed analysis of the day's sports, mixed with a healthy sprinkling of their own humor and insights. They described their attitude as "What do we have to lose? No one is watching anyway."[2] *SportsCenter* became an offbeat, fun place for viewers to catch the news of the day.

That offbeat style and risk taking permeated the network over time. ESPN did the unusual on a regular basis. Its broadcast of the finals of the America's Cup yachting race in 1983 was the first time yachting fans could watch their premier event on television. For good measure, they doubled down and covered the entire 1987 event, then added a new twist: ESPN placed a camera and live microphones on American skipper Dennis Conner's yacht to provide viewers with a personal and intense look at competitive sailing. Having a miked-up athlete was cutting edge in 1987; it later became the norm in sports television.

Chris "Boomer" Berman's arrival on the flagship *SportsCenter* program in 1980 transformed the show. With clever wordplay that turned, for example, New York Yankees star Darryl Strawberry into "Darryl Strawberry Shortcake" and Saint Louis Cardinals slugger Albert Pujols into Albert "Winnie the" Pujols, Berman's improvisational style transformed the program into thirty minutes of engaging sports reporting that garnered a huge and dedicated audience.[3] Berman anchored *SportsCenter* until 1986, and he remains one of the network's premier personalities today.

While Berman's linguistic imagination brought national prominence, Keith Olbermann and Dan Patrick metamorphosed *SportsCenter* into an American institution. The two men coanchored their first broadcast on April 5, 1992. Everyone in the Bristol studios, and likely millions of viewers, sensed a chemistry and unique relationship between Keith and Dan. Chemistry, combined with their innate talents as journalists and writers, created a *SportsCenter* about which one commentator wrote, "It had all the qualities of chocolate cake: rich, filling ingredients of news and highlights thickly frosted with humor." Bill Belichick, at the time the head coach of the Cleveland Browns, typified many fans and watched all six daily reruns. When Olbermann asked him why, Belichick responded, "I know all the punch lines by then. I get to do the jokes."[4]

ESPN continued its tradition of innovation throughout the next two decades. The *E* (entertainment) in ESPN expanded with the addition of ESPN Films, a studio dedicated to original documentary and dramatic content. The division kicked off with its *SportsCentury* series, fifty-minute documentaries on the top fifty athletes and events of the twentieth century. The celebrated series won both Emmy and Peabody awards for excellence in radio and television broadcasting. More importantly, *SportsCentury* turned a profit and highlighted the power of ESPNs integrated media empire in bringing content to viewers.[5]

A freewheeling culture at ESPN drove strategy and action, though not always in the best or most appropriate ways. Gayle Gardner, *SportsCenter*'s first female anchor, described life in Bristol: "Don't be surprised if you feel like you've reached the middle of nowhere, because that's exactly where you are. . . . It's very boring."[6] Geographic isolation, coupled with a testosterone-rich environment of sports junkies, made life difficult and uncomfortable for women working at ESPN. Bill Wolff, a producer at the network, explained, "The atmosphere was very tough on women, because in those days, it might have been a twenty-to-one or thirty-to-one ratio. . . . The men are all single, the men are all horny, and they are in Bristol where there is nothing to do, and you work all the time. So the women were objects of desire for just being there." Female employees faced exposure to everything from Hooters posters to pornography, requests for dates, and sometimes vulgar requests and outright propositions for sex.

Female reporter Karie Ross became the catalyst for cultural change, calling out her colleagues during an all-hands meeting. She shared from her own experience: "Men are acting like animals. When a woman walks into the building, it's like 'fresh meat.'" After the confrontation, the work environment did improve. However, the sad truth of the matter is that rooting out sexism and harassment has proven far more challenging than most of us ever imagined. Natural tendencies of some individuals toward these negative behaviors, especially when sanctioned and amplified by cultural norms and values, create deep ruts from which escape proves difficult.

Lee Leonard opened that initial broadcast in 1979 with these words: "If you're a fan . . . what you'll see in the next minutes, hours, and days to follow may convince you you've gone to sports heaven."[7] Three decades later, CEO George Bodenheimer described both the culture and the strategy of the network: "Sports fans serving sports fans."[8] The early culture of innovation and risk taking underpinned a strategy that led ESPN to find new ways to serve viewers and dominate sports television. It continues to evolve, mostly for good, but still ultimately subject to both human and organizational misbehavior.

ESPN shows us the power and role of culture in driving strategy and, frankly, everything else an organization does. Culture captures "the way things are done around here" for any organization. It takes shared values, worldviews, assumptions, and ideas about what's right and wrong and mixes them together in an (often) unspoken set of norms that govern behavior.[9] Culture is perhaps the most powerful shaper of organizational life. Management guru Peter Drucker graphically describes its power: "Culture eats strategy for breakfast."[10] If you don't like the meal metaphor, you can think of your organization as an iceberg. Strategy, marketing, logistics, and all the other functions are the one-eighth that is visible above the waterline, and culture is the submerged, but very real, seven-eighths below.[11] Culture dominates strategy and, at the end of the day, directs its movement. The upshot? Any new initiative that hopes to survive and succeed, including SRM, has to fit within the organization's culture or to help that culture adapt to create a fit. We'll rely on a well-worn strategy framework, the McKinsey 7-S model, for help in accomplishing this ambitious goal.

The Cultural Challenge: Alignment

The 7-S model is a compact diagnostic to enable executives to gauge potential alignment between current culture and proposed future states. It also prescribes changes that will strengthen organizational congruence. Put simply, *alignment* means people and processes are assembled and mobilized to point in the same direction and to support the same goals. Figure 8.1 displays the model, seven distinct elements of an organization and the systemic relations between them. Our main interest is in how well the other six elements consistently support, enable, and reinforce strategy, the true north of our SRM compass.

Understanding the 7-S Model

The origin of the 7-S model traces back to 1977, when McKinsey managing director Ron Daniel summoned a newly minted Stanford University organizational PhD, Tom Peters, to his New York office. Daniel tasked Peters with creating the next big thing for McKinsey's arsenal of consulting frameworks.[12] Bruce Henderson's new firm, the Boston Consulting Group, had seemingly stolen the McKinsey magic for developing new strategy models, and Daniel wanted McKinsey to regain its historic leadership role in the industry. Daniel invited Peters to focus on organizational effectiveness and implementation, as poor performance in these two areas often doomed even the best-devised strategies.

Peters traveled the globe collecting primary data, interviewing the leading minds in academia and business to find what worked. In 1978, Bob Waterman became Peters's boss, and the two continued to plow the implementation field. Sometime over the next two years, Peters, Waterman, and colleagues Tony Athos and Richard Pascale held a "two-day séance" in San Francisco, where they developed the essence of the framework. The elements of the model captured important drivers of organizational effectiveness and, coincidentally, barriers to strategy implementation.[13] Clever alliteration made the elements easy to remember for consultants and clients, gaining the tool traction and endurance. The seven elements are: strategy, structure, systems, staffing, skills, style, and shared values.[14]

Strategy captures the integrated plans, processes, and related activities that create and sustain a competitive advantage for a firm in its target markets. For our SRM purposes, strategy represents the vital *S* because it anchors organizational action and success eventually depends on the other *S*s aligning with and supporting strategy.

Structure resolves three basic issues in any organization: Who does what, who gets to tell others what to do, and who reports to whom. The boxes on an organization chart tell us who does what, the (vertical) lines between those boxes specify who has authority, and reporting pathways are indicated by both vertical and horizontal lines.

Systems describe important processes that coordinate and control the work of the different units on the organization chart. What is the easiest way to identify a system? Its eponymous quality, of course—information system, inventory control system, compensation system, performance review system . . .

Staffing covers human capital, or how an organization recruits, hires, trains, deploys, evaluates, promotes, retains, and compensates people.

Skills refer to the technologies, knowledge, and abilities of individuals and groups within the firm. Skills and staffing work closely together to drive strategy. Companies can make or buy talent; they may either hire people who have the required skills or develop in-house know-how through training.

Style captures the interpersonal qualities of the work environment—its overall atmosphere, attitudes, pace, and tenor—that contribute to a defined culture. Some style clues are visible. Formal clothing usually signifies much more than just a fashion preference, even as shorts and T-shirts are about more than just physical comfort. Other clues are below the surface but are nonetheless even more revealing; conflict resolution, confronting problems, and communication choices all are windows into style.

Shared values are the core written and unwritten standards that motivate the activities and behaviors within the organization. They are the fundamental building blocks for culture and will in large part define how the business is seen from the outside. Respect for every team member, community engagement, keeping the interest of the client first, and commitment to the highest quality of effort are but a few examples.

Figure 8.1 uses different tints for different *S*s. Strategy, structure, and systems, the three elements in white, constitute the *hard triangle*. *Hard* doesn't imply "difficult"; in fact, there's little that is easier than redrawing the organizational chart. Instead, *hard* identifies the tangible levers managers can pull for more immediate effect, to align or realign internal elements with external markets. Adjustments in strategy, for example, can lead to a structural reorganization, to deploy resources in other areas, and may require changes to management reporting and incentive systems.

The other four *S*s make up the *soft square* and form the essence of culture. We color staffing and skills light grey, as they embody the intrapersonal parts of culture, while shared values and style, darker grey, capture the interpersonal parts. The softness of these elements is driven by their intangible nature. It takes a long time to make these elements different enough to achieve productive alignment. Tom Peters's punch line for the guidance these distinctions give managers is "Hard is soft, soft is hard."

Another McKinsey alum, legendary CEO Lou Gerstner, validated this guidance as he described the turnaround at IBM during the 1990s: "If I

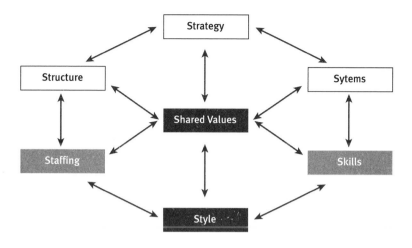

Figure 8.1   The 7 S Model

could have chosen not to tackle the IBM culture head-on, I probably wouldn't have. My bias coming in was toward strategy, analysis and measurement. In comparison, changing the attitude and behaviors of hundreds of thousands of people is very, very hard. [Yet] I came to see in my time at IBM that culture isn't just one aspect of the game—it is the game."[15] We agree with Gerstner on the vital role of corporate culture and how truly demanding is the work to move it in a different direction. We would add that sustainable cultural change requires the foundation of the soft square to be reinforced by the mechanisms of the hard triangle. All seven Ss must line up for change to stick.

With the 7-S framework in hand, we now have the tools to talk meaningfully and sensibly about how executives can create a culture that embraces SRM. We'll first consider certain actions that will move the process forward.

Creating Cultural Alignment

Chapters 3 and 4 featured organizations that, even with strong ERM programs, could not prevent disaster. MF Global established a state-of-the-art ERM structure that didn't align with, and in fact ran counter to, the leadership style of celebrity CEO Jon Corzine. Our belief is that if culture eats strategy for breakfast, then style eats structure for lunch. Wells Fargo survived the 2008 financial crisis in large measure because of its disciplined attention to risk management, reinforced by a solid structure, skills, and the right staff.[16] By 2015, however, those elements had been shouted down by compensation and evaluation systems, and employees mastered new skills and behaviors that pursued cross-selling at all costs, which included treating ethics and laws as inconsequential impediments. Skills and systems ate structure, staff, and strategy for dinner.

Our call for leaders to adopt SRM programs is accompanied by real challenges. Simple advice like "Focus on the soft square" or other sound bites trivialize both the scope of work required to create cultural room for SRM and the time needed to realize success. As we have pointed out, cultural change is not for the faint of heart. It is certainly achievable, but it requires coordinated, sophisticated, and systematic executive actions to align the seven Ss. These actions come in two interrelated flavors, which we call symbolic and substantive actions.

SYMBCLIC ACTIONS

We earlier invoked the metaphor of the organization as an iceberg, with the visible tip representing the substantive work of the firm, including strategic actions, marketing, logistics, and related functions. Culture—the accepted rules of behavior, assumptions, worldviews, priorities, and values contained in organizational symbols—is out of sight, beneath the waterline. If you want to move the one-eighth above water, get to work on the seven-eighths below. If you want to change how people conduct themselves on the job, address the symbols that encourage them to think, feel, and act in certain ways.

Symbols and artifacts (the physical manifestation of symbols) exist throughout companies, and they communicate outlooks, priorities, and values. The seven Ss we discuss here manifest themselves in a variety of ways, and our discussion won't exhaust all the possibilities. Sometimes symbols and artifacts stand alone, but symbol most often exists as the other side of the coin of substantive action. Staffing and skills provide a great example of this, as they have rich symbolic as well as substantive components. The size, centrality, and professionalism of market research groups, for example, determine the scale, scope, and quality of the market intelligence gathered. They also reflect and reinforce implicit assumptions about the utility of market feedback and its value in decision making. This truth holds for any work group.

Structure and systems behave in similar fashion. Where a work group lands on the organization chart symbolizes commitment and constraints. How that unit reports its works, both vertically and horizontally, and how the organization rewards those individuals, arises from and reinforces organizational worldviews, priorities, and value commitments. Over time, internal audit, with the help of outside accounting consultancies, subsumed most companies' ERM programs. As a result, ERM became, for the most part, a control mechanism to deal with compliance and management reporting regulations. Hemmed in by these management control processes, ERM professionals were hardly in a position to incorporate a strategic perspective into their work.

Shared values become concrete in the artifacts of mission, vision, and values statements. While always tangible, missions might be informal or formal. Gordon Moore developed his own law of semiconductor development, and he shaped the early culture at Intel with a plaque on his office wall that read "This is a profit-making organization."[17] That artifact communicated in crystal-clear terms what mattered in those early days. Intel's current, formal mission and vision statements do much the same. The mission statement is "Utilize the power of Moore's Law to bring smart, connected devices to every person on earth," and the vision statement is "If it's smart and connected, it's best with Intel."[18] Mission and vision clarify and specify the organization's most hallowed assumptions and values about making money, serving customers, and a host of other activities.

Style, the companion to shared values, brings culture to life. The tone at the top translates the norms, priorities, and values of the organization into everyday life. Jon Corzine's love for trading and lust for large-scale deals set the tone MF Global. He defined acceptable and exemplary actions, and his style marginalized smart or prudent risk taking as inconsistent with what he valued and rewarded. Tone at the top works because people look to leaders to define, in behavioral terms, what's appropriate and what's not, what will be rewarded and what will be punished. Corzine effectively killed risk management at MF Global. Without the right timbre and support from senior leadership, SRM programs have no chance of long-term survival.

When executives roll their eyes or scoff at the idea that current strategies may face shadowy future strategic risks, that eye roll will spread like wildfire throughout the organization, because people tell stories about what leaders do. Stories, legends, and myths act like flying buttresses that support culture. They transmit the real yet intangible culture—as opposed to the one in the mission statement or employee handbook—to new members *in time*, and the retelling of stories perpetuates norms and values *over time*. Unlike missions, visions, and handbooks, no one writes stories down; they survive and thrive as informal oral traditions that prove remarkably resilient to alteration or elimination.

Staffing, skills, structure, systems, shared values, style, and stories make up both the visible and the submerged parts of the iceberg. The substantive part of the *S*s matter, but executives who omit the symbolic fit of SRM to each *S*, and to strategy, hamstring their ability to align SRM, or any other initiative, with the culture. Substance matters as well, and we'll now consider how the substantive aspect of the *S*s create alignment.

SUBSTANTIVE ACTIONS

Substantive actions have, as the term suggests, heft and consequence. Physical, intellectual, and financial actions that people take lead to tangible effects, such as products, patents, or purchases. As we have outlined, but repeat for emphasis, each *S* has a substantive as well as a symbolic component, just as an iceberg has above- and below-the-waterline components. Let's start with staffing and skills. Who gets hired and how they get trained, retained, and promoted certainly signals values. It also makes the commitment real, through the actions that these individuals and groups take. A conscientiously selected SRM team filled with well-trained, curious polymaths will, quite simply, do better work than one to which minimal developmental effort was devoted.

We outlined in chapter 5 an ideal structure for the SRM team and the work of the CRO. Yes, this structural arrangement communicates a worldview, but it also enables high-quality work and, as we will describe, establishes accountability and facilitates rich communication. Mission statements reflect beliefs, values, and priorities; they also provide guardrails to guide action and decision making. Style sends signals; it also determines decisions.

Corzine's style drew upon a hearty (if not unhealthy) appetite for risk in the name of growth. Consequently, Eurobonds, and the loans incurred to purchase them, collected in large amounts on the MF Global balance sheet. Systems play an important and often outsize role in driving substantive action, because systems define a set of cause-and-effect relationships that inform behavior. All systems do this, but none more clearly or more powerfully than compensation incentive systems. Real behaviors, whether trades made at MF or fake accounts opened at Wells Fargo, will follow, with positive and negative rewards that people care about a lot. Commission carrots drove trading at MF, and the employment termination stick provoked Wells Fargo team members to falsify accounts and insurance policies.

These points may seem obvious, but many firms fail to realize that substantive action, the above-water part of the iceberg, shapes and reinforces culture. Culture isn't just symbol, and two realities explain this. Sociologists have a term for the first one: structuration.[19] It's an imposing expression to describe a pretty simple reality. Perspectives, thoughts, and worldviews, the symbolic part of culture, motivates and directs action, but those actions, particularly when they lead to positive outcomes, reinforce and strengthen individual and organizational commitment to those underlying perspectives, thoughts, and worldviews. Substance and symbol loop forward, each reinforcing and strengthening the other.

Our second reality follows from the first. Substantive action imprints culture and contributes to symbol because substance provides the content for stories, legends, and myths. The executive eye roll we noted above was a physical, substantive action, one with ramifications. An ocular gesture, then, will be mentioned time and again as representative of management's true feeling about SRM. Stories, in their most effective and enduring form, arise from the behaviors of executives and employees. The things they actually did and the attendant aftermath move from the world of tangible action to the realm of intangible (and immortal) legend, to be inculcated into the culture of every new generation of employees.

Six of the Ss in the 7-S model have symbolic and substantive components that create alignment with the seventh, strategy. You might believe that SRM, with its clear link to preserving and enhancing competitive advantage, naturally aligns with strategy. That may be the case, but it's not just alignment with strategy that matters. When SRM initiatives run counter to, and potentially threaten, other Ss in the model, those misalignments create frictions that impair the functioning of the SRM team. For SRM programs to work, the entire cultural apparatus of the seven Ss must reflect and respect a sensitivity to risk and uncertainty. Culture, and the elements of the 7-S model, play another significant role in sustaining SRM: they design and perpetuate a communication system that allows knowledge, monitoring, and management of strategic risks to spread throughout the organization.

Communication that Supports SRM

Strategic risk managers must resolve an important paradox: Those with the power to respond to strategic uncertainty are those least likely to see and understand it in a timely manner (depending on what they are told, and when). Conversely, those most likely to sense new uncertainty have the least power to mount a response. Robust communication systems transfer information about strategic risks from bottom to top—from those in direct contact with shifting markets, namely, line management and the SRM team, to senior managers and the board, who allocate resources to create and maintain competitive advantage.

The nature of the system itself matters greatly. Simple, periodic reporting of risks (such as monthly or quarterly), if not either linked to hard performance measures or requiring management action, will likely lack effectiveness.[20] Further, normal communication filters stymie the movement of early warnings about strategic risks, preventing them from moving up and increasing uncertainty absorption. Organizations employ two types of filters, one structural and rational, the other cultural and emotional. Each filter absorbs uncertainty at every level of the hierarchy. James March and Nobel Laureate Herbert Simon described the process and consequences of uncertainty absorption for communication:

> Through the process of uncertainty absorption, the recipient of a communication is severely limited in his ability to judge its correctness. Although there may be various tests of apparent validity, internal consistency, and consistency with other communications, the recipient must, by and large, repose his confidence in the editing process that has taken place, and, if he accepts the communication at all, accept it pretty much as it stands. To the extent that he can interpret it, his interpretation must be based primarily on his confidence in the source and his knowledge of the biases to which the source is subject, rather than on a direct examination of the evidence.[21]

The structural/rational response comes as organizations and decision makers accept strong signals and discard weak ones.[22] Strong signals, to borrow a phrase from author Tom Clancy, epitomize a clear and present danger—clear because everyone understands the threat or opportunity without much explanation or thought; present because it has the power to influence short-term results; and dangerous because a significant threat will be realized, or an opportunity foregone, if it is ignored. Strategic risk and uncertainty, as we know from chapters 2 and 5, fails the Clancy test. Weak signals lack clarity (they are hard to describe and understand), presence (these exposures may take years to come to pass), or danger (the nature of the threat or opportunity is ambiguous). Rational managers with lots of strong signals vying for attention will naturally discard the weak ones, or at least relegate them to the back burner.

The tools we describe in chapters 5 and 6 won't change weak signals into strong ones, which would defy the nature of strategic risk. However, the tools give organizations, from bottom to top, a common language to frame and understand weak signals. Those tools also help minimize uncertainty absorption by accommodating rather than shunning the uncertainty in weak signals.

In addition to the structural/rational problem, organizations and executives face a cultural/emotional barrier that can impede the flow of information about strategic risk. Intentionally or not, systems may indeed castigate people for moving weak signal information up the chain. Most of us learned in elementary school to never, ever make the teacher look dumb, whether through question or comment. Questions or answers that exceeded our teachers' knowledge may have been labeled "interesting," but as we observed body language, we knew that he or she did not really abide that sort of "interesting."

Fast-forward to adulthood and we see the same pattern repeatedly. Just knowing more than the boss, even without public demonstrations of the fact, puts you in an untenable situation. It can evoke the same response we saw from our teachers, only with consequences more serious than a note to your parents. Raises, opportunities to work on plum assignments, and promotions may be jeopardized by knowing more than the boss. When people in the field bring an emerging uncertainty or source of volatility to their manager, it means they now have keener insight into the business than the one to whom they report (which could make for a productive mini-scenario planning session). Unless the organization's culture and communication systems support this type of knowledge asymmetry, the default response—don't share information—kicks in. It's a recipe for strategic risk–laden weak signals to get discarded before they even move into communication channels. Effective SRM requires jumping both the rational and emotional hurdles that drive uncertainty absorption.

Our final tool, the Risk Reporting Matrix, provides the board, senior leaders, the SRM team, and middle managers throughout the organization with a template for clearly, comprehensively, and concisely sharing vital information about emerging strategic risks. Indeed, since communications with the board in particular may be limited to thirty or forty-five minutes per quarter, the ability to cut to the chase is gold. The matrix offers all participants a structured, stylized process that focuses on weak signals and emerging strategic risks—the rational challenge—and accepts the premise that those sharing information know more than those receiving it—the emotional one. Figure 8.2 displays the Risk Reporting Matrix.

The matrix crafts communications that serve diverse audiences, each with their own needs and concerns, which correspond to their respective decision portfolios. It frames both vertical communication to the board and senior leaders and horizontal interactions between the SRM team and managers in the business units. Directors are supplied with the information that assists them in performing their fiduciary and legal risk

Figure 8.2 The Strategic Risk Reporting Matrix

oversight responsibilities and making the associated decisions around strategic and tactical risks. Middle managers receive data and frameworks to make tactical decisions that support the day-to-day transactions of running the business.

The vertical dimension of the matrix separates information by timeliness, or more appropriately, by "time to impact." What constitutes "long term" will vary by organization, but it usually considers strategies and risks further than three years in the future. "Short term" comprises everything less, and may address only the upcoming quarter. Risk and strategy conjoin across the horizontal dimension. What is it that parses strategy and risk? Strategy defines and builds competitive advantage, while risk includes those things that impact the viability and sustainability of that advantage. Four distinct "conversations" occur in the quadrants, which we label to facilitate a sequenced, orderly report.

Long-Term Strategy (Quadrant I)

Communications here consider the current state of the firm's long-term sources of competitive advantage and accompanying strategic plans or budgets. These discussions evaluate the appropriateness of, and debate modifications to, the risk capacity statement, those key pillars of strategy the firm must protect to stay in the game and expand to win it. Finally, this quadrant encourages frank and open discussions about cultural alignment with strategy, in general, and with respect to the risk management culture, specifically, and the integration of SRM into the operating core of the organization.

Long-Term Risk (Quadrant II)

This conversation uses and builds upon the different models in the SRM tool kit, grounded by the strategic uncertainty map. Leaders at every level can understand the role of different PEST forces that turn weak signals into strategic risks, and get a sense of the maturation of each signal. The SRM team also uses this quadrant to share the results of scenario planning and wargaming exercises that push leaders to explore the implications of potential strategic risks for their future. Identification of "platform" investments that will pay off in multiple futures is the goal of these discussions.

Short-Term Strategy (Quadrant III)

These dialogues help leaders understand, monitor, and adjust risk tools that impact the day-to-day execution of strategy. Because SRM works hand in glove with TRM and ERM, it makes sense for stakeholders to understand the purview and concerns of these elements. Senior executives and the board should see risk appetite guidelines on a regular basis, not only for the whole firm but also for each business unit. Regular review of these documents allows modification and change, to ensure that risk appetite doesn't choke growth but nonetheless offers a set of defensible limits to keep activities from going off the rails, as we saw with MF Global.

Short-Term Risk (Quadrant IV)

A clear delineation of "who does what and when," via the Risk Ownership Map, grounds this discussion. As we noted in chapter 6, the added value of utilizing the map is that it narrows the gap between those making strategy, the board and senior leaders, and those individuals and units implementing it. We label this as quadrant IV to present a coherent temporal sequence. However, quadrant IV may be the first, most important conversation. If the business can't manage its impending strategic risks, discussions about longer-term challenges and opportunities make little sense.

A quality communications apparatus maximizes the value of SRM and paves a long runway for boards, executives, and mangers to respond to strategic risks. It also fortifies the alignment between SRM (and, by extension, the entire office of the CRO) with the rest of the organization. Having such conversations in and of itself signals a shared value commitment. In addition, well-managed risk dialogue will gradually give rise to its own system, skills, and style. It will capture the value generated by the diverse inputs of curious polymaths interacting with functional specialists throughout the organization. To be certain, SRM programs flourish in an environment of robust, horizontal, peer-to-peer communication.

When SRM becomes a true partner and collaborator with business units and functions, the firm will identify more—and more relevant—weak signals. Analysis becomes richer as functional partners share context, nuance, and theories. As strategic risks mature and management of the risk moves from the SRM team to individual unit or functional leaders, the lived history of active collaboration and open communication facilitates a seamless handoff of those risks and a greater likelihood that ownership will lead to action. Best practice horizontal communications lead to more precise, relevant, and timely assessment of strategic risks. Best practice vertical communication systems lead to more precise, relevant, and timely decisions about how to respond. Vertical communications also drive the creation and implementation of the Risk Ownership Map as the organization moves from monitoring to managing strategic risks.

SRM, Integrity, and Ethics

We close our discussion with one final cultural element, an organization's commitment to acting ethically and with integrity. We return to Jon Corzine and MF Global, as this case highlights the reality that SRM only complements, but can never replace, a company's commitment to integrity, courage, and ethical decision making. We can't lay the failure of MF Global on the lack of effective risk management. The company had checked the right ERM boxes; it had a dedicated and experienced CRO with direct access to the board and a board able to determine its risk capacity and appetite. Ultimately, the failure stemmed from a moral choice that prioritized current profits over sustainable ones. MF Global reminds us that no amount of risk management atones for a lack of integrity.

Integrity, in the moral sense, is defined by the *Oxford English Dictionary* as "soundness of moral principle . . . especially in relation to truth and fair dealing, uprightness, honesty, and sincerity." Some might argue that competing in the world of speculative financial products penalizes these virtues, but MF Global in fact engaged in fair dealing. Competing advice championed by Michael Roseman and Corzine was considered by the board, with full transparency. The board appeared sincere in its desire to return the firm to profitability and to build its stature. So the board acted with integrity, yes?

No, the board did not. A commitment to truth and honesty is the bedrock of integrity. Transparent processes and sincerity exacerbate rather than mitigate the problems that follow dishonesty and forsaking truth. MF Global chose to deny critical truths—two tactical realities that sank the firm and two strategic ones that aided and abetted the tactical errors. Tactically, the London Clearing House and its margin demands, not the European Financial Stability Facility, drove the price of the bonds. Second, the complexities of the RTM structure would have aggravated MF's lack of cash in any crisis.

The first strategic error was the board's willingness to bet the farm on Corzine and to accept the myth of the superstar CEO, which denies the truth that a single individual never saves an organization on their own. MF's board met in November 2010 to consider increasing the firm's exposure to European debt. Roseman, the CRO, argued that several plausible scenarios existed that could lead to a severe liquidity crisis at the firm. Corzine forcefully disagreed with the analysis and then played his nuclear option: if the board sided with Roseman, he would leave. Operating under the allure of Corzine's ability to save the firm, the directors rejected Roseman's argument. Corzine stayed, and in January of 2011 he fired Roseman. One headline about the event read "Jon Corzine Replaced MF Global's 'Risk Officer' with an 'Everything Is OK' Officer."[23]

The board's second strategic failure built on the first. It believed that the firm could transform overnight from a commodities broker, skilled at executing trades for its farmer and rancher retail customers, to a highflier in the world of speculative finance. To become a trading powerhouse, MF Global needed more cash on the balance sheet as well as sophisticated capabilities to fully assess opportunities, execute trades, and acquire real-time intelligence to actively track market volatility and risk. Surely, each part could be built or acquired. But only a long-term, focused, measured, and prudent entry into the high-yield debt market would bring the pieces together without an intolerable level of risk.

Put simply, the board accepted strategic untruths about its business model, its identity, and the time required for strategic transformation to occur. They also bought into the popular and amazingly recurrent notion of the superhero CEO who can, by defying all the laws of economic and organizational gravity, launch a firm to immediate success. With this core mental model at the heart of culture, no risk management system could carry the day. Absent a commitment to observing the fundamental laws of gravity that govern business—chief among them being that if something sounds too good to be true, it probably is—SRM becomes just another piece of window dressing. When it is constrained to doing no more than provide a thin veneer of prudence, as with MF Global, it only masks and perpetuates a corrupted mental map of the road to victory.

Conclusion

Peter Drucker understood quite well organizational appetite: culture eats strategy for breakfast. We began with the power of culture to enable strategy and competitive advantage at ESPN. Cultures at Disney, MF Global, and Wells Fargo all contributed to the success or failure of their strategic actions. Culture does matter.

The 7-S model is more than clever mnemonic device to sell consulting services. We use the model in our own work because it allows us to draw a clear, coherent, and concise picture of the culture of an organization, a simple picture that diagnoses misalignments between the different Ss and between each S, or all of them, and strategy. An accurate diagnosis leads to better prescriptions about which particular Ss, or combinations, need adjustment to realign the culture around strategy. Accurate diagnosis also closes the strategy–execution gap.

We've pitched SRM as the next big thing in helping executives and their organizations to create and sustain competitive advantage in a volatile and uncertain world. Chapters 3 through 6 provided a set of frameworks, issues to resolve, and tools to use to get SRM off the ground. This chapter is a final reminder that SRM cannot stand alone or get bolted on to the organization. Unless SRM programs fit with the culture or executives work to mold the culture to fit the logic of SRM, it may be the next big thing, but it won't last.

When boards and executives craft cultural change that supports and sustains SRM, this logic and these programs can help a firm prepare for and thrive in the highly dynamic, volatile, uncertain, and turbulent competitive environment of the twenty-first century. We live in a VUCA world, and SRM provides companies with a set of principles, processes, teams, and tools to survive and thrive.

CHAPTER 9

Concluding Thoughts: Currents, not Waves

Merritt J. (M. J.) Osborn crisscrossed the United States as a salesman in the early part of the twentieth century. He noticed that the hotels where he stayed always had rooms out of commission for carpet cleaning, which cost the hotel a couple weeks' revenue on each room. In 1923, Osborn developed a carpet cleaner—Absorbit—that cleaned carpets in less time and used less water, saving hotels money on cleaning and keeping rooms available for rent.[1] Osborn named his company Economics Laboratory—"Economics" because it saved customers time, labor, and materials costs, and "Laboratory" because laboratory research backed up his claims.

Over the next three decades, the company continued to bring innovative cleaning equipment and products to market. For example, the company entered the dairy industry in the early 1950s and developed the first clean-in-place system, which avoided the costly and time-consuming process of dismantling a dairy's production line to clean the system. Before clean-in-place entered the market, dairies just produced milk in dirty equipment, which resulted in a useful shelf life of only three days. Economics Laboratory's products doubled shelf life, saving dairies money and consumers the hassle of purchasing milk at three-day intervals.

Economics Laboratory, renamed Ecolab in 1988, established industry leadership in several industrial cleaning applications, products, and solutions over the decades since its founding. The company diversified along the value chain, looking for new markets where their expertise improved hygiene and lowered costs. In 2002, they launched their EcoSure business, an assessment, evaluation, and training service that expanded the company's offerings from "end of use" cleanliness and sanitation to "beginning of use" design and safety and "in use" process control. Ecolab was playing a larger role in its customers' operations, but over the next few years it kept hearing a consistent message: being a maker of high-quality and/or low-cost products and services was great, but customers now demanded "sustainable" cleaning products and services, ones that conserved and preserved inputs and resources.

As they spoke with customers about their major concerns, Ecolab learned that water treatment was a critical need for its institutional, food, beverage, and commercial laundry customers, all of whom used large amounts of water in their operations. By 2011, Ecolab's leaders realized that water was a business issue as well as a sustainability issue. Water is a limited resource. If customers could reuse and recycle water more efficiently, they'd cut their costs and become more sustainable—a double win. Ecolab needed to become "masters of water."[2]

The question became "Make or buy?"—whether to work internally to develop the capabilities or to buy someone who already knew water treatment. Angela Busch, senior vice president for corporate development, looked for acquisition targets and settled on market leader Nalco. She explained, "You can try to build Nalco 2 (which you can never do because they are the masters of water), or maybe you could buy them."[3] After some discussion the team realized that "you can't out-Nalco Nalco," and Ecolab executives began to explore an acquisition.

The company that would become Nalco began life in 1928, when the National Aluminate Corporation arose out of a merger between two Chicago companies that sold sodium aluminate, a chemical that prevented fouling and scaling in boilers and industrial pipes. The Chicago Chemical Company supplied sodium aluminate to industrial plants, while the Aluminum Sales Corporation targeted railroads, which used the chemical to keep their locomotive boilers running. National Aluminate changed its name to the Nalco Chemical Company in 1959, and continued to build expertise, skill, and market share in all types of industrial water treatment needs for manufacturing, mining, nuclear energy, oil and gas, and pulp and paper clients.

Nalco moved from the water market into industrial health and safety consulting and products following a large chemical spill at Union Carbide's plant in Bhopal, India, in 1984. Corporate executives needed to respond to the increasingly stringent industrial health, safety, and water use regulations that arose from the tragedy. Nalco helped companies meet these standards with cost-efficient solutions. For example, Nalco helped global oil giant Mobil develop and deploy a system that treated tanker sludge so that the resulting product could be sold for other uses. Nalco saved Mobile money and eliminated a hazardous waste by-product.[4]

Nalco survived a spectacularly failed acquisition and divestiture at the hands of Suez Lyonnaise, the French water giant, and in 2005 the company found itself independent again, but burdened with a crushing long-term debt level. Nalco limped along financially, but it never gave up its market-leading position and it continued to innovate. In 2004, the company brought to market a new, patented water management system, 3D TRASAR, a system that continuously monitors and adjusts water treatment levels without human intervention.[5]

Nalco had heard the same messages as Ecolab about customers' desire for sustainability, and by 2011 the issue had become an essential element in Nalco's value proposition. Customers loved Nalco's systems for their quality and cost-reducing properties, and they also loved that Nalco helped reduce their overall environmental impact. Customers began to see that Nalco offered "sticky" solutions, which reduced costs and improved a company's reputation over a number of years.[6]

Ecolab announced its intention to purchase Nalco on July 20, 2011, and the deal closed within a year. Angela Busch noted that "buying Nalco was like finding our long-lost brother." The Nalco acquisition represented the fulfillment of Ecolab's quest to offer a premium global water treatment solution. It also began a significant pivot, a large acquisition that could catapult Ecolab into new market spaces. By 2018, the combined company held leadership positions in the institutional (that is, hotels and hospitals), industrial, and oil and gas markets. The combined company continued its focus on sustainability in general and water in particular.

Ecolab's current strategy aims to profit from successfully managing four societal mega issues: clean water, safe food, abundant energy, and healthy environments. The company manages more than 1.1 trillion gallons of water each year, conserving enough to meet the drinking water needs of almost 600 million people. With Ecolab's help, its customers produce 24% of the world's processed foods and just under half of the global milk supply. Ecolab's energy customers produce 20% of the world's power, and Ecolab/Nalco products reduce water usage in 40% of the world's petroleum extraction and refining operations. Eight hundred million hotel rooms rely on Ecolab/Nalco products to be clean and pristine for guests.[7]

Each of these four mega issues represents a strategic risk, a long-term event or exposure that could potentially destroy Ecolab's competitive advantage, not to mention the quality of life for billions of people on the planet. Each issue also presents the company with an opportunity to grow and expand its strategic footprint, a way to cement and extend its competitive advantage. Ecolab and Nalco have been in these businesses for almost a century, and each couples technological innovation with a deep, abiding set of internal shared values to manage and profit from these long-term strategic uncertainties.

How does a company manage strategic risks for almost a century? How can an executive team focus almost fifty thousand global employees on uncertainties that may take decades to unfold, such as the transition away from petroleum to electric vehicles? Christophe Beck, Nalco's president, gave us one key to success: focus your people on currents, not waves.[8] Waves are short-term events, epiphenomena that come quickly and go just as rapidly—fads and fashions of the day, fast-burning crises, and events that dominate a news cycle. Currents, on the other hand, are long-term exposures driven by bedrock social preferences, physical laws, or deeply entrenched political and economic realities. The planet's finite freshwater supply combines with global population and economic growth to create lasting water scarcity, and the need to manage the resource effectively is a current. Annual floods and droughts, however, are waves. Beck's team at Nalco spends substantial time in the field to track currents, and the company trains its employees to differentiate between choppy waves and the relentless tug of underlying currents. The four pillars, as both strategy and values, help keep people attending to long-term, big strategic risks.

We like Beck's metaphor, and we conclude our book with advice to executives about how they and their organizations can focus on currents—we all already know how compelling and consuming waves can be. Currents beget and transport strategic risks; operating and tactical risks ride everyday waves.

SRM doesn't do so well with waves; it's designed to identify and navigate the underlying currents that drive strategic success or failure. We've asked John Bugalla to share, in conversational form, his thoughts about how executives can see through waves and catch the underlying currents.

A Road Map to an SRM Future

Paul Godfrey: How did you start thinking about strategic risk management?

John Bugalla: My entire career has been spent in the area of risk management. My first job was with the giant insurance firm Marsh & McLennan, and I learned about risk and risk management, but from a very traditional insurance perspective, really focused on hazard risks: people buy insurance for property casualty, and the like. I wanted to do something a little bit more, and I ended up going to another insurance broker called Willis, but the focus for me was really on consulting about risks—the beginnings of considering risk from the financial and strategy angles together. My third hitch was with the insurance broker Aon, where we really were focused on what we now call enterprise risk management.

I decided, in 2005, to form my own company, called ermINSIGHTS, that was going to focus exclusively on enterprise risk management, but more from a strategic perspective. Meaning, we know a lot about certain kinds of risks, but the risks that really cause the trouble, the risks that really are the ones that impact an organization, are strategic—and I did not think enough attention was being paid. That's how I got into it.

P. G.: In your consulting practice, you advise CEOs and boards of directors. What should boards, CEOs, and other senior leaders focus on as they navigate an increasingly volatile, uncertain, complex, and ambiguous world?

J. B.: Well, Paul, thinking about the waves and the forces of currents reminds me about one business sector that we wrote about, and it's a key component of the U.S. and, for that matter, the global economy. It's what I call the automotive-industrial complex. I believe the entire automotive sector's going to be transformed, not by a wave or even a storm but by a steady current or, perhaps more correctly, several interconnected currents that will move the industry along a path from the internal combustion engine to battery-powered electric vehicles. I think, because they're strong currents, we consumers are all going to be moved along with it along that path, and it's going to be within the next couple years, as we make the shift from gas stations to charging stations.

The giant automobile manufacturers like GM, Ford, Fiat, Chrysler, Daimler, Volkswagen are betting billions on the currents. I recently read a fascinating profile of Mary Barra, the CEO of GM. She describes her key roles as creating strategy, managing risk, empowering employees to execute, and holding people accountable.[9] To me, what she's focused on is taking GM's traditional core competencies, like making the cars we all grew up with, and reconfiguring those core competencies and building the company with the dynamic capabilities to adapt to and address a rapidly changing environment that moves from gasoline to electric to autonomous. Mary Barra has also stated that there's going to be more change in the next ten years than there has been in the last fifty. I think she's right.

So, to answer your question about what boards should be focusing on in the world of increased volatility, uncertainty, complexity, and ambiguity: developing leadership that embraces Mary Barra's key roles of creating strategy, risk management, empowering employees to execute, and holding people accountable. Going just a bit further, another question is how is she going to accomplish her objectives and make GM a leader in the future?

For a strategy and risk consultant like me, Mary's including risk management as a key role is gold. Strategy execution and talent management are obvious, but risk management's been the missing ingredient. The more important real question for all organizations will be: What kind of risk management? Will it be only about audit and compliance, as so many ERM programs are these days, or will it encompass strategy, execution, and talent management? Will they figure out that risk management is also about upside opportunities?

P. G.: Go just a little bit deeper, and tell me why—when Mary is including risk management in her key domains of activity—why is that gold to you, with your experience?

J. B.: Well, I think GM and all its competitors, and for that matter all organizations, have to figure out how to link strategy creation, execution, risk management, and talent management together. The reason why is that organizations are facing structural change in their industries and making a lot of decisions about their futures. Including SRM will improve the quality of those decisions. They need a strategic risk management approach that can provide them with the information, expertise, insight, and a road map about what those futures might look like—and be prepared to adapt or modify their existing strategies.

I haven't talked to a CEO or a CFO, or a chief risk officer for that matter, or anybody else in the C-suite, who doesn't think their current business model is being challenged by rapid change—and, in many cases, disruptive change. Disruption is coming from the really big, outside, uncontrollable forces that produce those deep-rooted currents like political, economic, technological, social, environmental, and legal shifts. Those able to see through the waves, and take advantage of the currents, need something to link everything together, and I think that ingredient is strategic risk management.

P. G.: In your experience, how good are executive teams and boards at really seeing currents versus waves? What percentage of the executives you deal with are sort of caught up in the day-to-day and never really get to seeing strategic risk?

J. B.: I think the important comment here is that everyone, every CEO that I've talked to, every CFO that I've talked to, wants to be engaged at the level of strategy. The problem is their current mental model of risk management, which tends to be more about compliance and control, does not include strategy. Their thinking gets buried by the waves coming from day-to-day things—which are incredibly important—but at the same time keep them from thinking about the future of their strategy and how it's being executed. And then, from the risk management perspective, most executives have a mental model that is clearly in the compliance and control mode. When I talk with them about the disruptive risks they face, a lot of them, they tell me they've developed and implemented ERM programs over the last ten years, they've now got some kind of risk register and a heat map, probably created with audit and compliance in mind.

They've gone even further and created a risk map that they present to the board on an annual basis, and the problem with risk registers is that they aren't strategic. They attempt to convey to the board a message that all their risks are known and have been measured and are being managed, and that the board, by this oversight process, has fulfilled its obligation to shareholders. Unfortunately, risks are being managed by their color on the map. The problem is that some very arbitrary decisions were made to place a particular risk on the map. Plus, upside opportunities are missed altogether. Traditional heat maps only include the downside. A multidimensional approach to risk and opportunity assessment should be presented to the board to improve their oversight and strategic decision making.

I saw a wonderful chart in *Harvard Business Review* in 2015 that showed that, over a recent ten-year period, about eighty-six percent of major drops in share price were because of strategic risks, but the auditors spend only six percent of their time on strategic risk.[10] The rest is spent on operational, financial, and compliance. Important, yes, but not necessarily that which is going to determine a company's future, or their strategic advantage.

P. G.: Okay, so this compliance mentality, this kind of accounting focus, is certainly a barrier to thinking about strategic risks. In your experience, what are some other barriers that you've seen that keep organizations from really incorporating a strategic view of risk?

J. B.: Well, one of the thoughts I've always had, and one of the themes I try to transmit to students or attendees at my speeches and in teaching, is about disruptive risks and opportunities that are going to impact their business, and potentially any competitive advantage that they have or they think they have. And what I always talk about is that the focus for boards and the C-suite needs to be on the quadrant in the Rumsfeld matrix of known unknown risks and uncertainties. These are the risks and uncertainties—we talk about them as weak signals in chapter five—that people in the company know about, and the opportunities as well. You know they're out there, but you don't know their impacts on the firm. They are known exposures with unknown impacts. For instance, we know that autonomous cars are on the horizon, but what we don't know is exactly when they will become commonplace, and how much our lives will be changed. Heck, we don't know what the entire industry will look like in 2030.

I think some organizations can better see the future when they get beyond a risk map and start using a tool like our strategic uncertainty map. The power of these tools is that they plot the known unknowns in a systematic way that gives real information about the potential impact on their strategy, good or bad. A good map, a road map, tells the board where risks are coming from, where they might be headed, and when they'll arrive. With that information, the board and C-suite can make a real plan about how and when to respond. You can't do that if all your strategic risk management tools monitor is compliance. To sum up and answer your question in a very simple way, I think a mental model that is in compliance is the biggest barrier to implementing SRM, considering how important strategic risk management could be to organizations.

P. G.: Let's assume that an organization is actually able to break out of that compliance mentality for a little while and adopt an SRM program like we've described. What's your experience about sustaining that program? How hard is it for an organization to really think about strategic risks, not only once every year but all the time?

J. B.: Well, I think there are a number of factors. One is—if you're really serious and considering implementing a strategic risk management program—one question that should be on your mind is where exactly is this function to be housed within your organization? So, if the SRM team is housed in a compliance function, whether it be legal or audit or something along those lines, it will focus on compliance. The result is that you will be compliant. The problem will be that there's really no chance of SRM that works from a strategic perspective ever being implemented.

If you want to keep SRM alive and really have a strategic view, it needs to be in a strategic function, ideally in the C-suite itself. You have to have a CRO with real executive authority and the opportunity to give input when strategy decisions get made, and even more so about when they are implemented. You also need a written board charter that says something to effect that "We're focused on not only compliance, financial, and operational issues but also strategic risks and opportunities." You need that clarity for when that person delivers some news others don't want to hear.

And keeping it alive—and again, I go back to Mary Barra, when she said, "I'm focused on creating strategy. I'm focused on risk management. I'm focused on people and making them accountable." To me, that sounds like she is reconfiguring GM's core competencies. They'll always make cars—they know how to do it, and they know how to do it well—but I think she's reconfiguring those core competencies so that they have the flexibility to anticipate and respond to the deep currents driving the automotive-industrial complex. For that, SRM becomes a critical competence. She's shifting the organization, I think, to one with dynamic capabilities that can stay ahead of competitors and produce superior financial results. She really needs to link all four elements: strategy, risk management, strategy execution, and talent management. And she needs to keep them linked together for GM to thrive in the new world.

If you accept the logic of the linkage, SRM can't just be something that your company does every six months, or every year, or part of their three-year, long-term strategic plan. SRM must be embedded in all of the strategic activities of an organization. Yes, strategic planning, but also mergers and acquisitions, new product launches, geographic expansion, and potential reorganizations of the company. All of these are really strategic activities, and I believe that SRM—because these things are ongoing, because organizations are reacting to a change in their business models—this is the way to keep SRM going and alive. It will also be a way to measure the results.

P. G.: You've been a consultant now for fifteen years, and before that you were an executive. When you think about good consulting or a good book that really helps you move forward, what should that book contain? What do you want to get out of a good consulting engagement?

J. B.:   When we started to write this book, one of the thoughts that we all had was "How do we make the book like a good consulting engagement?" To me, when you go to hire a consultant—or whether the chief strategy officer or the chief risk officer really is an advisor, an internal consultant, to an organization—I found that, over my career, a good engagement means delivering on four very basic but fundamental things. One, obviously, is information. The others are expertise, insights, and an execution road map that helps the organization better see the future and suggests ideas on to them how to get there.

I think in our book we've tried to provide the kind of information that the C-suite and other senior executives can use, in terms of "Wow, I didn't even know SRM existed. Here are the basic components of it. Here's how we begin to see it working in an our organization." We provide them with our collective expertise about what works and what doesn't, and some specific examples of how this stuff might work, for them to chew on.

We've tried to provide executive readers with insights about understanding their core values, how they get new customers, and how they can better compete in the marketplace. Traditional risk management questions are: What happened? Why? And how can we prevent this in the future? We've invited leaders to think about questions like "What might happen and how can we make it happen?"

Lastly, I think a good engagement ends with a clear road map. A good consultant doesn't just tell people what to do and walk away; he or she positions them to execute and to make things happen. I think our book gives people an early road map about how to get started down a new road, one that combines strategy and risk.

This book is certainly not the final chapter in strategic risk management, but we hope it's the first really good one that convinces them to go beyond compliance. To think about the future and what your competitive advantages will look like as weak signals turn into strategic risks. SRM is really an answer to questions most executives have: How can we see the future better? How can we respond more quickly, and better. Because, after all, the future ain't what it used to be.

We conclude by emphasizing the main current facing every business we see: a VUCA world and increasing volatility, uncertainty, complexity, and ambiguity on the horizon. No firm, no government agency, no nonprofit lives in what now appears to be (but did not appear as such then) the halcyon days of predictability and stability that existed a decade or two ago. We believe, based on our experiences with successful and unsuccessful companies, that the ability to link strategy and risk, in both formulation and execution, provides the best bet for success in a VUCA word. SRM, a set of principles, processes, teams, and tools for managing strategic risks, or those exposures that create threats to—or opportunities to expand—competitive advantage, provides the best way forward.

SRM offers another benefit: it helps close the gap between strategy and execution that destroys so much business value. The principles of SRM create and reinforce a mind-set that sees integration and close collaboration between those making strategy and those implementing it. The processes we've laid out provide structural and cultural supports to foster collaborative, integrative work across operating units. The SRM team has a natural affinity for, and skill in, taking a broad view of the future and its challenges, and the tools they employ—the Strategic Uncertainty Decision Map, scenario planning, and wargaming—communicate with and involve managers across functions and levels. The Strategic Risk Ownership Map and the Risk Reporting Matrix formalize the connection between strategy makers and implementers through a clear assignment of responsibility for action around strategic risks.

As John Bugalla emphasizes, the future ain't what it used to be. The ability to embrace VUCA provides the best defense, and the best offense, for surviving and thriving in changing markets and industries. Given all the uncertainty ahead, companies can ill afford to navigate by looking in the rearview mirror. The only way forward is to drive while looking out the front windshield. At the end of the day, that's what SRM allows a company to do.

APPENDIX A

Strategy in an Uncertain Age

W e've talked about strategy throughout the book. This appendix offers a deep dive into the logic and structure of the four-questions model that we wrote about in chapter 1. The four questions don't replace the traditional models and tools of strategy; they simply reorganize much of this thinking in a way that reflects how today's organizations ought to think about strategy. We begin, as we have done throughout the book, with a business story that highlights the importance of the topic.

By the time Walt Disney moved from Kansas City to Burbank, California, in 1923, he had already experienced stunning success and devastating disappointment—success from his Laugh-O-Gram cartoons, a series of short films that theaters ran before the main feature, to warm up the crowd, followed by the failure of *Alice in Cartoonland*, films featuring a live Alice interacting with Walt's cartoon characters. *Alice*, a technical wonder but a financial disaster, drove Walt's studio into bankruptcy in July 1923. Walt and his brother Roy headed West for a new start in the Golden State.[1] Within a year, the new Disney Brothers Studio contracted with local distributor Margaret Winkler to produce the *Alice Comedies*, a series based on Walt's failed *Alice in Cartoonland*. Three years and fifty-six triumphant episodes later, Winkler's husband, Charles Mintz, contracted with the Disneys to produce a new character, Oswald the Lucky Rabbit.[2]

Oswald quickly gained popularity, due in large part to Disney's insistence on quality drawing and animation sequences. Oswald didn't jerk about in fits and starts like other cartoon characters of the day; he moved like a live person and had the "illusion of life."[3] Mintz paid the Disneys $1,500 (more than $20,000 today) for each Oswald film, a price Walt felt was too low and Mintz felt was far too high.

In early 1928, Walt and his wife, Lilly, headed to New York to cut a new deal with Mintz that would expand the successful series. Walt failed again. Mintz held the legal rights to the Oswald character, and he had secretly negotiated with several Disney animators to join his studio. Mintz wanted to cut out what he perceived as an expensive and unnecessary middleman, and he fired Disney.

Crushed at the loss of their main character and sole income source, Walt and Lilly boarded the train to return to Hollywood. In the late 1920s, that was a multiday journey, and Walt began drawing to while away the long hours. Lilly recalled, "Walt showed me some of his sketches on the train coming home. They were cute little things; they could do anything. I asked him what he was going to call the character. 'Mortimer Mouse,' he said. I said, 'That doesn't sound very good,' and then I came up with 'Mickey Mouse.'"[4] Like a phoenix rising from the ashes, a mouse born in the midst of great crisis would transform the fortunes of Disney Brothers Studio.

Those fortunes turned with Mickey's portrayal of Steamboat Willie, in late 1928, when audiences first met an adorable, rambunctious mouse who made music while steering and stayed one step ahead of his cantankerous captain's ire. *Steamboat Willie* was a good story well told, and audiences loved it. Distributors did, as well, because Mickey incorporated the latest technical innovation in film: sound. The first full-length talking picture, *The Jazz Singer*, had appeared just a year earlier and promised to remake the industry. Technically, sound made high-quality films much harder to produce. Video and audio were recorded on separate reels, or tracks, and synchronizing the two would bedevil film editors and distributors for decades.

Steamboat Willie, however, featured a cutting-edge character whose movements on screen perfectly matched the audio track. Synchronous sound represented a major advance in motion pictures. The public, and critics, loved it, and the Disneys were on their way. Walt drove Disney, looking out the front windshield for ways to leverage the future, technological or commercial, for his company's benefit.

The Disney brothers released three more Mickey cartoons in the next six months. Mickey became the symbol of the Disney company and, over time, the stable of Disney characters grew to include a host of animals such as Bambi and Donald Duck, animated characters like Aladdin and Cinderella, and live-action favorites Jack Sparrow, Mary Poppins, Captain America, Ironman, and even Darth Vader and R2-D2. From a single cartoon short in 1928, Disney's Studio Entertainment unit grew into a $10 billion business by 2018.

In the fall of 1929, a year after *Steamboat Willie*, the Disneys licensed Mickey to a stationery company, which emblazoned the mouse on note cards. By the time World War II broke out, 10% of Disney's revenue came from licensing deals. The company expanded into children's books, clothing and apparel, toys and action figures. Today, Disney's consumer products business includes more than two hundred Disney stores, a dedicated Disney Princess business, as well as video games, YouTube channels, and a host of digital properties. The Consumer Products and Interactive Media unit contributed $4.6 billion to 2018 revenues.

In 1952, Walt extended his focus from the silver screen to the small one. On Christmas Day, he aired *One Hour in Wonderland* to promote the upcoming *Alice in Wonderland* film.[5] The first episode of *The Mickey Mouse Club* aired in 1955, and Disney has produced weekly television programming continuously for more than six decades. In 1995, the company moved from content producer into the distribution side of the television business with its purchase of ABC and a set of related media properties, including ESPN. Now grouped into the Media Networks unit, these businesses generated revenues of $24.5 billion in 2018.

Walt expanded into television because he needed money to realize another of his dreams: a destination theme park, something much different than the dirty, dingy, and dangerous amusement parks that dotted the United States and drew limited, local audiences. In 1954, the U.S. interstate highway system was only an emerging set of maps and diagrams—it would not be fully funded until 1956. Bankers and other investors did not share Walt's ambitious, forward-looking view and refused to underwrite the new venture. Walt turned to the new ABC network to finance his park. ABC needed programming to attract audiences to television; Walt needed cash, and a way to promote his new park. ABC offered both, and Disneyland opened in July 1955 to immediate success. Disneyland and eleven other parks across the world, a cruise line, and a set of vacation club properties produced $20.2 billion in sales for 2018.

Disney is a strategy success story. In 2018, the company came in at number fifty-five on the Fortune 500 and ranked fourteenth on Interbrand's list of the most valuable global brands. Success grew out of Walt's ability to see the future accurately and to answer the four key questions that, for us, define strategy: Why do we win with customers? How do we create value? Where should we compete? And what sustains our value over time? This appendix takes up these four questions that drive competitive advantage.

Why Do We Win with Customers? Creating Unique Value at a Profit

Companies that generate greater profits than rivals—a competitive advantage—do so because they understand and satisfy their customers' underlying needs better than their competitors do. Management guru Clayton Christensen frames customer needs within a job-to-be-done framework, in which customers "hire" products or services to do important jobs for them.[6] As marketing guru Theodore Levitt noted, "People don't want to buy a quarter-inch drill. They want a quarter-inch hole!"[7] When strategists understand and respond to their customers' job to be done, they can create a competitive advantage.

Doing Jobs Better: Differentiation

Differentiation means offering products or services that do more jobs for customers. That "doing more" happens in one of two ways: through superior products (or services) and/or through attention to the context in which that product or service gets purchased and used. Superior products either do more jobs for customers or they do a single job better than alternative offerings. Nalco, which we discussed in chapter 9, is the undisputed market leader in the unglamorous industrial water treatment industry. Water matters to most businesses—think about how important water is for Coca-Cola, Marriott Hotels, or Rio Tinto's mining operations—but most managers think of water as a commodity. Nalco garners a 10% to 20% price premium for its treatment systems, which is very unusual for a commodity product.

Customers pay more for Nalco systems because they outperform competitors on two critical water-related jobs: maximizing water cleanliness and minimizing overall costs. Nalco hardware and software automates decisions about water treatment, determines system-wide water quality every six seconds, diagnoses causes of changes in that quality in real time, and dispenses the right amount of treatment chemicals to rectify problems. That's faster and better than water engineers can do the same job. The company also helps its customers plan and implement programs to reduce the total amount of input water used, to reuse that water through several production cycles, and to clean wastewater before release back into the ecosystem.

Superiority may also come from better quality or reliability. Nalco's computer-controlled water treatment system measures and responds to microscopic changes in incoming mineral and microbial content (think of fewer mineral stains in glasses or on shower doors), in real time. That means more reliable and consistent water quality throughout a customer's operations. That consistency translates into higher machine uptime, lower repair costs, extended asset life, and lower capital costs for new equipment. Nalco's price premium captures some of customers' total cost savings.

The context in which customers use products offers opportunities for differentiation, through superior convenience or easy-to-access product support and customer service. Nalco uses a "lock and key" design that allows customers to easily and safely add a number of different treatment chemicals into the dispensing system. Each chemical, formulated to solve one or many water quality issues, comes in a hard block—just like solid dishwasher or laundry detergent. Each has its own unique shape (the key), which fits only one slot (the lock) in the treatment equipment.

Differentiation strategies increase a customer's willingness to pay for a product or service, which leads to higher selling prices and increased revenue. Companies usually incur extra cost to add features and benefits to products, but consumers pay more because they get more. Profit comes when the increased selling price exceeds the cost of additional features, but profit disappears if the cost of differentiation exceeds incremental revenue. Customers come first, but costs also matter.

Doing Jobs Cheaper: Cost Leadership

Sometimes, customers don't care about doing more or better jobs, they just want a job done as cheaply as possible. Cost leaders focus on understanding and streamlining their production process to reduce what it costs to produce and sell their offerings. This strategy relies on leveraging the behavior of fixed and variable costs, and how different stages in its value chain interact with one another.

Fixed costs have a unique property: as a firm sells more, fixed costs, as a percentage of total costs, fall. Walmart's fleet of company-owned trucks provides a great example. Walmart employs 7,200 full-time, salaried truck drivers and owns more than six thousand tractors (trucks), fifty-three thousand trailers, and 5,600 refrigerated trailers, or "reefers."[8] The crucial fixed cost metric: how many of the fleet's 900 million annual miles move merchandise. Every truck leaves the warehouse full, but many return empty. Walmart minimizes deadhead miles—miles with an empty trailer—by backhauling; trucks bring Walmart return merchandise back, and the company also rents its trucks to others wanting to move freight along its route. Walmart's trucks backhaul about 80% of the time, and the company earns more than $1 billion annually by renting out its empty trucks to other vendors.[9]

Variable costs, as the name suggests, vary with the level of output. At 900 million miles per year, fuel represents Walmart's largest trucking expense. In 2005, the company set an aggressive goal to double fleet efficiency by 2015. Walmart worked with trailer designers, engine manufacturers, and other vendors to design a futuristic concept truck, the Walmart Advanced Vehicle Experience. The company incorporated some elements of the concept vehicle into today's fleet, which helped Walmart surpass its goal of doubling fuel efficiency, a move that added another $1 billion annually to the bottom line.[10]

Cost interactions, or complementarities, provide the final pathway to cost leadership. Costs are complementary when reducing the cost of activity A, for example, lowers the cost of B. For Walmart, warehouses and trucks complement each other. The less time inventory spends in a warehouse, the less time it sits on Walmart's balance sheet and the sooner it gets loaded onto a truck, which increases the miles per year each truck drives, better amortizing its fixed cost.

Merchandise—say, a pallet of Crest toothpaste—arrives at a typical distribution center, which has 1 million square feet of space, ten to twenty miles of conveyors, and about one thousand employees.[11] Procter and Gamble prelabeled the pallet for a particular store, based on data shared by Walmart. The pallet moves from the P&G trailer to a conveyor system that routes each pallet to an outgoing bay, where it gets loaded onto a truck and shipped to the appropriate store. When the process works well, the toothpaste never stops moving. The system minimizes inventory holding, truck loading, and driver downtime costs.

Walmart translates its cost advantage into lower prices for customers, which drives up volume and total profit dollars. Others with a low-cost position may reinvest those savings into greater differentiation. These companies try to create a dual advantage of differentiation and cost leadership.

Cost Leadership and Differentiation

Many leading strategists see cost leadership and differentiation as mutually exclusive strategies; companies can't be true cost leaders when they layer on costs to create additional product benefits.[12] Toyota illustrates how a company can realize a dual advantage. Toyota's unique production system, which features strong relationships with its supply network, a Kanban system for inventory control, and Kaizen processes for continuous improvement, gives the company an estimated 30% cost advantage over its U.S. rivals.[13] Toyota plows those cost savings into higher-quality vehicles. The manufacturer's suggested retail price for a Toyota Camry comes in at about $2,500 more than that for a comparable Chevy Malibu, a price premium of about 10%. Toyota's return on assets was 3.14% in 2018, 64% higher than GM, which posted a return on assets of 1.91% for the same period.

Toyota wins in its market because it provides customers with a differentiated (higher-quality) product and does so at a radically lower cost of production than its rivals. In other words, Toyota has a different answer to the second question of competitive advantage: "How do we create value?"

How Do We Create Value?

How do Toyota, Walmart, Nalco, and Disney win? They engage in a set of coordinated activities, built on dedicated assets and organizational processes, that create differentiation or lower costs. These asset–process–activity combinations take years to develop, so these companies structure their long-term investment strategies around a clear set of priorities and values. The Company Diamond, a strategy tool developed by Paul Godfrey, offers a visual framework to think about how companies create value (figure A.1).

Activities

Activities sit at the top of the diamond; they create and deliver actual value to customers. Disney wins with customers, primarily, by doing an important emotional job for customers: making them feel good. Customers feel good because of what Disney employees and systems do every day, from creating the illusion of life in cartooning, to the training of cast members playing Cinderella or Mickey Mouse at Disneyland, to designing software code that runs *Kingdom Hearts* (a top-rated Disney video game). Activities have two key characteristics: they create value by "touching" the customer, and they fit together to deliver value in that customer touch.

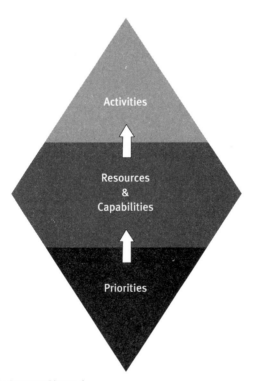

Figure A.1 The Company Diamond

Companies win when their core activities differ from what competitors do, or when they perform the same activities as competitors but in a different way.[14] The classic Disney movie performs a different set of core activities; it is animation instead of live-action production. That difference, combined with a penchant for timeless stories, creates a different type of value for Disney customers. Disney hotels engage in the same basic activities as Holiday Inn, but employees do them in a different way, with a lot more attention to detail and concern for the guest.

Activities have an organizational component as well. Executives and managers ensure that activities fit together into a clear and coherent value proposition. Disney's entails providing customers with a "magical" experience, one that transports them to a different world, ensures a fun and adventurous journey, and promises happiness and good feeling as the final destination. That value proposition defines other parts of the activity-based business model, from the market segments a company targets (for Disney, elementary school–age children), to how a company interacts with its customers (high levels of customer service and lots of smiles), to whom the company chooses as business partners (Hasbro produces Disney toys and action figures).

Resources and Capabilities

Resources and capabilities occupy the middle of the diamond, and they represent the intermediate and long-term investments that companies make to create competitive advantage. Resources (assets) and capabilities (processes) drive, energize, and give shape to the activities that create value. Some resources appear on a financial balance sheet, others on a strategic one. Disney's physical assets (worth almost $100 billion) appear on its financial balance sheet, but its $40 billion of brand equity does not.[15] Disney's brand evokes a certain set of emotions and feelings within a customer, even in anticipation of purchase; it also sends signals to that customer about the product's quality, price, and usefulness.

Strategic capabilities are the processes and routines through which companies deploy their resources. For the Disney brand, some capabilities are incredibly simple, such as a set of brand guidelines that help Disney's brand communicate the same messages across different venues. Some are more complex and dynamic and guard the brand's value, like Disney's legal department, which constantly looks for interlopers trying to unfairly leverage or infringe upon the brand. In fact, legend has it that the sign over the door to Disney's legal offices reads "Don't mess with the Mouse!" Some resources and capabilities have existed for decades (Disney's legal department has been excellent since the late 1920s), while some, such as the Disney Princess brand, are relatively new.

In 2000, Andy Mooney moved from Nike's marketing department to take over Disney's Consumer Products operation. Mooney "bundled" Snow White, Cinderella, Ariel, Belle, Jasmine, Mulan, Pocahontas, and Sleeping Beauty into a powerful extension of the core brand, the Disney Princesses. *Variety* noted the power of the new combination: "No longer were these characters identified only with their isolated fairy tales. They were an exalted sorority, a justice league for the sandbox set whose collective popularity was unrivalled by Barbies or Bratz."[16] The line sells dolls and clothes and even has a glass slipper line and adult wedding dresses priced at more than $1,000. Revenue from the Princess Line grew from $100 million in 2001 to $3 billion six years later, for a compound annual growth rate of almost 59%.[17]

Values and Priorities

Extending resources and capabilities might happen relatively quickly, but creating new ones may take several years and reflects a deep expression of a firm's values and priorities. Pixar Animation Studios, run by Apple founder Steve Jobs, created software called RenderMan, which produced sophisticated and lifelike computer-animated characters. Pixar's innovation rendered Disney's illusion-of-life techniques obsolete, and Pixar, taking a page from the Disney playbook, created a number of Academy Award–winning short films to highlight the new technology. In 1991, Disney and Pixar created an alliance to create three films (later changed to five). Pixar had the cool new technology and Disney would provide the marketing and distribution capabilities. The alliance produced five blockbuster movies: *Toy Story*; *A Bug's Life*; *Toy Story 2*; *Monsters, Inc.*; and *Finding Nemo*.

Disney had hoped to learn the new technique during the alliance, but it proved unable to master the skills, so it bought Pixar outright in 2006. The need to buy Pixar, and Disney's inability to master computer animation, exemplifies the importance of values and priorities, the base of the Company Diamond. Disney made its fortune in animated films, and by the time Walt died unexpectedly, in 1966, his company had leveraged those characters into a growing theme park business. The successors to Walt Disney had skills in developing theme parks but not in animation, and the post-Walt company failed to value animation; it valued the revenue growth and profit in the development of Disney World and other theme parks. Animation moved from a priority to an afterthought, and executives failed to invest in maintaining and developing the human, social, and organizational resources that produced great animation. When Pixar executives finally breached the castle walls and entered the animation studios, they found a unit with low morale, little flexibility to incorporate new ideas, and a management structure centered on minimizing cost.

Values can be defined simply as "what matters." Some values, such as honesty, fair dealing, or equal treatment of all, have a moral and ethical component; other values reflect deeply held business priorities. Some organizations value the short term, others prioritize longer time horizons. Promoting from within versus hiring from outside reflects more than a pragmatic choice; it describes whether stability or change matters more. Whether executives acknowledge them or not, values such as quality, cost, immediate return, growth, and innovation underlie strategy development and the organizational budgeting processes that give birth to the creation of strategic resources.[18]

Low-cost and differentiation strategies tend to be mutually exclusive because they build on different deeply held principles as much as on operational practices. Every low-cost company would love to add more features and garner higher prices, but adding features conflicts with minimizing costs. When push comes to shove, the default of keeping costs low wins those budget battles. An organization's resources and capabilities, and the activities they support, represent the survivors in a values-driven Darwinian process of bureaucratic survival.

Where Should We Compete?

MBA strategy courses usually begin with a discussion of where to compete, in homage to the historical origins of strategy as a discipline. Michael Porter's 1980 book *Competitive Strategy* ushered in the era of strategy and argued that the key to company profitability lies in the selection of industry, or where to compete.[19] For us, beginning with this question seems out of sequence; until a company figures out what value they deliver and how they deliver it, executives will struggle with this question and make poor decisions. Industry matters, but for us it only matters after a firm has developed the ability to deliver unique value to customers.

The "Industry" View

Industry matters, and the earliest strategy model, Porter's "five forces," helps executives compare industries they may want to enter. The five quantifiable economic factors that determine the underlying profit potential of any competitive setting—threat of new entry, supplier power, buyer power, threat of substitution, and competitive rivalry—also prove useful as executives consider moves they may take to make their own industry more profitable.

THREAT OF NEW ENTRY

New entrants increase the supply of product in the market place, which, absent any growth in demand, depresses prices for all competitors, or they may introduce new, differentiated offerings that better satisfy customer needs. Wise executives will invest in one of several factors that deter entry and preserve or enhance profitability: leveraging economies of scale and learning curves, deploying new technology that increases capital costs for entrants, developing brands and associated equity, or limiting access to key distribution channels, which raises marketing and sales costs for potential entrants.

SUPPLIER POWER

Suppliers increase their own profits by making their customers pay more. Paying more may happen through higher sticker prices, lower input quality, or less service and support. Whatever the cause, when a firm pays more (or gets less) from suppliers, they see their own margins decline. Suppliers with unique inputs have power over their buyers, as do those whose inputs add lots of value to their buyers' outputs. Power also shifts toward suppliers when inputs have few substitutes, when buyers lack alternative sources of supply, or when suppliers can forward integrate and compete directly with buyers.

BUYER POWER

Buyers want to maximize their own utility, which means getting the greatest benefit at the lowest cost. Lower prices for buyers mean, all else being equal, lower profits for firms. High-volume buyers negotiate price concessions; the same holds for buyers who can easily switch among suppliers or substitute products. Firms may have little power to influence volume discounts, but they can—and often do—create switching costs that deter buyers from migrating to other products or vendors. Products that lack significant proprietary features and benefits, brand identity, or substantial quality differences make customers extremely price sensitive.

THREAT OF SUBSTITUTION

Substitute products give buyers the same benefits, just in different ways. Skype represents a substitute for airline travel; sales staff can meet "face-to-face" with customers or others virtually instead of physically. Sporting events substitute for movies, as both meet a customer's need for entertainment. No substitute is perfect, but the closer a substitute comes in terms of customer jobs to be done, the more a firm must use the price of that substitute as a benchmark for its own offering. Smart executives think broadly and monitor adjacent industries for the rise of new, threatening substitutes.

COMPETITIVE RIVALRY

Rivalry provides the clearest, and usually the most present, threat to industry profitability. Rivals compete for share either by competing on price, which drives down revenue, or by competing on features and benefits, which raises costs. Either way, margins suffer and overall profitability declines. Several factors drive competition, including the rate of industry growth, real product differences and the ability of competitors to segment the market, and the cost of exiting a business—such as the cost of disposing of sophisticated technology or selling assets. Constructive rivalry keeps competing firms fresh and vibrant; destructive rivalry depresses profits and discourages innovation.

Prescriptively, the model suggests two courses of action for executives. First, they may deploy the firm's resources and capabilities in "attractive industries," those where the configuration of the five forces sustains high margins. Executives should seek out industries that are using commodity inputs (low supplier power), selling to a large number of price-insensitive customers (low buyer power), requiring significant economies of scale in production or brand (high barriers to entry), selling products that provide value in difficult-to-replicate ways (low threat of substitution), and, finally, carving up the market into clearly definable segments (low competitive rivalry). The first prescription of the model proves paradoxical, however, because these attractive industry settings, by definition, make entry difficult.

The second prescription tells managers to conduct business in a way that molds the competitive dynamic in their industry to their favor. Firms should, for example, always use second-source agreements and spread their purchases among multiple suppliers to reduce, if not eliminate, supplier power. Building a powerful brand diminishes the threat of substitute or competing products (customers don't get the same emotional connection), lowers buyer power (brands make customers less price sensitive), and reduces the threat of entry (creating a brand barrier that new competitors need to hurdle). The bottom line: if executives can't find an attractive industry to compete in, then they should make their own industry as attractive as possible.

The Job-to-Be-Done View

Every business student learns the "industry" answer to the "Where to compete" question. If we look back at Disney, however, we see that neither Walt nor his successors made expansion decisions consistent with the industry logic. If Walt had done a five forces analysis of the filmed entertainment industry in the early 1920s, he might not have entered. Several mega firms, including Metro Goldwyn Mayer and United Artists, had locked up the critical input—on-screen talent—and the distribution of films to theaters. The industry cranked out more than eight hundred films each year throughout the decade, a manifestation of intense competition.[20] Filmed entertainment hardly qualified as an attractive industry.

Walt Disney didn't ask "Where should I compete?" because he already occupied an industry niche—animated short films—where he had talent, skill, and some name recognition. Walt performed an important job for film distributors and movie houses: providing great opening content to set up the feature film. Walt got audiences laughing and feeling good by sprinkling his unique value—Disney magic. Disney grew his company by finding new ways and places to deploy that magic.

Feature films offered a new, longer format for customer experiences with Disney in the theater, while stationery and consumer products allowed fans to experience the Disney magic and brand at home (a new venue). Consumer products also provided fans with a tangible experience (through clothing, books, and the like), as opposed to a virtual one (the sight and sound of movies). The move to television brought the sight and sound of Disney entertainment into the home. Disneyland provided visitors with an immersive destination experience featuring sight, smell, sound, taste, and touch.

Figure A.2 illustrates the difference between the industry and job-to-be-done answers to the "Where to compete" question. The top line in the graph shows the industries in which Disney competes. Disney not only competes in a variety of industries but also appears to compete in entirely different sectors of the economy, as defined in the North American Industrial Classification System: Gift, Novelty, and Souvenir Stores; Motion Picture and Video Production; Educational Support Services; Amusement and Theme Parks; Hotels and Motels; and Full-Service Restaurants.

The job-to-be-done view, however, portrays Disney as a company with a clear focus and value proposition. "Disney magic"—the product or service that customers "hire" for their entertainment jobs—sits at the center

The "Industry View"

The "Job to be Done" View

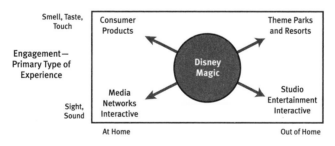

Figure A.2 Where Disney Competes

of all the company's businesses. It is the tie that binds disparate operations together. The vertical axis in figure A.2 captures how Disney magic gets delivered, which of the five senses customers use to experience the magic. The horizontal dimension tells us where the job gets done, in the home or outside of it. The job-to-be-done view differs dramatically from the industry one. Disney operates in several different sectors, but the company focuses on doing a single job for customers—satisfying their need for entertainment with Disney magic.

What Sustains Value over Time?

On that winter day in 1928, Walt Disney learned from Charles Mintz a hard truth about how to sustain a competitive advantage. Without clear ownership rights to Oswald the Lucky Rabbit, Walt lost his tangible intellectual property and the earnings stream that it garnered. Walt's company would never make that mistake again. Stories of Disney's aggressive protection of its copyrights abound; Disney pursues even the smallest, and often unintentional, infringements on its intellectual property. The company has protected its most valuable character, Mickey Mouse, with nineteen separate trademarks on his name, and the company went as far as the United States Congress, in 1988, to lobby for extending Mickey's copyright protection, originally set to expire in 2003. The effort succeeded, and Mickey now enjoys copyright protection until 2023.[21] Mickey's image and name, as well as that of most other Disney characters, appears safely ensconced behind a firewall of legal protections.

Mintz's experience, however, teaches us something else about sustaining a competitive advantage. Mintz captured the tangible image and name of Oswald, along with important human capital for Oswald's continued production, but Mintz failed to garner the essence of Oswald, the intangible elements that had made Oswald so popular. Oswald would appear in cartoons until 1943, but the Oswald in these cartoons lacked any deep or endearing character, and he faded from public consciousness, forgotten for more than six decades.[22]

Over that same fifteen-year stretch (1928–1943), Walt would win ten Academy Awards for his cartoon shorts, including a special award in 1932 for the creation of Mickey Mouse. During that time, the Disney stable of characters proliferated to include enduring favorites such as Minnie Mouse, Donald Duck, Goofy, Pluto, and a full-length feature character, Snow White. Mickey also became a licensing sensation in the midst of the Great Depression. In 1935, H. L. Robbins wrote in the *New York Times Magazine*, "The fresh cheering is for Mickey the Big Business Man, the world's supersalesman. He finds work for jobless folk. He lifts corporations out of bankruptcy. Wherever he scampers, here or overseas, the sun of prosperity breaks through the clouds."[23]

Mintz owned the tangible character of Oswald the Rabbit but not the intangible human capital inside of Walt Disney that enlivened Oswald. In the language of strategy, Mintz owned the asset (resource), Walt the process (capability). In the film industry, capabilities create far more value than resources. Walt could, and did, create new assets because he owned the underlying processes that created lovable characters. The loss of Oswald caused Walt pain and anguish, and it taught him a valuable lesson about protecting his valuable assets, but at the end of the day, the loss of Oswald proved to be a bump on Disney's road to riches. Mintz enjoyed the fruits of his victory in the short run, but Oswald—and the artists who executed Walt's vision—proved unable to sustain competitive advantage over the long term. Mickey Mouse illustrates the importance of protecting assets and continually building tomorrow's competitive advantage on top of today's assets.

Protecting Resources: Barriers to Imitation

Strategy scholars have invoked the term *barriers to imitation* as a correlate to Michael Porter's barriers to entry.[24] Barriers to entry preserve industry profitability by deterring profit-eroding entry, while barriers to imitation protect a firm's profit stream by forestalling direct competition. Barriers to imitation come in two varieties, hard and soft. Hard barriers arise primarily through legal protections and property rights. Patents, copyrights, and trademarks all shut down imitation of hard or tangible resources. Mintz snared Walt in a work-for-hire agreement that made Oswald his rightful property. Noncompete agreements protect against softer assets such as customer lists or trade secrets falling into the hands of competitors. Nondisclosure agreements keep trade secrets and other types of idiosyncratic knowledge from leaking across firm boundaries to competitors. Each of these legal mechanisms exists to encourage creativity and innovation by insulating that creative work from easy imitation.

Soft barriers arise through a series of path-dependent investments, each of which builds on previous ones and reinforces advantages. Imitation requires the duplication of the path—a daunting task for existing or potential competitors. Disney's brand represents a set of cognitive messages to, as well as an emotional connection with, both casual and die-hard fans. Those messages and connections prove difficult enough to replicate in time, but repeat that message often enough over almost a century and the brand takes on a multigenerational character that becomes almost impossible to imitate.

Organizational cultures represent the ultimate soft barrier to imitation. An organization's culture is a set of taken-for-granted assumptions about how the world works, what constitutes appropriate behavior, and what outcomes members should work for.[25] Culture determines how employees and managers interact with one another and how everyone values and treats customers, and it creates convergence and agreement about goals, objectives, and strategies. Disney's magic comes from a set of employees (cast members) acting according to written and unwritten scripts. That culture gives Disney access to great talent willing to work incredibly hard, and often at a discounted wage, just for the privilege of being associated with the company and its culture. Disney offers something that no other company can, and its culture attracts the creative business talent that contributes to the continued development and extension of the organization's capabilities and business processes.

Dynamically Deploying Capabilities

Disney depends on its legal team, its accumulated brand equity, and its powerful corporate culture to help protect and preserve its competitive advantage. While important, barriers to imitation play a lesser role in sustaining a competitive advantage. Walt's behavior upon losing Oswald surely reflected some level of desperation; he had just seen the company's largest revenue stream evaporate. However, that would only lead to developing and protecting a replacement for the rabbit. When the reception for *Steamboat Willie* signaled that Mickey Mouse could win the hearts and minds of the American public, Walt didn't rest on success. In the short run, the studio cranked out more Mickey cartoons, twelve in 1929 alone, to capitalize on and cement Mickey's emerging fame.

In the longer run, Walt pressed his advantage by introducing new personalities; he deployed and leveraged his strategic capability to produce winning characters. Each new character built on and reinforced the value of existing ones, and Disney had a full pipeline of cartoon shorts, a steady and growing revenue stream, and an emerging, unique connection with fans that became the Disney brand. By 1932, Walt's creative capabilities and his accumulated brand equity enabled another first: the first full-length animated feature, *Snow White and the Seven Dwarfs*, for which Walt would win an honorary Oscar in 1939. He took home eight statues that night—one large one and seven dwarfs. Walt continued to expand and exploit his stable of animated properties through television and theme parks.

Walt sustained his competitive advantage by continually building upon it. He and his company weren't satisfied with what they had achieved; they focused on achieving more. That ethos of continually moving forward and creating new characters and classic stories continues today. Oswald the Lucky Rabbit proves the point. The rights to Oswald remained with Universal Studios after 1943, when the Mintz-held copyright passed to its new owners. In 2006, sportscaster Al Michaels wanted to leave Disney's ESPN unit to work for NBC, a unit of Universal Studios. Disney CEO Robert Iger made a trade: Al Michaels for Oswald the Rabbit. Iger claimed that he wanted to bring Oswald home to the Disney family and complete Walt's vision; however, within months of Oswald's arrival at Disney, the company monetized its long-lost son through consumer products and video games.[26] Disney continues to press its competitive capabilities around character development, merchandising, and weaving its characters into projects and products throughout the company.

Conclusion

Strategy is the process of allocating resources in a very directed way and over time in order to create a sustainable competitive advantage: the ability to earn more than one's rivals. The four questions of strategy we've discussed in this appendix provide that direction for executive teams making resource allocation decisions. The early—and the most recent—experiences of Walt Disney's company illustrate how the interactive answers to these four questions can create a valuable and sustainable competitive advantage. The four questions offer a simple but not simplistic method for managers to think through the difficult issues of strategy.

APPENDIX B

How to Determine Risk Capacity and Risk Appetite

In chapter 3, we outlined the principle of understanding a firm's risk capacity and risk appetite, two terms that are often confused with each other. Returning to the poker player analogy we used earlier, *risk capacity* is the maximum loss that our player can absorb but still leave the game able to return and play another day. Sustainability as a going concern sets the upper bound on risk capacity. *Risk appetite*, on the other hand, describes the betting limit for any individual hand. The most critical relationship between these two elements is that risk appetite should never exceed risk capacity.

This is simple to see in the case of a poker player in a single game, but imagine if she were playing internet poker, with several hands going at one time. That makes our player more like a business with several competitive arenas, projects, and risks active at the same time. In this case, our player, or an executive team, would monitor the risk appetite in each hand to ensure that the total amount bet at any one time remains below the limit defined by risk capacity.

Risk Capacity

The first step in defining an organization's strategic risk capacity is to clearly understand the source of a firm's competitive advantage. Appendix A provided a primer on the foundations of competitive advantage, or why and how a firm wins with customers. The board, C-suite, and others in the strategy complex should clearly articulate the pillars of advantage. For cost leadership firms such as Walmart, the pillars might be logistics, operations, or store locations; for a differentiator like Disney, it might be brand, or customer service, or hiring/training.

With the pillars in place, the team then evaluates all major risk categories that business units or functions experience: operational, technological, financial, political, reputation, and so on. Teams consider these risks in their *inherent* state, without risk controls, and in their *residual* state, with risk controls and active management. The difference between the two states offers some insight into the ability of the firm to transfer, manage, or accept each risk, and how each risk impacts the strategic pillars. When risks respond well to active management, risk capacity may be set higher, but risks that can't be managed well, and their impact on pillars, call for a more conservative view of risk capacity.

Risk capacity will look different for every organization, because each organization builds its strategy on unique pillars and faces a different portfolio of risks. Given the complexity of risks, there is no cookie-cutter approach to determine an organization's risk capacity. A highly leveraged firm, for example, might have a lower overall risk capacity than a deleveraged competitor, because of its need to maintain a certain level of free cash flow. Diversified firms, with several business units, should design risk capacity around strategic pillars in each business but also account for synergies across businesses. Innovative companies will factor in the need for research and development–related risks as they think through their capacity.

Typically, risk capacity anchors around financial constraints, such as available capital, liquidity, or borrowing capacity. However, qualitative constraints, such as regulatory standing, risk management capability, or reputation and brand capacity, also warrant consideration to uncover the firm's true risk capacity. With a good sense of the overall capacity of the organization to take on strategic risk, both downside and upside, executive teams are wise to encapsulate this learning into a formal document to guide decision making.

Risk Appetite

Risk appetite sets the betting limit for each hand our poker player plays. Our most important advice is that, however the team thinks about risk appetite, whether for any project, function, or business unit, or spanning several of those, appetite should always be less than an organization's risk capacity.[1] The firm should never have more chips in the pot than it can lose and still stay in the game. Examples like MF Global and Wells Fargo show how risk appetite needs to be monitored and reported, not ignored.

Risk capacity is the upper limit, but risk appetite should capture the optimal amount of risk that an organization takes on to effectively execute strategy and build competitive advantage. Because risk appetite considers operations and operates within the executive framework of risk capacity, it's easy to think that risk appetite is a job for middle managers. It's not. They lack the broader view of the firm's operations. They'll live within the risk appetite parameters, but the board, particularly the risk management committee, has fiduciary responsibilities for risk oversight and has a broader vision of how strategic risks play out across the firm. Much like a risk capacity statement, risk appetite originates with the board.

We suggest a top-down approach from the C-suite to middle managers and functional units as the best way to define risk appetite. A top-down approach ensures that top executives understand the strategies and risk requirements of the various divisions and units they oversee. The process can also be used to engage board and non-executive directors on the subject of which risks are worth taking and which risks are better to avoid. The result is a robust framework that can be used to articulate appetite throughout the group and to internal stakeholders

A risk appetite process also helps leaders understand the relative tradeoffs between risks and returns. The risk appetite framework helps leaders make appropriate decisions regarding capital investment and allocations, as well as informing them about the level of emphasis to place on R & D and product development or what types of mergers and acquisitions fit best.

Unfortunately, far too many strategic decisions are made with an incomplete understanding of risks and the company's capacity to manage those risks.

Executives should focus on these factors as they develop an organization's risk appetite statement: context, design and content, implementation, accountability, and governance.

1. **Context** for risk appetite needs to be established prior to identifying it. The first component is the external business and market environment, followed by the internal context, including executive styles (think Jon Corzine) and the risk culture of the company (think Wells Fargo). The final context is the risk management process, including organizational and human capital around risk management, and the structure of the board's responsibility for overall risk appetite, capacity, and strategy.

2. **Design and content** of risk appetite. Risk capacity links risk categories to strategic pillars, and risk appetite statements should create the same links between risks, actions, and projects and how the unit contributes to a strategic pillar. Some statements need to be very specific, such as those related to hedging strategy for interest rates or other market risks, commodity pricing decisions, foreign currency exchange and interest rates, or credit risk and liquidity risk. Other statements, such as those around brand, customer relationships, or innovation, will be far broader in scope.

3. **Implementation** of risk appetite asks how the statement will actually guide decision making. Leaders need to think through the process and make sure milestones exist that force teams to consider their actions within the risk appetite framework. Managers also need to define other milestones that require updates to ensure that initial or subsequent actions of investments remain within the risk appetite.

4. **Accountability** for risk appetite and impact. Milestones provide the architecture, but functional leaders and business units need a clear chain of reporting and accountability for risk performance. Reporting plays two important roles. First, it ensures that risk appetite has teeth, that managers operate within the guardrails so that individual

projects don't take on too much risk. Second, accountability helps to validate the value in the risk management process and to strengthen the role of risk management within the firm. As more managers see that linking risk and strategy leads to positive outcomes, their willingness to use these tools in the future increases.

5. **Governance** of risk appetite. These statements need to be dynamic, living documents. Executive teams should design processes that update risk appetite as external and internal conditions change, but also as the firm's overall risk capacity changes. The board's risk committee plays a critical role here, and their regular meetings should include discussions about revisions to risk appetite content or the risk appetite process.[2]

Risk appetite statements work best when they are accompanied by both quantitative and qualitative key performance indicators and by key risk indicators that can be used to monitor risk appetite and risk capacity. Without key performance and key risk indicators, either statement will look more like a vague mission or vision statement, filled with great ideas but with no real way to account for performance.

Risk quantification methodologies will vary depending on the type of risk and the availability of data, such as metrics and loss history. Certain risks, such as credit and market risks, lend themselves to quantification better than others due to the availability of observable financial exposure data. Although there may be challenges in selecting and agreeing on the types of metrics to use to set credit and market risk appetite, there is generally observable data to support measurement. As an example of these measures, we consider three potential strategic risks related to loss exposure, sales scale and scope, and environmental sustainability (table B.1).[3]

Qualitative risk metrics help measure difficult to quantify risks such as reputational or political risks. Consider reputational risk, generally considered by traditional and enterprise risk management to be an unrewarded risk that is very difficult to quantify and manage. Risk appetite for reputational risk can be set qualitatively through consideration of the acceptable types of new business activities and customers and their potential reputational impact on the organization. Qualitative measures, such as interview

Risk Scenario	Quantitative Key Performance Indicator	Quantitative Key Risk Indicator
Loss exposure that threatens cash flow for R & D	Loss exposure to pretax operating should range from $10 million to $60 million	Sales declines of greater than 4% in any given quarter.
Scale and scope	Five major sales customers for each line of business	A single customer will account for no more than 10% of total sales
Environmental sustainability	Reduce energy usage by 40%	Energy costs increase by 5%

Table B.1: Quantitative Dimensions of Risk Appetite

or focus group data, help managers understand the impact of actions on the brand. Table B.2 provides some examples of qualitative risk appetite statements around brand.

Both key performance indicators and key risk indicators will vary by industry, corporate culture, and quantification capabilities, but they should always provide a consistent and comprehensive description of the firm's risk-bearing capacity, and these guidelines will need to be adapted to fit the pillars of each company's core competitive advantages.

Risk Scenario	Qualitative Key Performance Indicators	Qualitative Key Risk Indicators
Brand equity	Customer focus group results indicate strong emotional connection with the brand	Delays in product shipments or stock-outs during critical sales windows
Brand proliferation	Customers understand brand extensions and logic	New products create confusion and dissipate brand messages in focus group participants
Brand crises	Public relations or media coverage negative of the brand	Internal training and public relations proactivity and timing around negative events

Table B.2: Qualitative Dimensions of Risk Appetite

NOTES

INTRODUCTION. HOW WE GOT INTO THIS MESS, AND THE NEED FOR NEW TOOLS

1. Shaun Crawford, Luca Russignan, and Nilabh Kumar, *Global Insurance Trends Analysis 2018*, Ernst and Young, June 2018, www.ey.com/Publication/vwLUAssets/ey-global -insurance-trends-analysis-2018/$File/ey-global-insurance-trends-analysis-2018.pdf.

2. Gerry Dickinson, "Enterprise Risk Management: Its Origins and Conceptual Foundations,. *Geneva Papers on Risk and Insurance* 26, no. 3: 360–366. www.actuaries. org.uk/documents/enterprise-risk-management-its-origins-and-conceptual- foundation-gerry-dickinson.

3. The Committee of Sponsoring Organizations are the American Accounting Association, the American Institute of Certified Public Accountants, Financial Executives International, the Institute of Management Accountants, and the Institute of Internal Auditors. See www.coso.org/Pages/default.aspx.

4. Adam Davidson, "How AIG Fell Apart," Reuters, September 18, 2008, www.reuters.com /article/us-how-aig-fell-apart-idUSMAR85972720080918.

5. Michael Mankins and Richard Steele, "Turning Great Strategy into Great Performance," *Harvard Business Review*, July–August 2005, hbr.org/2005/07/turning-great-strategy -into-great-performance.

6. The number literally hits millions when we consider platforms such as YouTube, which allow individuals to own and run their own "channels," or miniature networks.

CHAPTER 1. STRATEGIC RISK MANAGEMENT: COMPETITIVE ADVANTAGE IN AN UNCERTAIN WORLD

1. "#ThrowbackThursday: Hartford Civic Center Roof Collapse," *Hartford Courant*, www.courant.com/courant-250/moments-in-history/hc-1978-civic-center-collapse -pg-photogallery.html.

2. Data on the 1977–1978 season is available at "1977–78 New England Whalers Roster and Statistics," *Hockey Reference*, www.hockey-reference.com/teams/NEW/1978.html.

3. For a richer description of Bill Rasmussen's career and the beginnings of ESPN, see Michael Freeman, *ESPN: The Uncensored History* (New York: Taylor Trade, 2001), especially chapters 1 and 2.

4. Freeman, *ESPN*, 61.

5. Robert Waterman McChesney, *The Political Economy of Media: Enduring Issues, Emerging Dilemmas* (New York: Monthly Review, 2008), 288.

6. Freeman, *ESPN*, chapter 4, provides the story of Getty Oil and its involvement in ESPN.

7. The actual footage of Lee Leonard's first performance is available at "1979—ESPN Commercials—First Day/3 Months: *SportsCenter*, NCAA," posted by Mancini TV Classics, March 15, 2015, www.youtube.com/watch?v=voed1dkqHZY&t=5s.

8. Forbes valued the ESPN brand at $16.9 billion in 2016. That valuation ranked ESPN as the thirty-first most valuable brand in the world at the time.

9. Don R. Fitzpatrick, "The Survival of the Three Original U.S. Television Networks into the Twenty-First Century as Diverse Broadcast Programming Sources" (master's thesis, Butler University, 1995), 4, digitalcommons.butler.edu/cgi/viewcontent.cgi?article =1030&context=grtheses.

10. Fitzpatrick, "Survival of the Three Original Networks," 5.

11. David B. Yoffie and Mary Kwak, *Judo Strategy: Turning Your Competitors' Strength to Your Advantage* (Boston: Harvard Business School Press, 2001).

12. Archy O. de Berker, Robb B. Rutledge, Christoph Mathys, Louise Marshall, Gemma F. Cross, Raymond J. Dolan, and Sven Bestmann, "Computations of Uncertainty Mediate Acute Stress Responses in Humans," *Nature Communications* 7, March 29, 2016, www .nature.com/articles/ncomms10996.

13. Harold and Margaret Milliken Hatch Laboratory of Neuroendocrinology, "Stress Effects on Structure and Function of Hippocampus," Rockefeller University, lab.rockefeller. edu/mcewen/stresshippo.

14. For an extended discussion of this phenomenon, see Richard E. Neustadt and Ernst May, *Thinking in Time* (New York: Free Press, 1986), chapters 3–5.

15. The United States did not formally declare war on Afghanistan. Congress passed, and President Bush signed, a joint resolution authorizing the use of force, which is something different from a declaration of war. See 107th Congress Public Law 40, Joint Resolution, www.govinfo.gov/content/pkg/PLAW-107publ40/html/PLAW-107publ40. htm.

16. James G. March and Herbert A. Simon, *Organizations* (New York: John Wiley and Sons, 1958), 186.

17. March and Simon, *Organizations*, 165.

CHAPTER 2. STRATEGIC RISK: UNCERTAINTIES THAT IMPACT COMPETITIVE ADVANTAGE

1. John Taylor, *Storming the Magic Kingdom: Wall Street, the Raiders, and the Battle for Disney* (New York: Ballantine, 1987), 220–221.

2. Chuck Schmidt, "Was 1964 the Most Significant Year in Walt Disney Company History? We Think So," SILive.com, February 8, 2013, blog.silive.com/goofy_about_ disney/2013/02/was_1964_the_most_significant_year_in_walt_disney_company_ history_we_think_so.html.

3. Data on Disneyland attendance can be found at "More Disney Theme Park Attendance Figures," Disneyland Linkage, www.scottware.com.au/theme/feature/atend_disparks. htm. Data on the population of California comes from "Historical General Population: City and County of Los Angeles, 1850 to 2010," Los Angeles Almanac, www.laalmanac. com/population/po02.php.

4. Data on the Florida land purchases can be found at Lou Mongello, "Walt Disney World History 101–'How to Buy 27,000 Acres of Land and Have No One Notice,'" WDW Radio, February 11, 2005, www.wdwradio.com/2005/02/wdw-history-101-how-to-buy-27000- acres-of-land-and-no-one-noticeq. See also Schmidt, "Was 1964 the Most Significant Year in Walt Disney Company History?"

5. Data in this paragraph found in Taylor, *Storming the Magic Kingdom*.

6. Michael A. Cusumano, Yiorgos Mylonadis, and Richard S. Rosenbloom, "Strategic Maneuvering and Mass-Market Dynamics: The Triumph of VHS over Beta," *Business History Review* 66 (1992): 51–94. Data on U.S. home penetration is from "Disney's Movie Vault: 1984–1998," *Pop History Dig*, www.pophistorydig.com/topics/tag/ disney-home-video-history.

7. Domestic box office revenues in 1983 were $2.66 billion. See "1983 Domestic Grosses," Box Office Mojo, www.boxofficemojo.com/yearly/chart/?yr=1983.

8. "The Jungle Book (re-issue) (1984)," Box Office Mojo, www.boxofficemojo.com/movies/ ?page=main&id=junglebook84.htm.

9. Jason Scott, "Disneyizing Home Entertainment Distribution," in *DVD, Blue-ray and Beyond*, ed. Jonathan Wroot and Andy Willis (London: Palgrave Macmillan, 2017), 15–33, esp. 18.

10. "HBS Professor Frank Aguilar Dies at 80," Harvard Business School Newsroom, February 21, 2013, www.hbs.edu/news/releases/Pages/aguilar-obituary.aspx.

11. Quotation taken from Frank Aguilar's book, cited in Philip Kotler "Book Review: *Scanning the Business Environment*, Francis Joseph Aguilar," *Journal of Business* 40, no. 4 (January 1967): 537–539.

12. Sony Corp. v. Universal City Studios, 464 U.S. (1984), 417.

13. Michelle Pautz, "The Decline in Average Weekly Cinema Attendance: 1930–2000," *Issues in Political Economy* 11 (2002), org.elon.edu/ipe/pautz2.pdf.

14. Data on the number of televisions comes from Pautz, "Decline in Average Weekly Cinema Attendance," and Tamara Tamazashvili and Adam Lefky, "Number of Televisions in the U.S.," *Physics Factbook*, 2005 and 2007, hypertextbook.com/facts/2007/TamaraTamazashvili.shtml.

15. Taylor, *Storming the Magic Kingdom*.

16. Data on the initial cost estimate of Disney World is from Mongello, "Walt Disney World History 101." The cost of Mary Poppins can be found at "Mary Poppins (1964)," *The Numbers*, www.the-numbers.com/movie/Mary-Poppins#tab=summary.

17. "Disney's Movie Vault."

18. See Adam Smith, *An Inquiry Into the Nature and Causes of the Wealth of Nations* (1776; New York: Modern Library, 1994). Book 1 takes up the topic of the division of labor.

19. Data from Box Office Mojo, www.boxofficemojo.com.

20. John Taylor, *Storming the Magic Kingdom*.

21. Kevin Archer, "The Limits to the Imagineered City: Sociospatial Polarization in Orlando," *Economic Geography* 73 (1997).

22. Estimate of market value found in Taylor, *Storming the Magic Kingdom*.

23. Thomas C. Hayes, "Disney Reaches Accord for Gibson Greetings," *New York Times*, June 7 1984, www.nytimes.com/1984/06/07/business/disney-reaches-accord-for-gibson-greetings.html.

24. See Cusumano, Mylonadis, and Rosenbloom, "Strategic Maneuvering."

25. Edward Epstein, "How Did Michael Eisner Make Disney Profitable?" *Slate*, September 27, 2005, www.slate.com/articles/arts/the_hollywood_economist/2005/04/how_did_michael_eisner_make_disney_profitable.html.

CHAPTER 3. SRM AT THIRTY THOUSAND FEET: ASSUMPTIONS, MENTAL MAPS, AND PRINCIPLES

1. Data on the stock gains found in Jessica Silver-Greenberg, "Jon Corzine Is Working at MF Global. Say What?," *Bloomberg*, May 12, 2010, www.bloomberg.com/news/articles/2010-05-12/jon-corzine-is-working-at-mf-global-dot-say-what.

2. Azam Ahmed, Ben Protess, and Susanne Craig, "A Romance With Risk That Brought On a Panic," *New York Times Dealbook*, December 11, 2011, dealbook.nytimes.com/2011/12/11/a-romance-with-risk-that-brought-on-a-panic.

3. Robert Stammers, "MF Global: Were the Risks Clear?" *Forbes*, December 12, 2011, www.forbes.com/sites/cfainstitute/2011/12/12/mf-global-were-the-risks-clear/#45ea0f0a50a6.

4. U.S. Commodity Futures Trading Commission, "CFTC Sanctions MF Global Inc. $10 Million for Significant Supervision Violations Between 2003 and 2008," release 5763-09, December 17, 2009, www.cftc.gov/PressRoom/PressReleases/pr5763-09.

5. Peter Elkind and Doris Burke, "The Last Days of MF Global," *Fortune*, June 4, 2012, fortune.com/2012/06/04/the-last-days-of-mf-global.

6. European Stability Mechanism, "Before the ESM," www.esm.europa.eu/efsf-overview.

7. This quote has often been attributed to John Meynard Keynes, but there is no evidence of such an utterance from him. See "The Market Can Remain Irrational Longer Than You Can Remain Solvent," Quote Investigator, quoteinvestigator.com/2011/08/09/remain-solvent.

8. Elkind and Burke, "Last Days."

9. Elkind and Burke, "Last Days."

10. Peter M. Senge, *The Fifth Discipline: The Art and Practice of the Learning Organization* (New York: Doubleday/Currency, 1990), 8.

11. Thomas J. Chermack, *Scenario Planning in Organizations* (San Francisco: Berrett-Koehler, 2011).

12. Cortez and his ships sailed into Baja after their initial work in Mexico. See "Discovery and Early Exploration of La Baja California," CA Genealogy, californiagenealogy.org/labaja/discovery_exploration.htm.

13. Elkind and Burke, "Last Days."

14. "DoD News Briefing—Secretary Rumsfeld and Gen. Myers," U.S. Department of Defense, news transcript, February 12, 2002, archive.defense.gov/Transcripts/Transcript.aspx?TranscriptID=2636.

15. Phillip Inman, "Greek Debt Crisis: Timeline," *Guardian*, March 9, 2012, www.theguardian.com/business/2012/mar/09/greek-debt-crisis-timeline.

16. Kailan Shang and Zhen Chen, *Risk Appetite: Linkage with Strategic Planning*, Society of Actuaries, March 2012, web.actuaries.ie/sites/default/files/erm-resources/research_risk_app_link_report.pdf.

17. Michael Porter. "What Is Strategy?," *Harvard Business Review* 74 (November/December 1996): 61–78.

18. "Strategic Planning Basics," Strategy Management Group, www.balancedscorecard.org/BSC-Basics/Strategic-Planning-Basics.

CHAPTER 4. SRM AT TEN THOUSAND FEET: ORGANIZATIONAL STRUCTURE, PROCESSES, AND ROLES

1. Kay Ryssdal, "Interview Transcript: John Stumpf," *Marketplace*, June 10, 2008, www.marketplace.org/2008/06/10/interview-transcript-john-stumpf.

2. Thomas Stanton, *Why Some Firms Thrive While Others Fail* (New York: Oxford University Press, 2012), 51–52.

3. Adam Lashinsky, "Warren Buffett on Wells Fargo," *Fortune*, April 24, 2009, archive.fortune.com/2009/04/19/news/companies/lashinsky_buffett.fortune/index.htm.

4. The most-valuable bank data comes from Oliver Staley, "Wells Fargo Just Became the Poster Child for When External and Internal Values Don't Match," *Quartz Media*, September 8, 2016, qz.com/777241/wells-fargos-fake-accounts-scandal-makes-it-the-perfect-poster-child-for-when-external-and-internal-values-dont-match. Morningstar, "Wells Fargo's John Stumpf Receives Morningstar's 2015 CEO of the Year Award," CISION PR Newswire, January 26, 2016, www.prnewswire.com/news-releases/wells-fargos-john-stumpf-receives-morningstars-2015-ceo-of-the-year-award-300209920.html.

5. The agencies were the Consumer Finance Protection Bureau, the Los Angeles City Attorney, and the Office of the Comptroller of the Currency. See Paul Blake, "Timeline of the Wells Fargo Accounts Scandal," ABC News, November 3, 2016, abcnews.go.com/Business/timeline-wells-fargo-accounts-scandal/story?id=42231128.

6. Paul Blake, "Wells Fargo CEO John Stumpf Told to Resign by Sen. Warren," ABC News, September 20, 2016, abcnews.go.com/Business/wells-fargo-ceo-john-stumpf-facing-senate-panel/story?id=42217002.

7. Halah Touryalai, "The Gospel According to Wells Fargo," *Forbes*, January 24, 2012. www.forbes.com/sites/halahtouryalai/2012/01/25/the-gospel-according-to-wells-fargo/#8d979927904c.

8. E. Scott Reckard, "Wells Fargo's Pressure-Cooker Sales Culture Comes at a Cost," *Los Angeles Times*, December 21, 2013, www.latimes.com/business/la-fi-wells-fargo-sale-pressure-20131222-story.html.

9. Wells Fargo and Company, Schedule 14-A, April 10, 2017, United States Securities and Exchange Commission, www.sec.gov/Archives/edgar/data/72971/000119312517118654/d375947ddefa14a.htm.

10. Wells Fargo and Company, Schedule 14-A.

11. "Interview: Diane Vaughan," *Consultant*, May 2008, www.consultingnewsline.com/Info/Vie%20du%20Conseil/Le%20Consultant%20du%20mois/Diane%20Vaughan%20(English).html.

12. Data on Wells Fargo is taken from Yahoo Finance for the period September 16, 2016, to September 14, 2018. Data on the Dow is from Google, same dates.

13. Robert A. Rennie, "The Measurement of Risk," *Journal of Insurance* 28, no. 1 (March 1961): 83–91.

14. Charlton Ogburn, "Merrill's Marauders: The Truth About an Incredible Adventure," *Harper's Magazine*, January 1957, harpers.org/archive/1957/01/merrills-marauders.

15. The early view, from industrial economics, can be found in Michael Porter, *Competitive Strategy* (New York: Free Press, 1980). The so-called resource-based view is best articulated in Jay B. Barney, "Firm Resources and Sustained Competitive Advantage," *Journal of Management* 17 (1991): 99–120. The idea of dynamic capabilities comes from David J. Teece, Gary Pisano, and Amy Shuen, "Dynamic Capabilities and Strategic Management," *Strategic Management Journal* 18 (1997): 509–533.

16. Teece, Pisano, and Shuen, "Dynamic Capabilities."

17. *Competence, Change, Future*, Allianz Group annual report 2017, www.allianz.com/content/dam/onemarketing/azcom/Allianz_com/investor-relations/en/results-reports/annual-report/ar2017/en-group-2017-annual-report-allianz-group.pdf.

18. Adapted from Michael Raynor, *The Strategy Paradox: Why Committing to Success Leads to Failure, and What to do About it* (New York: Doubleday 2007).

19. General Electric Company, Form 10-K, for the fiscal year ended December 31, 1993, United States Securities and Exchange Commission, getfilings.com/o0000040545-94-000003.html.

20. Public Law 107-204, Sarbanes-Oxley Act of 2002.

21. Committee of Sponsoring Organizations of the Treadway Commission, *Enterprise Risk Management—Integrated Framework: Application Techniques*, September 2004, www.macs.hw.ac.uk/~andrewc/erm2/reading/ERM%20-%20COSO%20Application%20Techniques.pdf.

22. Public Law 111-203, Dodd-Frank Wall Street Reform and Consumer Protection Act, www.govinfo.gov/content/pkg/PLAW-111publ203/html/PLAW-111publ203.htm.

23. Thomas Stanton, *Why Some Firms Thrive While Others Fail* (New York: Oxford University Press, 2012), 95.

24. Research shows that personal, informal power tends to be more effective in getting work done while preserving morale and organizational commitment. See Stephen Robbins and Timothy Judge, *Organizational Behavior*, 14th ed. (Upper Saddle River, NJ: Prentice Hall, 2011), 423.

25. Robbins and Judge, *Organizational Behavior*, 423.

26. Allen C. Amason and Harry J. Sapienza, "The Effects of Top Management Team Size and Interaction Norms on Cognitive and Affective Conflict," *Journal of Management*, August 1, 1997, doi.org/10.1177/014920639702300401.

27. Material here taken from "Fiduciary," in Henry Campbell Black and Bryan A. Garner, *Black's Law Dictionary*, 7th ed. (Saint Paul, MN: West Group, 1999).

28. David J. Teece, "Explicating Dynamic Capabilities: The Nature and Foundations of (Sustainable) Enterprise Performance," *Strategic Management Journal* 28, no. 13, 1319–1350.

CHAPTER 5. SRM AT GROUND LEVEL: WHY, WHO AND WHERE, AND HOW?

1. "William Shockley," Engineering and Technology History Wiki, ethw.org/William_Shockley.

2. Suzanne Deffree, "Intel Is Founded, July 18, 1968," *EDN Network*, July 18, 2018. www.edn.com/electronics-blogs/edn-moments/4390653/Intel-is-founded--July-18--1968.

3. Jeff Dyer, Paul Godfrey, Rob Jensen, and David Bryce, "Intel (A): Dominance in Microprocessors," in *Strategic Management* (Hoboken, NJ: Wiley, 2016).

4. Tim Jackson, *Inside Intel: Andy Grove and the Rise of the World's Most Powerful Chip Company* (New York: Dutton, 1997), 74.

5. Jerrold Siegel, "Moore's Law," lecture notes, University of Missouri–St. Louis, www.umsl.edu/~siegelj/information_theory/projects/Bajramovic/www.umsl.edu/_abdcf/Cs4890/link1.html. See also Carla Tardi, "Moore's Law," *Investopedia*, April 20, 2019, www.investopedia.com/terms/m/mooreslaw.asp.

6. Intel, *2005 Annual Report*, www.intel.com/content/dam/doc/report/history-2005-annual-report.pdf; Intel, *Intel Corporation Annual Report*, 1980, www.intel.com/content/dam/doc/report/history-1980-annual-report.pdf. The United States spends about 2.9% of its gross domestic product on research and development. If we use Intel as a guide and assume that about 2.9% goes to capital expenditures based on that R & D output, then we have 5.8%, roughly one-fifth of the 29% Intel spends. Data on U.S. R & D from Yoram Solomon, "Why R&D Spending Has Almost Nothing to Do With Innovation," *Inc.*, October 19, 2017, www.inc.com/yoram-solomon/dont-be-alarmed-by-us-4th-place-in-rampd-investment.html.

7. Dyer et al., *Strategic Management*.

8. "Global Apple iPhone Sales from 3rd Quarter 2007 to 4th Quarter 2018 (in million units)," Statista (accessed January 1, 2019), www.statista.com/statistics/263401/global-apple-iphone-sales-since-3rd-quarter-2007.

9. Alexis C. Madrigal, "Paul Otellini's Intel: Can the Company That Built the Future Survive It?," *Atlantic*, May 16, 2013, www.theatlantic.com/technology/archive/2013/05/paul-otellinis-intel-can-the-company-that-built-the-future-survive-it/275825.

10. Jeff Dyer, Hal Gregersen, and Clayton Christensen, *The Innovators DNA* (Boston: Harvard Business School Press, 2011). See also David C. Robertson and Bill Breen, *Brick by Brick: How LEGO Rewrote the Rules of Innovation and Conquered the Global Toy Industry* (New York: Crown Business, 2013), 268–269.

11. The correct wording for this quote is found at "Quotes Falsely Attributed to Winston Churchill," International Churchill Society, winstonchurchill.org/resources/quotes/quotes-falsely-attributed.

12. A. G. Lafley and Roger Martin, *Playing to Win* (Boston: Harvard Business School Publishing 2013).

13. Jim Collins, *Good to Great* (New York: Harper Collins, 2001).

14. Art Kliener, "The Life's Work of a Thought Leader," *Strategy + Business*, August 9, 2019, www.strategy-business.com/article/00043?gko=bcd57.

15. Joe Concha, "ESPN Loses 2M Subscribers in 2018." *The Hill*, November 23, 2018, thehill.com/homenews/media/418039-espn-loses-2m-subscribers-in-fiscal-2018.

16. Most watched TV networks in the United States, 2017, accessed through Statista, December 21, 2018.

17. Matt Honan, "Remembering the Apple Newton's Prophetic Failure and Lasting Impact," *Wired*, August 5, 2013, www.wired.com/2013/08/remembering-the-apple-newtons-prophetic-failure-and-lasting-ideals.

18. "PDA Sales Soar in 2000," *CNN Money*, January 25, 2001, money.cnn.com/2001/01/26/technology/handheld.

19. Stanley M. Besen and Robert W. Crandall, "The Deregulation of Cable Television," *Law and Contemporary Problems* 44, no. 1: 77–124. scholarship.law.duke.edu/cgi/viewcontent.cgi?article=3609&context=lcp.

20. David B. Yoffie and Mary Kwak, *Judo Strategy* (Cambridge, MA: Harvard Business School Press 2001), 103.

21. "Palm: The Rise and Fall of a Legend," Technobuffalo, March 31, 2011, www.technobuffalo.com/2011/03/31/palm-the-rise-and-fall-of-a-legend.

22. Chris Ziegler, "Ten Years of BlackBerry," *Engadget*, December 28, 2009, www.engadget.com/2009/12/28/ten-years-of-blackberry.

CHAPTER 6. SRM AT GROUND LEVEL: WHAT TOOLS TO ANALYZE AND MANAGE STRATEGIC RISKS

1. Data on the early history of Lego is from "About Us: LEGO History Timeline," LEGO Group, www.lego.com/en-us/aboutus/lego-group/the_lego_history.

2. "About Us: Timeline 1990–1999," LEGO Group, www.lego.com/en-us/aboutus/lego-group/the_lego_history/1990.

3. David C. Robertson and Bill Breen, *Brick by Brick: How LEGO Rewrote the Rules of Innovation and Conquered the Global Toy Industry* (New York: Crown Business, 2013), 43.

4. Data is found in the relevant annual reports from 2000 to 2005, available at "About Us: Annual Reports," LEGO Group, www.lego.com/en-us/aboutus/lego-group/annual-report.

5. "At LEGO, Growth and Culture Are Not Kid Stuff," *Boston Consulting Group*, February 9, 2017, www.bcg.com/publications/2017/people-organization-jorgen-vig-knudstorp-lego-growth-culture-not-kid-stuff.aspx.

6. Robertson and Breen, *Brick by Brick*, 241.

7. Stuart Collins, "Strategic Risk Management Helps Lego Find Route to Growth," Business Insurance, September 9, 2012, www.businessinsurance.com/article/20120909/NEWS06/309099999/Strategic-risk-management-helps-Lego-find-route-to-growth.

8. Emily Holbrook, "Not Just Child's Play: Strategic Risk Management at Lego," *Risk Management*, February 1, 2013, www.rmmagazine.com/2013/02/01/not-just-childs-play-strategic-risk-management-at-lego.

9. Mark Frigo and Hans Læssøe, "Strategic Risk Management at the LEGO Group," *Strategic Finance*, February 2012, sfmagazine.com/wp-content/uploads/sfarchive/2012/02/Strategic-Risk-Management-at-the-LEGO-Group.pdf.

10. Victoria Tozer-Pennington, "ORR Innovation Awards 2011: Corporate of the Year," Risk.net, March 2, 2011, www.risk.net/risk-management/operational-risk/2027159/orr-innovation-awards-2011-corporate-year.

11. Johnny Davis, "How Lego Clicked: The Super Brand That Re-invented Itself," *Guardian*, July 4, 2017, www.theguardian.com/lifeandstyle/2017/jun/04/how-lego-clicked-the-super-brand-that-reinvented-itself. See also Mark Frigo and Hans Læssøe, "Strategic Risk Management at the LEGO Group," *Strategic Finance*, February 2012, sfmagazine.com/wp-content/uploads/sfarchive/2012/02/Strategic-Risk-Management-at-the-LEGO-Group.pdf.

12. Tozer-Pennington, "ORR Innovation Awards 2011."

13. Emanuel V. Lauria Jr., "Downside–Upside Duality: The Role of Ambidexterity in Enterprise Risk Management" (PhD diss., Georgia State University, 2015).

14. Collins, *Good to Great*.

15. Robert A. Rennie, "The Measurement of Risk," *Journal of Insurance* 28, 1 (March 1961): 83–91.

16. Stuart Collins, "Strategic Risk Management Helps LEGO Find Route to Growth," *Business Insurance*, September 9, 2012, www.businessinsurance.com/article/00010101/NEWS06/309099999/Strategic-risk-management-helps-Lego-find-route-to-growth.

17. Rich Horwath, "Scenario Planning: No Crystal Ball Required," *Strategic Thinker*, 2006, www.strategyskills.com/Articles/Documents/ST-Scenario_Planning.pdf.

18. Matt Honan, "Remembering the Apple Newton's Prophetic Failure and Lasting Impact," *Wired*, August 5, 2013, www.wired.com/2013/08/remembering-the-apple-newtons-prophetic-failure-and-lasting-ideals.

19. Hans Læssøe, "Imagine and Prepare for 2030," February 9, 2018, www.linkedin.com/pulse/imagine-prepare-2030-hans-l%C3%A6ss%C3%B8e.

20. Thomas C. Schelling, "Red vs. Blue," in *Zones of Control: Perspectives on Wargaming*, ed. Pat Harrigan and Matthew G. Kirschenbaum (Boston: MIT Press, 2016), 229–239.

21. "The History of SaaS," BeBusinessed.com, bebusinessed.com/history/the-history-of-saas.

CHAPTER 7. "THE FUTURE AIN'T WHAT IT USED TO BE!"

1. "Yogi Berra," National Baseball Hall of Fame, baseballhall.org/hall-of-famers/berra-yogi; Nate Scott, "The 509 Greatest Yogi Berra Quotes," *For the Win*, September 23, 2015, ftw.usatoday.com/2015/09/the-50-greatest-yogi-berra-quotes.

2. For the early history, see Daniel Yergin, *The Prize* (New York: Free Press, 2008), chapter 1.

3. "The DARPA Grand Challenge: Ten Years Later," Defense Advanced Research Projects Agency, March 13, 2014, www.darpa.mil/news-events/2014-03-13.

4. "DARPA Grand Challenge."

5. Data for LiDAR and radar is from Ann Neal, "LiDAR vs. RADAR," Fierce Electronics, April 24, 2018, www.sensorsmag.com/components/lidar-vs-radar.

6. Benjamin Gomes-Casseres, *The Alliance Revolution: The New Shape of Business Rivalry* (Boston: Harvard University Press, 1996), 93. Information on Canon's history is from "The History of Canon 1976–1987," Canon, global.canon/en/corporate/history/01.html.

7. Data on market shares and sales a half century ago is sketchy, but professional photographers remember Canon's entry and changes. See "Camera Market Dominator in 1960s, 70s and 80s?," Photo.net forums, www.photo.net/discuss/threads/camera-market-dominator-in-1960s-70s-and-80s.431046. Data on Canon's 2017 market share is from "2018 Canon, Nikon and Sony Market Share (Latest Nikkei, BCN and CIPA Reports)," Photo Rumors, photorumors.com/2018/08/01/2018-canon-nikon-and-sony-market-share-latest-nikkei-bcn-and-cipa-reports.

8. Dunja Djudjic, "Camera Sales Report for 2016: Lowest Sales Ever on DSLRs and Mirrorless," *Photography*, March 2, 2017, www.diyphotography.net/camera-sales-report-2016-lowest-sales-ever-dslrs-mirrorless.

9. Jack Karsten and Darrell West, "The State of Self-Driving Car Laws Across the U.S.," Brookings, May 1, 2018, www.brookings.edu/blog/techtank/2018/05/01/the-state-of-self-driving-car-laws-across-the-u-s.

10. Information about Uber is from Dan Blystone, "The Story of Uber," *Investopedia*, August 9, 2018, www.investopedia.com/articles/personal-finance/111015/story-uber.asp.

11. Lauren Feiner, "Uber Ends Its First Day of Trading Down More Than 7%," CNBC, May 10, 2019, www.cnbc.com/2019/05/10/uber-ipo-stock-starts-trading-on-the-new-york-stock-exchange.html.

12. Ryan Lawler, "Lyft-Off: Zimride's Long Road to Overnight Success," *Techcrunch*, techcrunch.com/2014/08/29/6000-words-about-a-pink-mustache.

13. Kevin Kelleher, "Lyft Rises 9% on First Day of Trading for a Market Cap of $26.5 Billion," *Fortune*, March 29, 2019, fortune.com/2019/03/29/lyft-stock-today-ipo-market-cap-26-billion.

14. "State Farm Mutual Automobile Insurance Company History," *Funding Universe*, www.fundinguniverse.com/company-histories/state-farm-mutual-automobile-insurance-company-history.

15. Financial and operating data taken from "State Farm Announces 2017 Financial Results," State Farm, March 1, 2018, newsroom.statefarm.com/2017-state-farm-financial-results.

16. Alexa Lardieri, "Report: Two-Thirds of World's Population Will Live in Cities by 2050," *U.S. News and World Report*, May 17, 2018, www.usnews.com/news/world/articles/2018-05-17/report-two-thirds-of-worlds-population-will-live-in-cities-by-2050.

17. "Who Invented the Automobile?," *Everyday Mysteries*, U.S. Library of Congress, www.loc.gov/rr/scitech/mysteries/auto.html.

18. Information on the history of electric vehicles is from Rebecca Matulka, "The History of the Electric Car," Energy.gov, September 15, 2014, www.energy.gov/articles/history-electric-car.

19. Maxine Joselow, "The U.S. Has 1 Million Electric Vehicles, but Does It Matter?," *Scientific American*, October 12, 2018, www.scientificamerican.com/article/the-u-s-has-1-million-electric-vehicles-but-does-it-matter. Data on the number of charging stations is from "Number of Public Electric Vehicle Charging Stations and Charging Outlets in the U.S. as of December 2018 (in Units)," Statista, www.statista.com/statistics/416750/number-of-electric-vehicle-charging-stations-outlets-united-states.

20. "Soft Drinks Target of a Changing Market," *Convenience Store Decisions*, March 26, 2018, cstoredecisions.com/2018/03/26/soft-drinks-target-of-changing-market.

21. "The Coca-Cola Company," *Encyclopedia Britannica*, www.britannica.com/topic/The-Coca-Cola-Company.

22. Data for 1997 is from Elena Holodny, "The Epic Collapse of American Soda Consumption in One Chart," *Business Insider*, March 10, 2016, www.businessinsider.com/americans-are-drinking-less-soda-2016-3; 2017 data is from "Per capita Consumption of Carbonated Soft Drinks (CSD) in the United States from 2010 to 2017 (in 8-Ounce Servings), Statista, www.statista.com/statistics/306841/us-per-capita-consumption-of-csd-by-state.

23. Phil LeBeau, "Americans Buying Fewer New Cars in Lifetime," CNBC, October 22, 2012, www.cnbc.com/id/49504504.

CHAPTER 8. SRM FOR THE LONG TERM: CULTURE, COMMUNICATION, ETHICS, AND INTEGRITY

1. Weather report, *Hartford Current*, September 7, 1979, 2.

2. Anthony Smith, *ESPN the Company: The Story and Lessons Behind the Most Fanatical Brand in Sports* (Hoboken, NJ: Wiley, 2009), 112.

3. Michael Akelson, "The 20 Best Chris Berman Nicknames of All-Time," *Bleacher Report*, March 29, 2010, bleacherreport.com/articles/370557-the-20-best-chris-berman-nicknames-of-all-time#slide0.

4. Michael Freeman, *ESPN: The Uncensored History* (New York: Taylor Trade, 2001), 115.

5. Smith, *ESPN*, 152.

6. All direct quotes here come from Freeman, *ESPN*, chapter 9

7. Smith, *ESPN*, 11.

8. George Bodenheimer, pers. comm., January 2013.

9. Edgar Schein, *Organizational Culture and Leadership* (San Francisco: Jossey-Bass, 2010).

10. The history of the phrase and its rich history can be found at "Culture Eats Strategy for Breakfast," Quote Investigator, quoteinvestigator.com/2017/05/23/culture-eats.

11. For an explanation of why this is the case, see "How Much of an Iceberg Is Below the Water," Navigation Center, U.S. Department of Homeland Security, www.navcen.uscg. gov/?pageName=iipHowMuchOfAnIcebergIsBelowTheWater.

12. The material in these two paragraphs comes from Tom Peters, "A Brief History of the 7-S ('McKinsey 7-S') Model," Tom Peters! blog, January 9, 2011, tompeters. com/2011/03/a-brief-history-of-the-7-s-mckinsey-7-s-model.

13. Robert H. Waterman Jr., Thomas J. Peters, and Julien R. Phillips, "Structure Is Not Organization," *Business Horizons* 23, no. 3 (June 1980): 14.

14. Jack Weber, "A Leader's Guide to Understanding Complex Organizations: An Expanded '7-S' Perspective," Darden Case No. UVA-OB-0659.

15. Peters, "A Brief History."

16. Thomas Stanton, *Why Some Firms Thrive While Others Fail* (New York: Oxford University Press, 2012), 51–52.

17. Tim Jackson, *Inside Intel: Andy Grove and the Rise of the World's Most Powerful Chip Company* (New York: Dutton, 1997).

18. Intel's mission and vision statements are from "What Are Intel's Mission Statement, Values, and Objectives?," Intel, www.intel.com/content/www/us/en/support/ articles/000015119/programs.html.

19. For a complete description, see Anthony Giddens, *The Constitution of Society: Outline of the Theory of Structuration* (Berkeley: University of California Press, 1984).

20. Hans Læssøe, pers. comm., June 30, 2019.

21. James G. March and Herbert A. Simon, *Organizations* (New York: John Wiley and Sons, 1958), 186–187.

22. C. K. Prahalad, "Weak Signals Versus Strong Paradigms," guest editorial, *Journal of Marketing Research* 32 (August 1, 1995): 3–6.

23. Ben Walsh, "Jon Corzine Replaced MF Global's 'Risk Officer' with an 'Everything Is OK' Officer," *Business Insider*, February 3, 2012, www.businessinsider.com/jon-corzine-replaced-mf-globals-risk-officer-with-an-everything-is-ok-officer-2012-2. See also Hersh Shefrin, *Behavioral Risk Management* (New York: Palgrave Macmillan, 2016), 267–279.

CHAPTER 9. CONCLUDING THOUGHTS: CURRENTS, NOT WAVES

1. "Celebrating 75 years of History," Ecolab internal company document, 1998, 5–6.

2. Christophe Beck, pers. comm., October 11, 2017.

3. Angela Bush, pers. comm., October 12, 2017.

4. Nalco Chemical Corporation History," Funding Universe, www.fundinguniverse.com/ company-histories/nalco-chemical-corporation-history.

5. Gabriel Zoratti, "B-1435 Galaxy 3D TRASAR Automation Cooling Water PDF," Nalco Water, www.scribd.com/document/384022770/B-1435-Galaxy-3D-TRASAR-Automation-Cooling-Water-PDF.

6. The previous paragraphs use data from Emilio Tenuta, pers. comm., October 11, 2017.

7. Ecolab's 2017 sustainability report, page 4. Sustainability reports are available at www.ecolab.com/sustainability/download-sustainability-reports.

8. Christophe Beck, pers. comm., October 22, 2018.

9. See Rick Tetzeli, "GM Gets Ready for a Post-Car Future," *Fortune*, May 23, 2018, fortune.com/2018/05/23/gm-general-motors-fortune-500.

10. See "How to Live with Risks," *Harvard Business Review*, July–August 2015, hbr.org/2015/07/how-to-live-with-risks.

APPENDIX A. STRATEGY IN AN UNCERTAIN AGE

1. "Walt Disney," Biography.com, www.biography.com/people/walt-disney-9275533. For more on the Laugh-O-Gram Studio, see "History," Thank You, Walt Disney, Inc., thankyouwaltdisney.org/history.

2. Bob Thomas, *Building a Company : Roy O. Disney and the Creation of an Entertainment Empire* (New York: Hyperion, 1998), 46–47.

3. J. P. Telotte, *The Mouse Machine: Disney and Technology* (Urbana: University of Illinois Press, 2008), 27.

4. Thomas, *Building a Company*, 57–58.

5. "Walt Disney and Television," JustDisney.com, www.justdisney.com/features/disney_tv/index.html.

6. For an excellent introduction, see Clayton Christensen, "The 'Jobs to be Done' Theory of Innovation," *Harvard Business Review*, December 8, 2016, hbr.org/ideacast/2016/12/the-jobs-to-be-done-theory-of-innovation.

7. Clayton M. Christensen, Scott Cook, and Taddy Hall, "What Customers Want from Your Products," *Working Knowledge*, Harvard Business School, January 16, 2006, hbswk.hbs.edu/item/what-customers-want-from-your-products.

8. Clara Lu, "Walmart's Successful Supply Chain Management," *Tradegecko*, October 4, 2018, www.tradegecko.com/blog/incredibly-successful-supply-chain-management-walmart.

9. The 80% figure comes from a conversation one of the authors had with a Walmart logistics executive. The revenue figure is for 2014 and comes from "The Real Secret to Wal-Mart's Success," *DC Velocity*, July 1, 2004, www.dcvelocity.com/articles/20040701inbound_the_real_secret_to_walmarts.

10. "Walmart 2017 Global Responsibility Report," Walmart, corporate.walmart.com/2017grr.

11. For the size of Walmart's distribution centers, see "The Walmart Distribution Network in the United States," MWPVL International, www.mwpvl.com/html/walmart.html.

12. See, for example, Michael Raynor, *The Strategy Paradox: Why Committing to Success Leads to Failure, and What to Do About It* (New York: Doubleday 2007).

13. Jeffery H. Dyer and N. Nobeoka, "Creating and Managing a High-Performance Knowledge-Sharing Network: The Toyota Case," *Strategic Management Journal* 21 (2000): 345–367.

14. The activity-based view of strategy was first developed by Michael E. Porter. See Porter, "What Is Strategy?," *Harvard Business Review* 74 (November–December 1996): 61–78.

15. Disney's 2018 10-K filing can be found at *Fiscal Year 2018 Annual Financial Report*, The Walt Disney Company, www.thewaltdisneycompany.com/wp-content/uploads/2019/01/2018-Annual-Report.pdf; the $40 billion brand value estimate comes from "Best Global Brands 2018 Rankings," Interbrand, interbrand.com/best-brands/best-global-brands/2018/ranking.

16. Jonathan Bing, "Marketing Is King for Disney's Princess Line," *Variety*, December 12, 2005, variety.com/2005/scene/columns/marketing-is-king-for-disney-s-princess-line-1117934460.

17. Vincent Ng, "How Disney Princesses Became a Multi-Billion Dollar Brand," MCNG Marketing, March 18, 2013, www.mcngmarketing.com/how-disney-princesses-became-a-multi-billion-dollar-brand/#.WV4VHYgrI2w.

18. Peter Drucker, "Managing Oneself," *Harvard Business Review* 83 (2005): 100–109.

19. Michael Porter, *Competitive Strategy: Techniques for Analyzing Industries and Competitors* (New York: Simon and Schuster, 1980).

20. Tim Dirks, "The History of Film in the 1920s," AMC Filmsite, www.filmsite.org/20sintro.html.

21. Steve Schlackman, "How Mickey Mouse Keeps Changing Copyright Law," *Art Law Journal*, February 15, 2014, alj.artrepreneur.com/mickey-mouse-keeps-changing-copyright-law.

22. "The Unbelievable History of Oswald the Lucky Rabbit," Oh My Disney, ohmy.disney.com/insider/2016/09/05/oswald-the-lucky-rabbit.

23. Quoted in "Disney Dollars: 1930s," *Pop History Dig*, www.pophistorydig.com/topics/disney-dollars1930s.

24. See Richard Reed and Robert J. Defillippi, "Causal Ambiguity, Barriers to Imitation, and Sustainable Competitive Advantage," *Academy of Management Review* 15 (1990), 88–102.

25. See Edgar Schein, *Organizational Culture and Leadership* (San Francisco: Jossey-Bass 2010).

26. Ng, "How Disney Princesses Became a Multi-Billion Dollar Brand."

APPENDIX B. HOW TO DETERMINE RISK CAPACITY AND RISK APPETITE

1. Edward Hida, "Establishing Risk Appetite Statements for Stronger Risk Management," *Wall Street Journal*, December 22, 2014.

2. Institute of Risk Management, *Risk Appetite Statements* (London: Institute of Risk Management, 2017).

3. "Risk Appetite Statement Examples," Proviti, www.protiviti.com/US-en/insights/key-questions-consider-risk-appetite-dialogue.

CREDITS

Cover photo	Getty Creative
Figure 3.1	Herman Map of North America, 1712 Library of Congress, Geography and Map Division.
Figure 3.2	How ERM and SRM Create Value © Strategic Risk Insights, LLC . Paul C. Godfrey
Figure 4.1	The Strategic Uncertainty Frontier © Strategic Risk Insights, LLC. Manny Lauria
Table 4.1	The Complementary Roles of the CRO and CSO Paul Godfrey and Manny Lauria Adapted from *The Strategy Paradox* , Michael Raynor, 2007
Figure 5.1	SRM and the Risk Function Paul C. Godfrey
Table 5.1	A PEST Analysis of Three Weak Signals Paul C. Godfrey
Figure 5.2	The Strategic Uncertainty Map © Strategic Risk Insights, LLC. Paul C. Godfrey and John Bugalla
Figure 6.1	A Traditional Heat Map Paul C. Godfrey
Figure 6.2	Potential Scenarios in Mobile Computing, ca 1996–8 Paul C. Godfrey
Figure 6.3	The Risk Ownership Map © Strategic Risk Insights, LLC. Paul C. Godfrey and John Bugalla
Figure 7.1	The Impact of Changes in the Automobile Paul C. Godfrey and John Bugalla. Photo Wikimedia commons/Grendelkhan
Figure 8.1	The 7 S Model © John Wiley and Sons, 2015. Used with permission
Figure 8.2	The Strategic Risk Reporting Matrix © Strategic Risk Insights, LLC. Paul C. Godfrey, Kristina Narvaez and John Bugalla
Figure A.1	The Company Diamond © John Wiley and Sons, 2015, used with permission
Figure A.2	Where Disney Competes © Strategic Risk Insights, LLC.Paul C. Godfrey
Table A.1	Quantitative Dimensions of Risk Appetite Kristina Narvaez
Table A.2	Qualitative dimensions of Risk Appetite Kristina Narvaez

INDEX

March, James, 20–21, 156
margin calls, 50
Mary Poppins, 40
McKinsey 7-S model. *See* 7-S model; cultural alignment.
McKinsey and Company, 69
Mecherle, George Jacob "G. J.," 136
meltdown of 2008. *See* Great Recession of 2008.
mental maps
  competitive advantage, 60–62
  definition, 52
  description, 52
  embedding with ERM, 59–62
  failure of, example, 53–54
  focus on knowns *vs.* unknowns, 55–57
  integrating SRM into the strategy complex, 62–64
  risk appetite, 57–59
  risk capacity, 57–59
Merkel, Angela, 57
MF Global (Man Financial Global). *See also* Corzine, Jon.
  bad mental maps, 54
  bankruptcy, 51
  Bernie Dan as CRO, 48
  financial blunders, 48–52, 56
  focus on knowns *vs.* unknowns, 55–57
  Great Recession, 48
  Greek debt crisis, 57
  irrationality and solvency risk, 50
  liquidity risk, 51
  margin calls, 50
  Michael Roseman as CRO, 48–50
  Michael Stockman as CRO, 50
  risk appetite, 57–59
  risk capacity, 57–59
  sovereign debt, 49–50
  time to liquidate, 50
  UROs (unidentified risk objects), 57
Michaels, Al, 197
Mickey Mouse, 180–181, 195
The Mickey Mouse Club, 181
microcomputers, 88
Miller, Ron, 30
Mintz, Charles, 179–180, 194–195
mission and vision, cultural alignment, 153
mobile computing market, Strategic Uncertainty Decision Map, 103–104
Monsters, Inc, 188
Mooney, Andy, 188
Moore, Gordon, 88, 153
Moore's Law, 88–89
Morgan Stanley, CDS (credit default swaps), 4

Morris, William, 139
Mortimer Mouse, 180
movies and television. *See also* Disney, movies and television.
  A Bug's Life, 188
  Finding Nemo, 188
  Monsters, Inc, 188
  Toy Story, 188
  Toy Story 2, 188
myths, cultural alignment, 154–156

N

Nalco, 166–168, 183
Nalco Chemical Company, 166
National Aluminate. *See* Nalco.
NBC network, origin of, 14
network television. *See also* cable television; satellite television; *specific networks*.
  audience statistics (1976), 14
  FCC protections, 14
New England Whalers, 9–11
Newton
  introduction of, 98–99
  Strategic Uncertainty Decision Map, 103–104
Newton, PEST filter
  economic forces, 100, 100*f*
  political forces, 99, 100*f*
  social forces, 100, 100*f*
  technological forces, 100*f*, 101
NM Electronics, 88
Noyce, Robert, 88

O

Ogburn, Charlton, 72
Olbermann, Keith, 146
One Hour in Wonderland, 181
operating capabilities, SRM, 72
operational risks, 9–10
Oracle of Omaha, 68
Osborn, Merritt J. (M. J.), 165
Oswald the Lucky Rabbit, 179–180, 197
Otellini, Paul
  creating the SRM team, 91–96
  iPhone sales, 90–91
  wargaming, 121
Ovesen, Jesper, 108–109
ownership, indicating, 123

ABOUT THE AUTHORS

Paul C. Godfrey, PhD currently serves as the William and Roceil Low Professor of Business Strategy in the Marriott School of Management at Brigham Young University. His academic research has appeared in *Academy of Management Review, Strategic Management Journal, Journal of Business Ethics,* and *Journal of Management Inquiry.* His book *More than Money: Five Forms of Capital to Create Wealth and Eliminate Poverty*  garnered an Axiom Business Book's silver medal in 2016. Dr. Godfrey is also a co-author of *Strategic Management: Concepts and Cases.* He consults with a variety of businesses and not-for-profit organizations on economic impact analysis, mission and vision development, organizational change, and strategy. Dr. Godfrey received a bachelor of science in political science from the University of Utah and MBA and PhD degrees from the University of Washington.

Emanuel V. Lauria, DBA, is chief executive officer of KB Risk Solutions, a specialized insurance broker dedicated to serving the managed healthcare industry. KB Risk provides sophisticated reinsurance transactions, data analytics, and financial risk management advice to physician groups, hospital systems, and accountable care organizations nationally. The launch of KB Risk was the culmination of a multiyear consulting project conducted by Dr. Lauria at Risk Strategy Dynamics, where he was managing principal. His client base included a wide range of financial and professional services

firms, whom he advised in the areas of strategic options for growth and increasing risk management effectiveness. Dr. Lauria was formerly executive vice president and chief client officer at Crawford & Company, a global claims management firm. He was also cochair of its enterprise risk management executive council. Prior to joining Crawford, Dr. Lauria held senior management positions with Wells Fargo Insurance Services and Marsh. His innovative work at Wells Fargo brought the company's insurance brokerage and banking capabilities into an integrated risk advisory platform for the benefit of its major corporate clients. Dr. Lauria has more than thirty years of risk management and insurance industry experience. He earned a doctorate in business administration from Georgia State University, where he was the first Huebner Foundation executive fellow for risk management research. He is an instructor in the university's Robinson College of Business, and chair emeritus of its Risk Management Foundation. He holds a BA in economics from Villanova University, and a professional certificate in strategic decision and risk management from Stanford University.

John Bugalla has been a strategic risk management consultant for twenty years, following a twenty year career working for leading firms in the risk management industry. He is currently principal of ermINSIGHTS, a consulting firm dedicated to linking strategy and risk. One of Mr. Bugalla's consulting assignments was leading the team that designed and implemented the breakthrough enterprise risk management program for United Grain Growers. The program was hailed as the "deal of the decade" by *CFO* magazine and a "revolutionary advance in corporate finance" by the *Economist*. He also is an active author and presenter. Mr. Bugalla most recently authored two chapters in the book *Implementing Enterprise Risk Management*. Some of his recent articles appear in *The Corporate Board*, *Boardmember.com*, *CFO.com*, *Risk Management* magazine, *National Law Review*, and *Journal of Risk Management for Financial Institutions*.

Kristina Narvaez is owner of ERM Strategies, an enterprise risk management/strategy research and consulting firm. She also serves as an adjunct professor at Brigham Young University and the UCLA Extension. Ms. Narvaez teaches strategy and enterprise risk management, helping the next generation of professionals master the tools of each discipline. She received a bachelor's degree in environmental  risk management from the University of Utah and an MBA from Westminster College, where she earned the Risk and Insurance Management Society Spencer Education Foundation's graduate scholar award. Ms. Narvaez has authored two other books: *Success Stories: Public Entities Adopt ERM Practices* and *Implementing Enterprise Risk Management: Case Studies and Best Practices*. She has published more than sixty articles on Enterprise risk management and strategies risk management and related topics.

Dear reader,

Thank you for picking up this book and welcome to the worldwide BK community! You're joining a special group of people who have come together to create positive change in their lives, organizations, and communities.

What's BK all about?

Our mission is to connect people and ideas to create a world that works for all.

Why? Our communities, organizations, and lives get bogged down by old paradigms of self-interest, exclusion, hierarchy, and privilege. But we believe that can change. That's why we seek the leading experts on these challenges—and share their actionable ideas with you.

A welcome gift

To help you get started, we'd like to offer you a **free copy** of one of our bestselling ebooks:

www.bkconnection.com/welcome

When you claim your **free ebook**, you'll also be subscribed to our blog.

Our freshest insights

Access the best new tools and ideas for leaders at all levels on our blog at ideas.bkconnection.com.

Sincerely,

Your friends at Berrett-Koehler